STORY TIME

This book has been supported by the Jockey Hollow Fund, established by Betsy Beinecke Shirley to enable projects related to American children's literature.

STORY TIME

Essays on American Children's Literature
from the Betsy Beinecke Shirley Collection

Edited by Timothy Young

Beinecke Rare Book & Manuscript Library, Yale University
Distributed by Yale University Press, New Haven and London

Table of Contents

Juvenile Amusements.

Ned and Ann looking at pictures through a glass.

Flying the kite.

Spinning.

Introduction

Children's books can be full of energy and joy, as they reveal the world to young readers. When viewed through the lens of history and the attendant changes in culture, books we read and enjoyed as children can be seen in very different ways. This change in distance—from the immediate, engaged child reader to the mature, consciously informed adult critic—is at the heart of the academic study of the history of children's literature. Stories that were intended and read as charming, gentle, and innocent—or even terrifying, subversive, and knowing—when examined by scholars and critics, are opened to examination and interpretation for what they say about subjects ranging from the history of the book to challenging questions of representation.

A collection of historic books for juvenile audiences presents a rich field for scholars to investigate—to examine how young minds were taught and entertained and what changes can be seen over time. Betsy Beinecke Shirley, the daughter of one of the brothers who funded and endowed the Beinecke Rare Book and Manuscript Library, saw this as the principal value of her collection, which grew from a group of her own childhood favorites to a much more expansive archive that includes important books, manuscripts, and artwork. The collection that Betsy Shirley created is now a solid research trove. Since her passing in 2004, it has grown with the acquisition of significant groups of authors' and artists' papers and many rare printed volumes. The 2007 volume, *Drawn to Enchant*, featured many of the striking pieces of artwork in the Shirley collection. This new volume explores the scholarly approach to the

(*opposite*) Some of the many "Juvenile Amusements" from the so-titled book published in Albany, NY, by G.J. Loomis and Co., 1822.

9

collection. A group of writers who specialize in the study and teaching of the history of children's literature were invited to explore topics of interest to them.

Most of the contributors began with a particular author, artist, publisher, or theme found in the Shirley collection, then expanded their work with research, often in other rare book and manuscript libraries—in several instances citing connections and discoveries among different collections. All of the writers represented here have spent time in residence at the Beinecke Library—as fellows, lecturers, and researchers—and their voices, heard in the impressive variety of subjects covered, make us attentive to the possibilities of understanding the history of children's literature.

The one broad limit that can be found in these essays was imposed by the nature of the Shirley Collection. By definition, it is about American children's literature. However, as any scholar knows, we cannot talk about American children's books without the need to refer to English books, French books, German books—and the other forebears and contemporaries that provide context and comparison. One other observation will also inform the reader. The books discussed are those that have achieved some form of acclaim and longevity. While there are thousands of picture books and novels that have had strong effects on readers, those in the Shirley Collection are mainly those that survived because they were identified as having long-lasting importance. So then, knowing that this deck of essays is slightly stacked—due the curated nature of the Shirley Collection—you, dear reader, are invited to enjoy the many paths to understanding the literature of childhood offered by the assembled cast of talented writers.

One entryway to the world of children's literature is to understand the cultures of the publishing industry and the prevailing educational philosophies that were contemporaneous with specific books. Pádraic Whyte takes a look at the mythology books of Padraic Colum and provides ways to understand why this genre was extremely popular in the early twentieth century. In his essay on Margaret Wise Brown and Leonard Weisgard's *Noisy Book* series, Leonard Marcus reveals the philosophy behind a new type of book intended for a changing mid-twentieth-century audience. A pair of more personal essays approaches the effect of reading and a life of scholarship. Gregory Maguire's meditation on his own childhood reading provides a key to how books became his path to writing. In his wide-ranging essay, Brian Alderson offers a look back at important titles and striking images that he encountered during his career as a scholar of children's literature.

A revival of the study of the history of the book informs a trio of essays in this volume. Elizabeth Frengel uses the approach to look at illustrations in several of Ludwig Bemelmans' early books to investigate his working technique and life story. Beverly Clark's research shows how the graphic depictions of the March sisters and their mother in *Little Women* were a crucial part of how that classic novel was parsed by a reading public. My own contribution is a look at what was once an immensely popular theme of children's books in centuries past: happy deaths of pious infants.

Research into children's literature can also afford an opportunity for scholars to look closely at archives and discover little known histories and treasures. Laura Wasowicz's examination of original artwork for books published by McLoughlin Bros., based on her consultation of several different archives, shows how these books were constructed for a quickly expanding nineteenth-century market. Patrick Kiley's survey of nineteenth-century books about farming gives us a look at some rare volumes that provide insight into American cultural practices. Sandra Markham, the archivist who has worked most closely with the Shirley Collection, examines a group of eighteenth- and nineteenth-century copybooks that turn out to have deep connections to American history.

The academic practices of close reading and analysis are well represented in a group of essays that look at what can be discovered in the words and pictures of children's books. Jill Campbell's connection of

Robinson Crusoe to the work of Karl Marx shows the value of understanding an author's early reading. Katie Trumpener gives three important works by Robert McCloskey a close examination to understand what they say about home, family, and motherhood. Heather Klemann looks at the most contemporary topic in this collection—parenting in the works of Mo Willems—and reveals emotional complexities in this celebrated author's works.

A pair of essays addresses topics that are—to use a word that is increasingly in wide use in academia—"problematic." Books for children are sometimes filled with presentations of culture and depictions of the world that can be seen, at a remove, to be awkward, insensitive, or offensive. Because they were created to give simplistic rules for navigating what are, in truth, very complicated social relationships, many books for children do not age well as society becomes increasingly more diverse and as readers mature. In short, children's literature is problematic in the same way that childhood itself is problematic—full of conflicting messages about complex concepts. While most of the contributors to this collection address some aspects of the problematic nature of children's literature, two writers confront the subject quite directly. In her essay on Langston Hughes's and Arna Bontemps's *Popo and Fifina, Children of Haiti*, Michelle Martin recovers the book as one of the first to present black lives sympathetically to a broad audience. JoAnn Conrad's essay on the work of the d'Aulaires makes us realize that biographies of authors who wrote about national cultural mythologies can be invented in ways similar to the books they made.

The assembled contributors represent a variety of perspectives for looking at the history of children's literature. There are academics who use the language of critical inquiry; there are librarians and archivists who focus on information we can glean from rare materials; there are aficionados who infuse their essays with the still vibrant passions that were sparked in them as young readers. All of the writers in the collection begin at the point of passion and then explore. That's one of the great aspects of children's books—while they can be read for deeper meanings now that we are adults, they can continue to provide the joy we found in them on first reading.

The authors and I hope that you will learn a lot from this collection, and perhaps be able to read and see well-known books in new, exciting, and even challenging ways.

Timothy Young

A NOTE ON THE EDITORIAL PROCESS: While a general approach was taken to bring the essays into a standard format, some stylistic choices particular to each author, including citation formats (e.g. some page number are cited in the text, while others are cited in footnotes) have been left unchanged. Notably, some individual choices governing capitalization and punctuation have also been retained. Thus, the essays, in the way they appear in print, convey something more of the voices of the authors.

———⊱⊰———

Gratitude is expressed for support during the creation of this book to Betsy Michel, Nancy Kuhl, Megan Mangum, Christa Sammons, E.C. Schroeder, John Hill, the wonderful staff of the Beinecke Library and to all of the talented authors who contributed.

GREGORY MAGUIRE

The Haunted Stacks
or A Reader's Guide to Writing Fiction

I'm told, by my husband, that I have an unusual capacity for remembering my dreams. Now, I concede that recounting one's dreams over breakfast is impolite. That practice can overtax the marital dull-o-meter, and one's dreams are *de facto* dull to others because dreams are composed in a private language of images and secret codes. So I do try to control myself. But things slip out.

My patient husband is an artist, a painter of abstracts and landscapes. Of his own nocturnal visions, at dawn he remembers bupkis. In response to my recitations, he wonders if the capacity to recall one's dreams in narrative form is a characteristic of the fiction writer. I can hardly take in a word he says. I have to lumber away and shower to try to escape the weight and significance, the *influence* of a midnight mood or *une aventure de rêve*. A picture book by Harve Zemach, *Awake and Dreaming*, begins, "There was once a young man who might have been happy had it not been for his dreams, which were so wild and strange and terrifying that a night's sleep left him more exhausted than a day's work." I am that man. That man be me.

The recurring dream I'll describe (briefly) isn't one of the terrifying ones. Rather, it's one of my favorites, but it leaves me with a sense of longing, something like divine discontent. "Heavenly hurt, it gives us..."

I am a child, or anyway, child-like in my needs and appetites. I'm alone in a room lined with bookshelves. As I type this out for you to read, I want to revise, upscale the space into a room with oak paneling,

(*opposite*) Detail of dust jacket, *Green Knowe* by Lucy Boston. Illustration by Peter Boston, 1954.

15

with light slanting through mullioned windows, but that's my waking mind taking over. Really, the dream doesn't pay attention to the setting. What is important is the presence of books on the shelves.

I'm pawing through favorite books, arranged alphabetically as in a proper library. While in some iterations of this dream, the books seem to be by Virginia Woolf or E.M. Forster, the first time I experience it, the most powerful time, I am reveling in the books of a favorite children's author, Jane Langton. I adored her books as a child and I read her spooky, cerebral fantasies over and over. In the dream, I'm tenderly fingering the beloved volumes—*The Diamond in the Window*, *The Swing in the Summerhouse*, *The Fledgling*, and others, with their gorgeous covers by Erik Blegvad—when I spy a heretofore unknown companion volume. For some reason this addition to the canon has never been advertised on any dustjacket featuring "Other books by Jane Langton." The secret treasure-book has all my favorite characters in it, and new line drawings by Blegvad. It's familiar and foreign at once. I have discovered it. My hands tremble to touch it.

When I awake, the realization that such a book doesn't exist is a dreadful comedown. Akin—and I mean this—to dreaming of a deceased lover, and having to endure the refreshed pain of separation by daylight.

The notion of the ideal library is very Borges. "I have always imagined that Paradise will be a kind of library," is a popular if shaggy translation of a line from his "Poema de los Dones." When I consider the research collection amassed by Betsy Beinecke Shirley, I'm drawn into the dream library of the mind. Not only the thrill over what *has* been written, what *has* been published and cherished and preserved for us, but also what might have been done, or what might yet be done. Proof to point: behold, here, a sample drawing Maurice Sendak worked up for a proposed reissue of *The Hobbit*. Gandalf, by Sendak! In my dream library, the whole book exists, and I can almost open it to study an inspired collaboration. My dream library allows me access to the idea of this impossible edition.

We think of mentors and muses as individuals, but the idea of the library itself is a kind of mentor, or anyway a residence hall of mentors and muses.

As a new graduate student at Simmons College in 1977, I wrote a college paper on the figure of the mentor in children's fantasy novels. I don't recall everyone I considered, but here are a few: Uncle Freddy, from those Jane Langton books, a kind of addled, rattled intellect with transcendentalist leanings;

the three guardian witches from *A Wrinkle in Time* (Mrs. Who, Mrs. Whatsit, and Mrs. Which); Gandalf; Merlin; and Ogion from *A Wizard of Earthsea*; perhaps Mary Poppins. It wasn't a very organized paper and I don't recall any thesis or conclusion. Perhaps the intent was merely catalogic. Or reverential. Or aspirational.

Maurice Sendak, Study of Bilbo Baggins and Gandalf for *The Hobbit*, 1967.

Now I see the presence of those wise adult figures in children's books as being stand-ins for their creators: Gandalf and his ilk are shape-shifting versions of Tolkien & Co. So I now regard the library as a sanctum sanctorum rather than a moratorium, a fever-powered pantheon where influential writers live on in the guise of their fictional dramatis personae.

As I recall, the first novel I read entirely on my own, when I was about seven, was L. M. Boston's *The Children of Green Knowe*. The queer, almost *Twilight Zone* story takes place in Cambridgeshire, England. A lonely boy goes to stay with an elderly relative. He finds her ancient stone house occasionally visited by the friendly phantoms of children who died of the plague in the seventeenth century. It is so convincingly told that, at the time, I could hardly believe it wasn't true. My virgin exposure to prose style.

Many years later, I realize my child self responded with a kind of thrill to this novel not so much because of the ghost story, which is gentle and, like dreams, unresolved, but because of the literary atmosphere conjured by the author. You see, even before the ghosts materialize, the story is haunting in a deeper sense, from the first page. Here's the isolated child, Tolly, arriving at the house, which has stood a thousand years. Terrible rains and floods require him to be delivered the last leg of his journey in a rowboat. Listen to this small Odysseus making his first landfall.

> Mr. Boggis handed him the lantern and told him to kneel up in the bows with it and shout if they were likely to bump into anything. They rowed round two corners in the road and then in at a big white gate. Toseland waved the lantern about and saw trees and bushes standing in the water, and presently the boat was rocked by quite a strong current and the reflections of the lantern streamed away in elastic jigsaw shapes and made gold rings round the tree trunks. At last they came to a still pool reaching to the steps of the house, and the keel of the boat grated on gravel. The windows were all lit up, but it was too dark to see what kind of a house it was, only that it was high and narrow like a tower. (p. 15).

The cover art conveys the same moment. Consider this boy's experience of the world: it is strange, elastic, recognizable but weird, glowing in the dark. Everyone arrives in life with a similar curiosity and apprehension.

Perhaps, if we all thought of the earliest books in our reading memories, we could sift and find in them some aspect of the *Odyssey*, because that epic of Ancient Greece is also an epic of Life, and the waves that spread out from the bow of the ancient triremes touch all our shores.

Nor do we know where our journeys will take us. Due to my compulsive childhood reading, I respected from early days the power of a great writer to change lives. L.M. Boston—called Lucy—and her writing colleagues changed mine. As I never fell out of love of the power of story over children, even when I was grown, my profession brought me to write for children and adults and to start and run nonprofits that fostered literacy in the young. To that end, nearly 30 years after reading *The Children of Green Knowe*, I was in England, to arrange for a Cambridge college to host an international literary conference. My English hosts brought me out to the old house in the fens that had been the inspiration for the Green Knowe story. The writer, now in her 90s, lived there still. She was the very picture of the old crabbity woman who had greeted Tolly in her novel. The house was the same—the graveled drive, the topiary yews, the stone fortress. It's known not as Green Knowe but as the Manor House at Hemingford Grey. The oldest continually inhabited house in England, they say. But venturing, with very American shyness, not only into the home of the author who had taught me about literary magic, but into the setting of that very ghost story—well, I was now Tolly, and the laughing child—unseen on the staircase, or within the stand of bamboo in the garden where, in another story, an escaped gorilla had sought refuge—well, that child was me. I was the ghostly child reader in a house of ghosts:

> As they rested there, tired and dreamy and content, he thought he heard the rocking-horse gently moving, but the sound came from Mrs. Oldknow's room, which opened out of the music room. A woman's voice began to sing very softly a cradle song that Tolly had learnt and dearly loved:
>
> *Lully Lulla, Thou little tiny child*
> *By by, Lully, Lullay.*
> *O sisters too, how may we do*
> *For to preserve this day*
> *This poor youngling*
> *For whom we sing*
> *By by, Lully, Lullay.*
>
> "Who is it?" he whispered.
>
> "It's the grandmother rocking the cradle," said Mrs. Oldknow, and her eyes were full of tears.
>
> "Why are you crying, Granny? It's lovely."
>
> "It is lovely, only it is such a long time ago. I don't know why that should be sad, but it sometimes seems so."
>
> The singing began again.

"Granny," whispered Tolly again with his arm through hers, "whose cradle is it? Linnet is as big as I am."

"My darling, this voice is much older than that. I hardly know whose it is. I heard it once before at Christmas."

It was queer to hear the baby's sleepy whimper only in the next room, now, and so long ago. "Come, we'll sing it too," said Mrs. Oldknow, going to the spinet. She played, but it was Tolly who sang alone, while, four hundred years ago, a baby went to sleep. (132-33)

I've been writing and publishing now for nearly forty years. Are there figures of beneficent mentors in my own fantasy novels? Of enchanted libraries? Perhaps not as many as you'd expect given my childhood and my dreamy adulthood. In *Wicked*, my wizard of Oz is not only a charlatan but a despot. In that adult book and in my YA novel *Egg & Spoon*, my witches—the Wicked Witch of the West and Baba Yaga, respectively—are failed insurrectionists or loopy grandees of non sequitur. True, the Grimmerie in *Wicked* is a magic book—maybe that counts. A current project I'm monkeying about with is the life of Drosselmeyer, the mysterious godfather who gives the enchanted Nutcracker to Clara in the weird-ass E. T. A. Hoffmann story that inspired the more famous Tchaikovsky ballet. I doubt, though, that my Drosselmeyer will be as Chiron to Achilles, as Socrates to Plato, as Merlin to Wart. In his own frail and compromised way, Drosselmeyer may be a little bit of Gregory Maguire, more resolutely uncertain than benignly wise. As I conceive of Drosselmeyer today, I realize—through writing this piece—that he will also be a little bit haunted. But by what? I shall have to go back to my story in a moment, to lift the lamp higher, to find out.

It does occur to me, as a result of writing this essay, that the nature of my own creative interests are, indeed, related to the notion of the imaginary library. In writing *Wicked* and its three sequels, I have added to the limited number of books about Oz in the ur-children's library of the mind. *Confessions of an Ugly Stepsister* and *Mirror Mirror* are my homages to Grimm, rooting those childhood stories into my more adult understanding of European history and the significant values of the cultures in which those stories became immortalized by collectors and retellers. *Matchless* is my short story wrapped around Andersen's "The Little Match Girl." And what if Lewis Carroll had gone back to Wonderland? *After Alice*, published in 2015 on the 150th anniversary of the original publication of *Alice's Adventures in Wonderland*, is my attempt to satisfy for others the need I have, the need I dream about. To discover yet more dream books in the library of the mind.

Do you remember (if you are a certain age) what it felt like to come upon *The Once and Future King* for the first time? Ah, there's Merlin, that miracle-man, living backwards in time, comically capable of all kinds of spouting anachronisms that fly over the heads of Wart and the rest of Camelot—but not of us. T.H. White took the Arthurian cycle and bravely, heretically, retold the story as if no one had ever heard of it before. The truth of my childhood reading is that I sailed from *The Children of Green Knowe* to *The Once and Future King*. Though I stopped at a thousand other enchanted islands along the way, those two volumes bracket my magic ten years of reading. From age seven to seventeen, everything I could imagine was somehow possible, and was present in prose, however codified or secret. I am still a reader of fiction a half-century later because I was freely persuaded by T.H. "Merlin" White to trust in his authority. To trust, and, I guess, to emulate his nerve, as a worthy way to spend a life.

For at this end of my life, I am no longer the orphan boy in the rowboat, approaching the lighted haven of the library. I have become the hoary old boatman, lifting my own lamp and trying to indicate, if not benefits of my own hard-won wisdom, at least my conviction that to find one's self in a haunted library is not to find one's self alone. Oh no. In dreams we are alone. In a library we are citizens and comrades, in association with one another and with the mentors and muses who beckon us home.

They all drew to the fire, mother in the big chair, with Beth at her feet; Meg and Amy perched on either arm of the chair, and Jo leaning on the back. — PAGE 12.

BEVERLY LYON CLARK

The Writer, the Family, or the House?

Visualizing Jo March's Genius in the Nineteenth Century

Some years ago, Betsy Shirley generously shared with me a transcript of a letter whose original she'd given to the Beinecke Library, an 1883 letter from Louisa May Alcott to Thomas Bailey Aldrich, editor of the *Atlantic Monthly* and author of *The Story of a Bad Boy* (1870). In it, Alcott mentioned that her publisher "once told me that you 'hated' me because my little works sold well."[1] In the mid-nineteenth century, having works that sold well might lead to some professional jealousy but was not yet divorced from being highly esteemed as a writer; Charles Dickens, after all, was both successful and esteemed. When Alcott published *Little Women* in 1868, in short, one could have both a genius for success and genius as a writer; one could also have a genius for a particular set of skills, perhaps even for domesticity—as nineteenth-century illustrators of the novel implicitly recognized.

Within the text of *Little Women* the idea of genius plays out in varied ways. Little Demi Brooke, for instance, "early developed a mechanical genius which delighted his father, and distracted his mother, for he tried to imitate every machine he saw."[2] In contrast, the artistic Amy, the youngest of the four March sisters, says, "talent isn't genius, and no amount of energy can make it so" (317). Of the various meanings of *genius* in the nineteenth century, I'm going to focus on two: one that indicates that one possesses a natural bent or ability, like Demi; the

(*opposite*) FIGURE 1. Perched indeed. May Alcott, 1868.

other, that one is extraordinarily gifted, the meaning implied by Amy's differentiation between talent and genius.[3] With reference to the genius of Jo March, the second oldest sister and the author's surrogate in this loosely autobiographical novel, the question might be whether she is sufficiently gifted as a writer to be considered a genius in our usual modern sense, or else simply has a natural bent for something, such as domesticity or family.

Since women were often seen as innately domestic in the nineteenth century, then, perhaps, Alcott's Jo has a genius for domesticity. Well, okay, maybe not Jo, given that she's likely to overcook asparagus and sprinkle strawberries with salt instead of sugar. Yet she does seem to have a genius for—a natural bent for—family connectedness. Jo is the one who wishes she "could marry Meg [her]self, and keep her safe in the family," instead of seeing her older sister leave and start a separate household (161).

On the other hand, with respect to *genius* as meaning extraordinarily gifted, consider the description of Jo's writing process. From time to time she falls into what she calls a vortex, closeting herself and "writing away at her novel with all her heart and soul." Members of the family occasionally venture to ask, "Does genius burn, Jo?" (211). The description is partly humorous, poking fun. Jo wears a "scribbling suit," for instance, which includes "a black pinafore on which she could wipe her pen at will, and a cap of the same material, adorned with a cheerful red bow, into which she bundled her hair when the decks were cleared for action" (211). "She did not think herself a genius by any means," the narrator assures us, but she happily abandoned herself to this blissful state when the fit came on—for the week or two that the "divine afflatus" lasted—emerging from it "hungry, sleepy, cross, or despondent" (211). In short, her divine inspiration is deflated, somewhat, by its aftermath.

As Keren Fite has argued, Jo negotiates between Transcendentalist ideals of the solitary inspired artist and a more communal and contextual approach to literary creation, implicitly recognizing that "a work of art is the product of the artist's complex negotiations of personal aspirations, familial conditions, commercial tastes and demands, and social constraints."[4] I'd contend that Jo, like Alcott, draws strategically on Romantic tropes of divinely inspired genius: she writes in a garret and can become engrossed in a frenzy of writing that lasts for weeks. Doing so frees her from household chores and gives her space in which to write—even as Alcott's writing celebrates the family connectedness from which the frenzy frees her.

So how do nineteenth-century artists illustrate these varied understandings of genius? First, a few words on how illustrations function in books for young readers. In a well-made picture book, both words and images are necessary for the narrative. There is a synergy between the two; neither alone communicates what both together do. In contrast, in an illustrated book—a novel whose text is illuminated by an occasional image—the images can have an ironic relationship to the words or otherwise amplify the text but they are usually less integral to the narrative. As a result, critics generally treat images as subordinate to the words, even if not always appropriately.[5]

With respect to illustrations in *Little Women*, Jo's genius can be depicted in at least three ways. One way of expressing her natural bent for family connectedness is through a direct image of the four March sisters, with or without their mother, Marmee. A more indirect way of figuring the family, or of figuring domesticity, is to depict the domicile. And as for the other meaning of genius, that of being extraordinarily gifted, Jo's genius can be visualized as Jo writing.

In the nineteenth century and since, artists have often accentuated family togetherness in *Little Women*. In the first edition of Part 1 of the novel (1868), the frontispiece, opposite the title page, features the four sisters and Marmee (FIGURE 1).[6] The artist, May Alcott, Louisa's youngest sister, corresponds to the artistic Amy in the novel. Her much-criticized frontispiece pictures what many readers would consider the heart of the book; it was the first rendition of a scene that would become iconic, the clustering sisters evoking family togetherness. One critic has read this image, together with another one of Meg looking in a mirror, as May's critique of the "disfiguring vision of the feminine ideal,"[7] but here it's not just the individual bodies that are out of kilter. For despite the somewhat harmonious circular family cluster, the five figures are disproportionate with one another and are also gazing in odd directions. Just what is it that Meg, on the right, is looking at behind the chair? Nor is the image fully coordinated with its caption, which states that Meg and Amy perch on arms of the chair. What perch? Indeed, what arms? As for May's other images, one shows Amy (or possibly Jo) skating. In the text, Jo is angry with Amy for having burned her manuscript and fails to warn her sister of thin ice, so Amy falls through the ice and nearly drowns. May's image, however, simply shows a stylish, serene skater; she was the first of numerous illustrators who have promoted fashion over action and ignored the undercurrent of anger. May likewise chose not to depict the other outlet for Jo's genius: Jo's writing. Still, it's relatively rare for illustrated editions of *Little Women* to feature an image of Jo writing. More often they have focused on romance or, like May, on fashion and domesticity.

The next illustrator for the novel was apparently Hammatt Billings; he produced six new images, four of them for Part 2 of *Little Women* (1869). Alcott was not pleased with his illustrations, especially his renderings of Amy and the neighbor Laurie,[8] but she is not on record as complaining about the images of Jo. Billings was the first artist to provide an image of Jo in a vortex (FIGURE 2). Jo's writing may be thematically important in the novel, but it does not offer visual opportunities for depicting a key turning point in the plot, or a dramatic action, or even the delights of fashion—common motives for artists' choices when illustrating *Little Women*. An additional challenge is how to capture a vortex visually and depict genius burning. How does one create something other than a static image of a woman at a desk? Billings included some of the trappings of conventional womanhood. Jo appears to be wearing an earring, not what one would expect of someone so cavalier

JO IN A VORTEX.

Every few weeks she would shut herself up in her room, put on her scribbling suit, and
"fall into a vortex," as she expressed it. — PAGE 44.

about dress (indeed, such an ornament is deemed vain in Alcott's *Eight Cousins* [1875]). She has the tiny feet common in nineteenth-century images of dainty women, and even if her facial expression seems focused, it seems more placid than intense. Nevertheless, her cap is perched back on her head, strands of hair have broken free, she leans forward, and pages have scattered. Billings has captured the disarray and some of the frenzy of the vortex. Jo is also facing left, and in the grammar of illustrations for books in languages that read left to right, having figures face left encourages us to pause over the image and may suggest some impediment to forward movement, some disarray, if you will. I find Billings's picture one of the more effective images of Jo in a vortex. Of the four main illustrators of *Little Women* in the nineteenth century, fully half of them, including Billings, attempted to depict Jo's genius burning—a much higher percentage than for the more than a hundred artists who have illustrated the novel since.[9]

The next significant illustrations are for the 1880 *Illustrated Edition*, for which Frank Merrill eventually created more than 200 images. In a letter to her editor, Alcott praised his drawings as "capital" and as displaying "a fertile fancy and quick hand," "improving on my hasty pen-and-ink sketches. What a dear rowdy boy Teddy [Laurie] is."[10] Although I'm not especially impressed by Merrill's depiction of faces, his images are technically—or at least anatomically—the best of the nineteenth-century illustrations of *Little Women*.

Given the enormous number of illustrations in the 1880 edition (the modal number in subsequent illustrated editions is probably eight), it's not surprising that Merrill addressed scenes that later artists have often depicted: the family tableaux, fashionable young ladies, and romantic moments, such as Jo and Professor Bhaer under their umbrella. But Merrill also spotlighted humor and drama more than other illustrators have. When a group of young people plays a storytelling game, for instance, Jo tells of a knight who took a pinch of snuff and then "sneezed seven times so violently that his head fell off" (107). Merrill illustrated the knight with his head flying off, depicting the whimsically violent fruits of Jo's invention.[11] In the skating scene, Merrill anticipated later illustrators who have been willing to explore the consequences of Jo's anger, a character trait that counters whatever genius she might have for tranquil domesticity. His image shows the rescue, thus engaging directly with the accident, even if he provided a relatively reassuring view. For his Laurie has already reached Amy to rescue her, and the near-horizontal lines of the image convey some stability and mitigate some of the danger of her fall through the ice. In the last few decades—after critics started excavating the novel's subtexts of anger, aggression, and ambition, in the wake of the republication of Alcott's pseudonymous sensation stories, starting in 1975—illustrators have been more will-ing to show anger and danger. They have done so, in part, by focusing directly on Amy's fall. The accident underscores the dangers of female independence. For Jo's ambition and anger have clouded her judgment, and Amy could die. Merrill may attenuate some of the danger, but he still gives some play to what have since been seen as the violent under-currents raging beneath the benign surface of the story—another kind of vortex, if you will.

Yet another refreshing choice by Merrill has to do with height. Recent scholars have pointed to the changes that the publisher made in the text of the 1880 edition that Merrill illustrated, probably with-out Alcott's explicit approval.[12] The language is less colloquial than in the first edition and the characters conform somewhat more to gender ideals. In Part 1, for instance, Jo's comrade and would-be suitor, Laurie, is no longer described as the same height as Jo but taller than she is. Critics who study visual images often pay attention to who is higher on the page—who, in effect, dominates. So how does Merrill place Jo and Laurie, especially in Part 1, now that the textual Laurie, in 1880, is taller than she is? Visually, the two figures are still often on a par, and sometimes Jo is somewhat higher. Even in Part 2, after the textual Laurie has grown to be about six feet tall, the visual Laurie towers above Jo and others when we first see him, but in later illustrations, there's more parity—even when he sprawls and dominates the horizontal space

on a sofa, he's not higher on the page. In Merrill's romantic and domestic pairings, in contrast, the men tend to dominate their partners. Laurie is given visual dominance over his eventual wife Amy more often than not; John Brooke dominates Meg in a conventional courting scene; Professor Bhaer is generally higher on the page than Jo (except when both are hidden behind that umbrella). Merrill seems attuned to the power relationships in the novel. When Jo and Laurie are comrades, they often are visually on a par, but in romantic relationships the man tends to dominate. Surprisingly few subsequent artists have managed such visual equality between Jo and Laurie.

Merrill also provided three images of Jo (or perhaps Alcott) writing. The first appears at the head of the Table of Contents in many of the post-1880 editions issued by Roberts Brothers. I'd often paused, while examining what turned out to be a later edition, over the tailpiece for the Table of Contents. Some of Merrill's images function as emblems or allegories, and thus the key that a nude child is holding in the tailpiece is emblematic: the list of chapter titles is a key to the book.

Yet the image still struck me as a little off-key, as it were. It was only when I finally looked at an 1880 edition that the nude child seemed fully apt. In that early edition, at the head of the Table of Contents, is an image of three nude children investigating the contents of a trunk (FIGURE 3)—so it follows that in the second image, with its single child, the key is to unlock the book's contents. Now the Victorians were generally more tolerant of images of nude children than our present generation is, despite their reputation for prudery. They tended to see such images, pre-Freud, as innocent. Still, it's possible that the image was replaced out of a sense of decorum; the child with a key may have seemed close enough to a wingless Cupid (and a couple of Cupids do appear later in the book) to remain. Then again, I can't object to the image that replaced the headpiece. The nude figures that cluster about the chest evoke a cuteness that is ultimately condescending to children, I would argue, in a way that the text rarely is. The replacement is not condescending but rather respectful of Jo (or Alcott) as a writer. It shows a thoughtful figure gazing to the right as if contemplating what we readers will encounter in the rest of the book. Whatever disarray is caused by genius burning is signaled by the billowing of her skirt and the odd cap perched on her head.

Another image of a young woman writing appears in Part 1 and shows Jo in a garret, where she is "seated on the old sofa writing busily, with her papers spread out upon a trunk before her" (121). Jo leans forward, absorbed, and the slight disarray of the papers hints at her creative vortex, also perhaps the way she is positioned somewhat off-center in the image, throwing us slightly off balance, but the disarray of the vortex is not yet in full force in either text or image. In Part 2 of *Little Women*, in the context of the vortex-and-genius discussion, Merrill again shows Jo writing. Here, his gesture toward the disarray of the vortex is what looks like a nightcap, her "scribbling cap," with its jaunty salute. Yet otherwise, despite her intent focus on her writing, neither she nor her papers are in conspicuous disarray, unlike in Billings's earlier illustration.

Then there are the variant frontispieces for this illustrated edition. As the first image that we encounter after opening the book, the frontispiece sets the tone for the novel, provides a context, and perhaps gives a foretaste of pleasures to come. I've identified three different ones for nineteenth-century printings illustrated by Merrill and issued by Roberts Brothers. These show, variously, a portrait, a house, or a five-some. Each memorializes a different aspect of genius. The frontispiece in the earliest version is a portrait of Alcott. Newspaper notices commented at the time that a portrait "has never before found place in any of her books" and that "Miss Alcott herself graces the frontispiece, her face beaming with kindness and good will, while an expression of deep thought lights up her features as if she were far away in some fancy flight in the land of dreams."[13] This portrait might in part be a concession to fans who clamored for a photograph and an autograph (reproduced below the portrait in facsimile), but it also validated Alcott as a writer, for authors accorded the honor of a portrait frontispiece had stature. The image might not capture the creative vortex of the writing process, but its presence attests to the achievement of something like genius in the sense of being extraordinarily gifted.

In subsequent editions, especially the less expensive trade editions with only a few illustrations, the frontispiece is an image of the Alcotts' Orchard House in Concord (FIGURE 4)—for instance, in copies of *Little Women* that I have located dated 1885, 1893, and 1916. Of the dozens of houses in which Alcott lived during her lifetime, Orchard House is the one most closely associated with her. Now a museum, it was where she wrote at least some sections of the novel, and it provided much of the architecture for the March family's house in *Little Women*. This frontispiece, not by Merrill but by Edmund H. Garrett, memorializes the genius for domesticity. The house becomes, in effect, a metonym for the labor of women within the domicile and also for the family, viewed at a distance. Entering the book becomes a way of entering the house of the Alcotts, and, indeed, Garrett's image includes a bright path inviting us to ramble from the bottom of the image to the house in the middle.

(*opposite*) FIGURE 1. Fencing in Orchard House. Edmund H. Garrett, 1880.

Home of the Little Women.

"They all drew to the fire, mother in the big chair, with Beth at her feet." —Page 9.

FIGURE 5.
Nostalgically domestic?
"They all drew to the fire,
mother in the big chair,
with Beth at her feet."
Frank T. Merrill, 1880.

Yet the path is barred by a gate, the house fenced off. The caption reads "Home of the Little Women"; the shapes in the fence almost spell out "Orchard House," an alternate caption.[14] The captions invite us to conflate the fictional Marches and the Alcott family, as does the decision not only to include but also to give pride of place to an illustration of the Alcotts' Orchard House.

In general, house images are static and self-contained. Here and in subsequent editions of *Little Women*, illustrated houses are both inviting and a bit remote. The illustrators, largely male, who have provided the images, whether of Orchard House or of a dwelling not particularly associated with the Alcotts, seem to position themselves like Laurie early in the novel, on the outside: "I can't help looking over at your house," he tells Jo; "you always seem to be having such good times. I beg your pardon for being so rude, but sometimes you forget to put down the curtain at the window where the flowers are" (46). Garrett's image of Orchard House frames the domestic arena and the invisible family, the house in turn framed by two overarching trees. The picture is almost a keepsake, as if to hint that the book too, a dozen years after first publication, is a treasured memento.[15] Both portrait and house images are static, inviting us to pause before plunging into the book. One is a kind of imprimatur, urging us to reflect on the author; the other, an emblem both of domesticity and of the Concord that bespoke literary culture in the nineteenth century.

In contrast, the third variant of the frontispiece depicts a scene from within the novel, less overtly staking out a kind of eminence for *Little Women*, although this image too has emblematic functions. Merrill shows the four sisters and Marmee reading a letter from Father, who is away at war (FIGURE 5). The illustration appears internally in 1880 but was moved to the front in some editions from 1896 and later. This foregrounding hints at the ways in which, at the turn of the twentieth century, the novel was increasingly associated with a kind of traditional domesticity, embodying "the simpler ideals of life when girls stayed at home; embroidered book marks for Christmas presents, baked cakes and sent valentines unsigned"[16]—not precisely activities pursued by the March sisters. This inventive, nostalgic list suggests how the novel was increasingly positioned in the national imagination, a positioning signaled and fostered by the new frontispiece.

Of the many foursome and fivesome images by various artists, I find Merrill's quite effective. The accouterments with which the scene is graced are not knitting and sewing baskets but books and playful cats, and thus the sisters aren't totally subsumed by traditional domesticity. The right triangle formed by the figures gives the image a solid base yet also a sense of rising to the right—a sense of uplift, if you will, that is nevertheless well anchored, and an invitation to proceed to the rest of the book to the right while providing abundant detail to dwell on before doing so. All five figures gaze at the letter from Father, giving him an absent presence. Jo is behind the rest, slightly separated from them by the back of the chair and by the negative space outlining her head, even if she does lean toward them. She is also higher than the others, giving her a dominance that is aptly in tension with the figures' focus on Father's letter. Yet making this image the frontispiece, like the many subsequent March family portraits that serve as frontispieces or cover images in twentieth- and twenty-first-century editions, ultimately reinforces traditional domesticity. By the turn of the twentieth century, *Little Women* had become associated with a nostalgically constructed past, presumably evoking the traditional family—not the somewhat atypical March family, with its largely absent father, nor the very atypical Alcotts, who had attempted communal living at Fruitlands.

For a long time I thought that these comprised all the nineteenth-century illustrated editions of the novel, while the publisher and the Alcott heirs controlled it under copyright. But then I located another nineteenth-century illustrated edition, a British one that might have been pirated, which is to say, not officially granted copyright permission. It was published by the London Sunday School Union in 1897. In 1868, an occasional evangelical periodical had deemed *Little Women* insufficiently religious for Sunday school libraries—it offered "religion without spirituality, and salvation without Christ"[17]—but by the end of the century it was more fully accepted in religious circles.

The illustrator of the 1897 edition, Jessie T. Mitchell, provided eight illustrations for *Little Women*. Her choice of scenes might now seem idiosyncratic; then again, certain scenes had not yet been established as standard. Instead of a sickbed scene with the dying Beth, one that I'd have thought ideal for a Sunday school audience, there's Beth mourning the death of her bird. Instead of a skating scene just before or after Amy falls through the ice, there's Jo and Meg musing, early on, what to wear to the Gardiners' dance. Like May Alcott, Mitchell was more interested in the embellishments of fashion than in action scenes.

Mitchell did not include an image of Jo writing, but the frontispiece shows the character announcing that she's the author of a published story that her sisters have just listened to with appreciation (FIGURE 6). We see the fruits of Jo's genius, if not genius in the process of burning. This is Mitchell's one image of the four sisters, instead of the usual tight cluster that underscores Jo's genius for family connectedness. The sisters still overlap and look at one another, but it's a looser grouping than most visualizations of the four together, allowing each character somewhat more independence. The caption—"Your sister!"—reminds us of their family relationship but also reveals the author of the story that Alcott's surrogate, Jo, has been reading them, and thus the scene is a metaphor for the publication of Alcott's autobiographical novel, whose title page two sisters are looking toward. Meg may be knitting, and there may be a sewing basket near Amy's feet, but there's a book on the stand next to Meg. Women thus have access to learning while pursuing their domestic activities. Mitchell has updated the sisters' dress; they wear muttonchop sleeves from the 1890s rather than fashions from the 1860s.[18] Three sisters look at Jo, who holds a story paper. Jo and, to a lesser extent, her story, are thus their focus. It's Jo's writing, not Father's letter, that governs the novel in Mitchell's visualization. Her images later in the book are more conventional, yet this frontispiece establishes the framework for our reading. In the scores of illustrated editions that I've examined, I know of no other frontispiece that alludes to Jo's genius for writing.[19] And this one does so while invoking family togetherness, thus contextualizing said genius, in keeping with one of the nineteenth-century ideas of genius as not solitary but communicative and communal.

Thus, with respect to visualizing Jo's genius, a few nineteenth-century illustrations depict Jo writing; others foreground domesticity, featuring a family grouping or, indeed, the house. In the scores of illustrated editions of *Little Women* that have been published since 1868, most artists have stressed Jo and her sisters' genius for domesticity and for contributing to a

"YOUR SISTER!"

Frontispiece.] [*See page* 120.

FIGURE 6.
Kudos to the author, whether Jo or Alcott. Jessie T. Mitchell, 1897.

family, whether the family of origin or family by marriage. Sometimes the artists hint at disruptions of such domesticity, through humor or through depictions of anger and danger. Sometimes they distance themselves from the family by offering an exterior view of the house, perhaps hinting at an inviting coziness, and sometimes they try to convey Jo's and Alcott's genius for writing—although not as often as they depict the delectable fashions of the sisters, or the family harmony, or the heartache and triumph of romance. When illustrators do depict Jo writing, they usually simply show her seated at a desk or table and rarely capture the frenzy of her vortex. Yet the nineteenth-century illustrators who depicted some aspect of Jo's genius for writing did so with a prominence and insight that later illustrators have rarely emulated.

I am grateful to Lis Adams and Jan Turnquist for the opportunity to present an earlier version of this essay at the Summer Conversational Series at Orchard House in 2014 and to Ken Davignon for reproducing the image by Jessie Mitchell.

1 Alcott to Thomas Bailey Aldrich, 23 Oct. 1883, Yale Collection of American Literature, Beinecke Rare Book and Manuscript Library.

2 Louisa M. Alcott, *Little Women; or, Meg, Jo, Beth and Amy: Authoritative Text, Backgrounds and Contexts, Criticism*, ed. Anne K. Phillips and Gregory Eiselein (New York: Norton, 2004), 358. Subsequent references appear parenthetically in the text.

3 For additional discussion of the meanings of *genius* in the nineteenth century, see Anne E. Boyd, *Writing for Immortality: Women and the Emergence of High Literary Culture in America* (Baltimore: Johns Hopkins Univ. Press, 2004), 128.

4 Keren Fite, "The Veiled, the Masked, and the Civil War Woman: Louisa May Alcott and the Madwoman Allegory," in *Gilbert and Gubar's "The Madwoman in the Attic" After Thirty Years*, ed. Annette R. Federico (Columbia: Univ. of Missouri Press, 2009), 178.

5 For discussion of how illustrations by an artist like Mark English (1967) can function more like paintings inspired by the novel, works of art in their own right, counterpointing the text, see Beverly Lyon Clark, *The Afterlife of "Little Women"* (Baltimore: Johns Hopkins Univ. Press, 2014), 190-98.

6 Lauren Rizzuto has astutely discussed this image, likewise Hammatt Billings's of Jo in a vortex, in "Illustrating *Little Women*, or, Louisa, Jo, May and Amy," paper presented at the meetings of the Children's Literature Assn., June 2012. As Susan R. Gannon aptly observes, May's four amateurish illustrations are sometimes allegorical but also interestingly at odds with the text ("Getting Cozy with a Classic: Visualizing *Little Women* [1868–1995]," in *"Little Women" and the Feminist Imagination: Criticism, Controversy, Personal Essays*, ed. Janice M. Alberghene and Beverly Lyon Clark [New York: Garland, 1999], 105-112).

7 Sara R. Danger, "Wounded by Culture: Reading May Alcott's Illustrations for *Little Women* in Context," *Interfaces* 26 (2006–2007): 157.

8 Alcott to Elizabeth B. Greene, 1 April [1869], *The Selected Letters of Louisa May Alcott*, ed. Joel Myerson and Daniel Shealy (Boston: Little, 1987), 126.

9 There have probably been close to two hundred artists for editions in all languages.

10 Alcott to Thomas Niles, 20 July 1880, *Selected Letters*, 249.

11 Alcott's comment on this image: "Very good" ("Frank Thayer Merrill Drawings to Illustrate Roberts Brothers 1880 Edition of Louisa May Alcott's *Little Women*, [1880]," Finding Aid, Concord Public Library Special Collections, www.concordlibrary.org).

12 See Daniel Shealy, "Note on the Text," in *Little Women: An Annotated Edition*, by Louisa May Alcott, ed. Daniel Shealy (Cambridge, MA: Belknap Press of Harvard Univ. Press, 2013), ix-x; Anne K. Phillips, "Quinny-Dingles, Quirks, and Queer-Looking Men: 'Regularizing' *Little Women*," in *Critical Insights: "Little Women"*, ed. Gregory Eiselein and Anne K. Phillips (Ipswich, MA: Salem, 2015), 90-93.

13 Review of *Little Women*, *Boston Evening Transcript*, 22 November 1880, 6, reprinted in *Louisa May Alcott: The Contemporary Reviews*, ed. Beverly Lyon Clark (Cambridge: Cambridge Univ. Press, 2004), 88; review of *Little Women*, *Providence Daily Journal*, 22 December 1880, [5], reprinted in *Contemporary Reviews*, 90.

14 See also my discussion in *Afterlife*, 24.

15 In editions with one of the other frontispieces, this image is in the middle, between Parts 1 and 2; its distanced view of domesticity is thus less prominent, although one could argue that the image becomes the heart of the novel in yet another way.

16 To quote a review of the 1912 hit Broadway production of *Little Women* (Isma Dooly, "'Little Women' Dramatized," in In Woman's World, *Atlanta Constitution*, 28 January 1912, C6 [ProQuest]).

17 Review of *Little Women*, *Ladies' Repository* (Methodist), November 1868, 472, reprinted in *Contemporary Reviews*, 65. The Universalist journal with the same name, however, recommended the novel (December 1868, 472, reprinted in *Contemporary Reviews*, 66).

18 Relatively few illustrators dress the young women in clothes from the 1860s; most give them fashions from a slightly earlier time than the artist's own or choose eclectic items that simply seem old fashioned and charming.

19 Though the title pages of some later printings include the image that had been added as the headpiece to the late nineteenth-century Table of Contents.

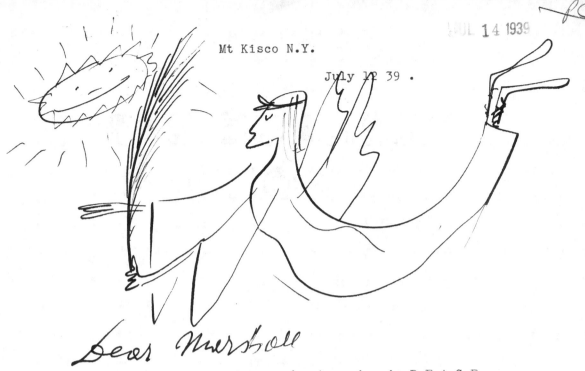

Mt Kisco N.Y.

July 12 39 .

Dear Marshall

ah - how good , how nice is P E A C E ,

the croix de guerre with palms for you . I am glad I sent

the letter , almost tore it up , because it seemed silly to me

too ,one should never write ,but I would have never heard the

wonderful news , why doesn't anybody tell me anything ? .

Incidentally , I think a superb news item will
be that in one year , <u>Victor</u> has been published in :

Town and Country ,
Life Class
Omnibook
and Readers Digest , A record I think ,

For gods sakes , have my correspondence destroyed
a volume of my letters even after my demise is nothing to look
forward to . In case you need any of my penwork , my adress for
the next three weeks is :
care of Mrs Bennet Bishop
Pudding Hill
East Hampton .L.I.

L'enfant du Malheur .

ELIZABETH FRENGEL

Ludwig Bemelmans
from *The Castle No. 9* to *Madeline*

"For gods sakes, have my correspondence destroyed [--] a volume of my letters even after my demise is nothing to look forward to."

—Ludwig Bemelmans to Marshall Best,
Bemelmans' editor at Viking Press. July 12, 1939.

What a shame it would have been if Best had heeded this directive. The letter is typical of Bemelmans' style: wry, witty and illustrated. In a glance it suggests something about Bemelmans as a writer and illustrator, even if the gist of the letter is obscure. The letter hints at Bemelmans' sense of humor and it displays his ability to set an illustration against a backdrop of text in a way that shows each to its best advantage. An earnestness of character is apparent, too.

The beauty of archival materials left behind by artists, musicians and writers rests in these revelations of artistic temperament. Archives are important, too, for the way in which they document the creative process. Fortunately for scholars, Betsy Beinecke Shirley made it her business to collect correspondence, original artwork, manuscript drafts, book dummies, and ephemera from the working papers of some of the most accomplished authors and illustrators working in children's book publishing in the twentieth century. Because of her visionary collecting and generous gifts, the Beinecke Rare Book & Manuscript Library now holds a range of materials that allow for important insights into the working life of Bemelmans, including published works, sketches and watercolor drawings, correspondence (much of it illustrated) and, the

(*opposite*) Letter from Bemelmans to Marshall Best, July 12, 1939.

41

jewels of the collection, book dummies for *The Castle No. 9* and *Madeline and the Bad Hat*. Like the letter that Bemelmans bade Best to destroy, these archives provide a unique vantage point from which to consider the life and work of an author and illustrator who proves to be much more complex than he may appear at first acquaintance.

Although Bemelmans holds a place among some of the most admired children's authors of the twentieth century, success did not come easily. In his childhood, especially, he experienced many turns of fortune and endured harrowing personal loss, but he showed resilience by applying the most vivid of his childhood memories to his art. He is best remembered as the creator of the yellow-hatted heroine, Madeline. How many of us wouldn't recognize, even today, these signature lines?

> *In an old house in Paris*
> *That was covered with vines*
> *Lived twelve little girls*
> *In two straight lines.*
> *They left the house at half-past-nine*
> *In two straight lines, in rain or shine.*
> *The smallest one was Madeline.*

However the Madeline books, seven in all, are by no means the sum total of Bemelmans' artistic and authorial achievement. Aside from the Madeline series, Bemelmans wrote some thirty works of autobiography, humor, travel, and memoir along with many other titles for children, including *Hansi*, his first published book, and the Newbery Honor book *The Golden Basket*. Bemelmans also published cartoons and was a frequent contributor to *The New Yorker*, distinguishing himself by landing his artwork on the cover and his prose inside the magazine. He exhibited his works on canvas in galleries in New York and Paris. Bemelmans was versatile, and he had a keen sense for the commercial, which led to a long and successful career.

Bemelmans seemed to do nothing half way. He sunk to the lowest depths and scaled amazing heights personally and professionally.

The barest biographical facts of Bemelmans' life read something like a picaresque novel. He worked as a waiter and restaurateur, did a stint in the U.S. Army, had a narrow miss with the law in Austria, worked in advertising, was a cartoonist, nearly lost his arm in a bicycling accident, married twice and maintained a wide circle of friends and produced lively correspondence. His autobiographical works, especially *My Life in Art*, are touched with colorful abstraction, not unlike his works on canvas, and are a delightful departure from the staid and sometimes sterile recitation of facts found in so many memoirs.

It is almost impossible to consider the work of Bemelmans without taking into account the interesting and sometimes traumatic events that shaped his imagination. Born in 1898, Bemelmans spent his earliest years in the town of Gmunden in the Austrian Tyrol, known for its scenic lakeside and riverfronts, swans, gardens, and pine-covered hills. Bemelmans never forgot the idyllic beauty of the Tyrol. Indeed it propelled him, indirectly, to his first success in children's book publishing.

In *My Life in Art*, Bemelmans recalls the sensory and seasonal delights of the first six years of his life. Gmunden, where his father owned a hotel called "The Golden Ship," seemed to Bemelmans like a set designed for a Viennese operetta. Without the distractions of television or radio, the days turned like the pages in a children's picture book, and they left a startling visual impression. "Large trees, whose leaves throbbed with color and who reached up to the sky—black tree trunks, sometimes brownish black and shining in the rain, with the leaves smelling—young in spring, and yellow in autumn, when each leaf in the light of afternoon was like a lamp lit up. Pink and violet clouds, and flowers very clear and close, for when one is small one can put one's face to them easily and breathe in their fragrance."[1] He writes of the snowmelt in spring, when icicles would fall from the eaves and the birds would drink in puddles made by the dripping water, the sun reflected in their pools. He recalls the last days of autumn, "the park cleared of the ochre leaves, the promenade swept, the trees now bare and the leaves sunk down to the bottom of the lake."[2]

Bemelmans' father, Lampert, was born in Belgium. He was an artist as well as an hotelier, and clearly he held influence over his son. Bemelmans describes him in *My Life in Art* as "an impatient perfectionist." These few words say plenty, and with hindsight they hint at the tragedy that was to come.

Bemelmans recorded comparatively few recollections or impressions of his mother, Franciska, from his childhood in Gmunden. Bemelmans spent these early years almost exclusively in the company of his young French governess. Because he could not pronounce the word *mademoiselle*, he called her "Gazelle"—and the name stuck. Bemelmans adored her, a feeling made apparent in his recollections. When he once fell into Lake Traunsee while playing with a swan, Gazelle jumped right in to save him. Bemelmans recalls the warmth of Gazelle's brown eyes in his memoirs. His father sometimes would come to the park to sketch Gazelle in various costumes and in various seasons.

But this idyll did not last long, as he recalled in his memoir: "And then one autumn the leaves in the park were not raked, the swan stood there forlorn and it was all over—all had come to an end. Papa was gone and so was my governess, and I wished he had run away with Mama and left me Gazelle."[3]

This abstract expression of the events that affected young Bemelmans' life suggest that they caused more pain than he could put into words, even some fifty years later.

Lampert Bemelmans left his wife, Franciska, and his son for a woman named Emmy, who would eventually become his second wife. At the time that he did this, Franciska was pregnant by Lampert—and so was Gazelle. Gazelle committed suicide. Franciska, a virtual stranger to Ludwig, fled with him to her parents' home in Regensberg, Germany.

In Regensberg, Bemelmans felt out of place. He spoke only French, and the clothes that he wore and the style of his long, blonde curls drew attention to his outsider status at the German public school he attended. Worse still, Franciska's father insisted that she divorce Lampert, an act that marked both her and her son with scandal, even though neither were to blame for their state of affairs. Franciska tried to fill the void in Ludwig's life left by Gazelle, but she was so shattered over her husband's desertion that she had little comfort to spare.

In the wake of this upheaval, Bemelmans did poorly at the public school and was eventually sent to a boarding school for underachieving students. He bridled against the German style of discipline, and felt wounded by his mother's attempts to obliterate an unhappy past.

Ludwig's situation in Germany seemed hopeless to Franciska, and she sent him back to the Tyrol to learn the hotel business from his Uncle Hans and Aunt Marie. While the project seemed to succeed at first, a now teenaged Bemelmans began drinking and got into a serious altercation with another hotel employee. He found himself faced with the choice between a military-style reform school or moving to America. Bemelmans chose America.

The sixteen-year-old Bemelmans arrived at Ellis Island on Christmas Eve, 1914, and his father Lampert, who was now living in America with his second wife, neglected to meet his son at the immigration inspection station. When the two finally met, they were not immediately reconciled. Bemelmans chose to make his own way, using letters of introduction from his aunt and uncle to get work at some of New York's best hotels, ultimately landing a post at the Ritz-Carlton.

Throughout this difficult period of his life, Bemelmans sketched and painted, an enthusiasm that never palled, even though his aunt and uncle scoffed at the idea of their nephew pursuing artistic ambitions. Bemelmans nearly lost his job at the Ritz-Carlton when a character sketch he had made on the back of a menu was accidentally handed to an important client. In the end, however, this close scrape led to a promotion, and Bemelmans found himself in the banquets department of the hotel, earning more money than he ever had before and finding himself with more leisure time to devote to drawing and painting. He thought of becoming a cartoonist, and in 1926 contributed "The Thrilling Adventures of Count Bric a Brac" to the *New York World*. The comic strip was short-lived, however.

Front endpapers from *Hansi*. New York: Viking, 1934.

Despite this upturn in his fortunes, Bemelmans' personal difficulties were not yet over. His short marriage to the English ballet dancer, Rita Pope, was tempestuous and ended in divorce. In 1929, Bemelmans resigned from the Ritz-Carlton to work exclusively as an artist but the timing couldn't have been worse, and the Depression forced him back to the hotel, where he had to endure derision from his co-workers.

In 1931, Bemelmans' younger brother, Oscar, died when he fell down an elevator shaft at the Ritz-Carlton. Ludwig felt intense remorse for having urged Oscar to leave Regensberg, which Oscar did reluctantly, to join his older brother in the hotel business in America.

Bemelmans was in a low point in his life when his luck turned around. May Massee, a children's book editor for Viking, came to a dinner party that Bemelmans hosted at his six-room apartment in New York. To brighten up the dreary view from his apartment, Bemelmans

46

painted scenes from the Tyrol on his window shades. When May Massee saw them, she encouraged Bemelmans to consider writing for children. He took Massee at her word and used his nostalgia for his childhood home of Gmunden to inspire his first book for children, *Hansi*, published by Viking Press in 1934.

Bemelmans' simplicity of style is readily apparent in this first book. The loose lines and choice of colors infuse a sense of joy to even the chilliest winter scenes of *Hansi*, which tells the story of a boy whose unexceptional career at school is happily interrupted by a visit to his Uncle Herman's house in the Austrian Tyrol. Although there are several sweeping double-page illustrations in full color, the text is heavy and dominates the storytelling. For the most part, the pictures embellish the tale and do not actively advance the narrative on their own account. The endpapers are the exception. Beneath the covers of *Hansi*, readers encounter an inviting cross-section of Uncle Herman's house, revealing the look, feel and character of the house and its inhabitants. The endpapers function like a pictorial signpost, pointing the way into the fictional narrative in a way that is welcoming and warm. They literally and metaphorically help the reader feel at home in the story.

Hansi sold reasonably well and gave Bemelmans the extra bit of confidence he needed to ask Madeleine Freund to marry him. Madeleine was a novice who had left her convent to pursue work as a model. Her unconventional path through life attracted Bemelmans, who nicknamed her "Mimi." The modest success of his first publication and the start of a happy marriage encouraged Bemelmans to work on his second book, *The Golden Basket*, which Viking published in 1936. *The Golden Basket* won critical acclaim, receiving the Newbery Honor in 1937. The story, which follows two little girls on a visit with their father to the Hôtel du Panier d'Or in Bruges, marks the first appearance of "Madeleine" and the "two straight lines" image that would become so famous in his later books. However, the idea for the Madeline books can be traced to the unhappiest period in Bemelmans' life, when his mother tried so desperately to make up for the loss of Gazelle. Through half-hidden tears, she would tell Ludwig stories about her childhood, specifically about life at the convent school in the Bavarian town of Altötting. She described how the schoolgirls would sleep in little beds arranged in two straight lines; how they would walk out, each dressed like the other, two-by-two, in two straight lines. Franciska's tales left an impression that Bemelmans visualized unforgettably in *The Golden Basket*, and later, in *Madeline*.

After *The Golden Basket* came Bemelmans' third book for children, *The Castle No. 9*, published by Viking in 1937. This eccentric story centers on "the good Baptiste," a servant, retired before his time and feeling at a loss. The quest for a new post takes him on a picturesque journey through the Tyrol to the home of Count Hungerburg-Hungerburg and the Castle Number Nine. It is a cautionary tale of sorts. The Count, bored with life in a way that mirrors Baptiste's ennui, decides to devise a new language, where objects are described literally rather than metaphorically. "I am worried about how wrongly all things are named in this world!," the Count says to Baptiste one languid afternoon. "What does 'dog' mean? It means nothing, and besides it is an insult!" And through a labored logic, the dog becomes "Friend-at-Both-Ends." Baptiste becomes "Bring-me."[4]

Not surprisingly, this language leads to great confusion. When the Castle Number Nine is accidentally set ablaze and Baptiste runs to the fire chief for help, the firemen cannot understand what the emergency is, as Baptiste tries to explain using the Count's new vocabulary. By the time the language is sorted out, the Castle Number Nine has been lost to the flames. Better to speak plainly, seems to be the message of this rollicking tale.

The artist's dummy for *The Castle No. 9*, which Betsy Beinecke Shirley acquired for her own collection before she gave it to the Beinecke Library, opens up the possibility for critical study of Bemelmans' working methods. The production of an artist's dummy is an integral step in the children's book publishing process. When an author is also the illustrator of a book, he or she will submit a dummy to the editor to consider it for publication. A dummy is essentially a map that shows the publisher how the text and the illustration will flow, and how the book will be constructed. The artist's dummy may seem to be a minor part of the process but it is, in fact, a crucial test of whether and how well a children's picture book will work. Often, the author uses a dummy to work out for himself or herself how the text and pictures fit together. In some cases, a dummy can make clear which parts of the text need illustrations, or what, if any, illustrations can be dropped. Likewise, illustration can sometimes take the place of text and vice-versa. Getting that balance perfectly pitched is no small feat.

The modern consideration of how illustrations work with texts to convey stories to children took shape in the nineteenth century when artists such as Randolph Caldecott began to examine their interrelation. Since then, scholars of children's literature have been theorizing about what makes a picture book grab hold of a child's imagination. Barbara Bader's 1976 survey, *American Picturebooks: From Noah's Ark to the Beast Within*, and Perry Nodelman's 1988 study, *Words about Pictures*, are excellent resources on the subject. Research suggests that a successful children's book rests on subtly nuanced interplay between text and illustration—a quality that can be difficult to pin down. Maurice Sendak calls this interplay "counterpoint," or the gold standard of harmony between text and illustration. For Sendak, the best children's books have pictures that supply information that is deliberately withheld from the text—and text that supplies information that may supersede or even contradict the imagery. "Words are left out—but the picture says it. Pictures are left out—but the word says it."[5] Successful picture book authors create a narrative that is hinged on the flow of text and imagery, where the reader finds surprise and pleasure in turning every page.

Bemelmans' dummy for *The Castle No. 9* provides material evidence for how he thought about the relationship between text and image. Using the old-fashioned cut-and-paste method, Bemelmans glued strips of cut-up typescript onto the pages of a blank book (hence the term *dummy*) and used pencil to sketch in rough illustrations, most of which appear in the final printed version. The archival evidence from the dummy in the Shirley collection suggests that Bemelmans strove for a kind of counterpoint in this early work. In the opening scene of the first chapter, the reader is introduced to Baptiste, and his closet full of fine liveries and shoes. In the dummy version, the text describing the liveries hanging over the shoes is placed neatly beneath the wardrobe and above rows of shoes, presenting the same information visually that is supplied verbally. In the printed version, however, the text that mentions the shoes shifts to the next page, creating the kind of contradictory counterpoint that makes a picture book interesting.

Other editorial changes are evident, too. Immediately apparent from a comparison of the dummy with the printed book is the change of the title of the work from *The Castle No. 1* to *The Castle No. 9*. The reason for this change is not made explicit through marginal notes or other instructions, though further archival research into Bemelmans' correspondence might reveal an answer.

Although it is not Bemelmans' most popular work, *The Castle No. 9* contains a number of remarkable illustrations. "Where is the Castle Number Nine?" Baptiste asks at the start of chapter two. Bemelmans answers with a visual montage, presented over a double-page spread. In the first picture, a tavern keeper points Baptiste to a bridge in the far right corner of the scene. In the second picture, just beneath the first, a watchman directs Baptiste past a church, which occupies the foreground. Baptiste is directed to pass through the city gate, which is shown at the picture's vanishing point. In the last scene, Baptiste learns from a shepherd that he'll find the castle on the "second hill to the right," but the hills are cleverly obscured by pine trees, and the Castle Number Nine is nowhere to be seen on the page, giving it an air of mystery and helping to increase the pacing of the story. The four pictures each have only a line or two of text beneath them, and work together in perfect harmony to move the story forward—and to move Baptiste further along in his quest.

Other illustrations are notable for their suggestion of action, movement, speed, and panic. The illustration that opens chapter four, for

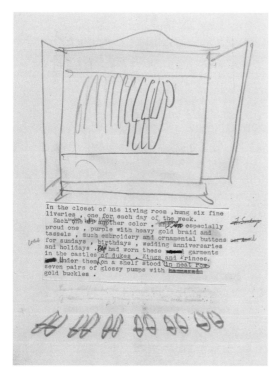

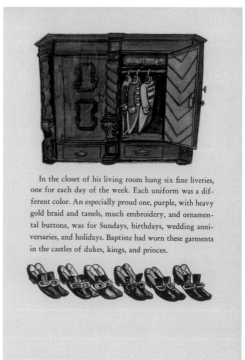

In the closet of his living room hung six fine liveries, one for each day of the week. Each uniform was a different color. An especially proud one, purple, with heavy gold braid and tassels, much embroidery, and ornamental buttons, was for Sundays, birthdays, wedding anniversaries, and holidays. Baptiste had worn these garments in the castles of dukes, kings, and princes.

example, shows Baptiste fleeing the flames that have already begun to spread through the castle, and he runs out in search of help. The mood of the scene is conveyed by image, rather than by description. The figure of Baptiste is flattened and shown striding forward. He is colored in yellow, like a streak of lightning. The Count's poodle leaps after him, flattened and elongated in the same way, which infuses the scene with the feeling of a chase and a great sense of urgency.

In 2002, the Beinecke Library had the opportunity, with Betsy Beinecke Shirley's support, to acquire the artist's dummy for *Madeline and the Bad Hat*, which was published by Viking Press in 1956. Bemelmans hits his artistic and authorial stride with the Madeline books, the first of which was published in 1938, the year after *The Castle No. 9*. There is a noticeable shift from the text-heavy narratives of *Hansi* and

Comparison of artist's dummy and printed page of *The Castle No. 9*, Bemelmans, 1936.

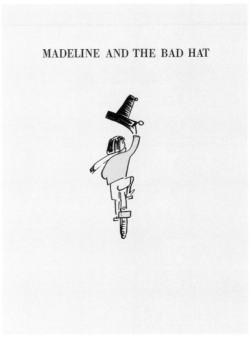

Comparison of half title in dummy and printed versions of *Madeline and the Bad Hat*. New York: Viking, 1956.

The Golden Basket to the spare, rhyming couplets that characterize the *Madeline* books. Still present are the loose lines, joyful palette, and the simplicity of style that defined Bemelmans' earlier works, but, beginning with *Madeline*, Bemelmans allows the pictures to bear more of the weight of the storytelling.

It is exciting to see evidence of this in the editorial decisions Bemelmans makes from the dummy to the printed version of *Madeline and the Bad Hat*. The half-title of the book, which introduces Pepito, otherwise known as The Bad Hat, provides a striking example. In the dummy version, the half title presents a cluttered scene that centers on a fountain, and shows Pepito heading towards a collision with Miss Clavel's two straight lines of schoolgirls. In the printed version, Bemelmans decided to eliminate the architecture that dominates the background, the fountain at the center, and even Miss Clavel and Madeline. What's left is a singular image; the elimination of all of the extraneous scenery in the half title leaves only The Bad Hat, seen from the rear, cycling away from the viewer, tipping his symbolic hat at a jaunty angle. The simplified scene allows for a much more powerful expression of character. Even though we do not see The Bad Hat face-to-face, we get a very clear idea of his mischievous nature. With no words at all, Bemelmans conveys the depth of genius he has for story-telling and art.

Using archival documents is only one of many possible critical approaches to the work and life of Ludwig Bemelmans. Examining the relationship between text and its material forms, however, is an approach that can shine light on the complexity and elegance that underpins the way that authors use materials to make meaning. For scholars inter-ested in taking a material-historical approach to the work of Ludwig Bemelmans, the Betsy Beinecke Shirley Collection of American Litera-ture is an excellent place to start. Additional collections directly related to the work of Ludwig Bemelmans and held at the Beinecke Library include:

Ludwig Bemelmans letters and other material, 1938–1962. (GEN MSS 686)

A Tale of Two Glimps. Artist's dummy for a 1947 Columbia Broadcasting System publication. (GEN MSS VOL 603)

The Borrowed Christmas. Illustrated typescript, circa 1952. (GEN MSS 1345)

Ludwig Bemelmans illustrations for *Madeline and the Bad Hat*, circa 1956. Includes artist's dummy. (GEN MSS VOL 876)

1   Bemelmans, Ludwig. *My Life in Art*. New York: Harper & Brothers, 1958, 7-8.

2   Ibid, 21.

3   Ibid, 22.

4   Bemelmans, Ludwig. *The Castle No. 9*. New York: Viking, 1937.

5   Sendak, Maurice. *Caldecott & Co.: Notes on Books & Pictures*. New York: Farrar, Strauss & Giroux, 1988, 21.

MICHELLE H. MARTIN

Black Childhood Abroad
Popo and Fifina: Children of Haiti

Langston Hughes and Arna Bontemps, friends and erstwhile collaborators for some forty years of their successful and varied careers, placed a high value on literature for children—particularly literature that would speak to all children that featured children of color. *Popo and Fifina: Children of Haiti*, published in 1932, one such story, was unusual for its time. While most children's books written by African American writers during this time were published through small Black presses like Carter G. Woodson's Associated Publishers for use primarily in educational settings, Hughes and Bontemps published this entertaining heavy-text picture book with a mainstream (White) press with the intention of reaching a mixed-race child audience. It is difficult for contemporary readers to appreciate what Langston Hughes and Arna Bontemps accomplished in writing and publishing *Popo and Fifina: Children of Haiti* in the early 1930s without some basic knowledge of important texts that comprised the context into which they were writing.

The Ten Little Niggers tales proliferated in the U.S. and abroad from the 1860s to the mid-1900s in the form of children's books, nursery rhymes in edited collections, stage plays, songs, and black-face minstrel shows. The plot of this rhyming ditty involves each of ten identical-looking, gaudily-dressed Black boys being "frizzled up" in the sun, squeezed to death by a bear at the zoo, swallowed by a fish, and suffering other equally gruesome demises. One version of the tale ends in this way: "One little nigger boy left all alone; / He went out and hanged himself and then there were None" (Anderson). These stories

(opposite) The boy on the boat by E. Simms Campbell, 1932.

portray African American boys as disposable while they invite White readers to laugh at this disposability.

In the early twentieth century, the negative portrayal of Black children continued but shifted from outright destruction to making them the subject of ridicule. In 1938, Sara Cone Bryant published *Epaminondas and his Auntie*, illustrated by Inez Hogan, permutations of which still persist in American children's literature today as in *Epossumondas* (2002) and its sequels, written by Colleen Sally, illustrated by Janet Stevens, which feature a possum protagonist instead of an African-American boy. In Bryant's version, Epaminondas visits his Auntie "'most every day, and she nearly always gave him something to take home to his Mammy" (3). When she gives him a big piece of "nice, yellow, rich-gold cake" (3) to transport, Epaminondas "took it in his fist and held it all scrunched up tight, and came along home. By the time he got home there wasn't anything left but a fistful of crumbs" (4). He successively fails at every courier task, ultimately prompting this response from Mammy: "O Epaminondas, Epaminondas, you ain't got the sense you was born with; you never did have the sense you was born with; you never will have the sense you was born with!" (14). This noodlehead tale—with a decidedly pickaninny flair—concludes with Epaminondas's misunderstanding Mammy's directive about her six mince pies: "you be careful how you step on those pies!" Epaminondas steps "right—in—the—middle—of—every—one" (16), affirming not only his simple mindedness but also his inability to understand anything but literal speech.

In this same tradition, Blanche Seale Hunt's 1940 *Stories of Little Brown Koko*, illustrated by Dorothy Wagstaff, tells of the protagonist who "…was the shortest, fattest little Negro you could ever imagine. He had the blackest, little wooly head and great, big, round eyes, and he was the prettiest brown color, just like a bar of chocolate candy" (n.p.). But he has a single bad habit: greed. "Why, compared with little Brown Koko, a pig should be called a well-mannered gentleman." Like Epaminondas, Little Brown Koko has a problem with cake. He cannot resist eating not *some* of the cake that his "nice, good, ole, big, fat, black" Mammy has made but *all* of it….in one sitting. "And all the time his little, round tummy kept pooching out, and pooching out, and pooching out, and POOCHING OUT until it does seem to me that it should have burst." As if this were not enough, Little Brown Koko then licks the plate. The incredulous narrator announces: "Honestly he did" (n.p.).

Popo and Fifina: Children of Haiti, a quiet story about Haitian siblings named Popo and Fifina from a poor and loving family, combats the pervasive negative images of Black children that White writers had promulgated in American children's literature for far too long. Early in the story, Popo and Fifina sit beside one another on a rock, looking out at the bay. They spot both steamships and sailboats, and Popo exclaims: "Aren't they fine!" (Hughes and Bontemps 26). Fifina agrees. But when Popo asks what the smaller boats are that he sees, Fifina points out that these sculling boats have sculls "that the men wiggle like tails" that are "as good as oars" (27). Popo spots a boat carrying mangoes, bananas, and a green parrot, then notices a naked boy about his size, carrying a chicken under each arm. "Popo jumped to his feet and threw up his hands, waving at the other youngster. When he saw that the boy was looking at him, he called at the top of his voice, "Say, where are you going with the chickens" (27)?

Hence, while the Birn Brothers and the McLoughlin Brothers wrote of *Ten Little Niggers* in the late 1800 and early 1900s, and Emery I. Gondor wrote (the new and improved) *Ten Little Colored Boys* in 1942 in which the ten brothers are successively found instead of destroyed, Hughes wrote "Winter Sweetness," his first published poem that appeared in *The Brownie's Book Magazine* in 1921. This simple, four-lined poem features a little sugar house with a snowy roof, out of the window of which "Peeps a maple-sugar child" (Johnson 53). A child made of maple sugar emphasizes both the sweetness and the amber color of the child—an unassuming way to represent children of color in the literature positively.

E. W. Kemble, well known for illustrating Mark Twain's *Adventures of Huckleberry Finn* (1884), wrote and illustrated a number of so-called humorous picture books about Black children being maimed, humiliated, and destroyed in a plethora of different ways as he did in his 1898 *A Coon Alphabet*. Bontemps, on the other hand, told the story of the Dozier Brothers: Rags, Willie, and Slumber, in his 1937 novel, *The Sad-Faced Boy* (1937), who hop a train from their poor farm in Alabama, to visit their Uncle Jasper Tappin, also from Alabama. Despite their unfamiliarity with city ways, the talented brothers end up making money playing and singing on the streets of Harlem in the midst of the Harlem Renaissance—the same music they often sing and play in the fields at home.

And while Blanche Seale Hunt wrote of Little Brown Koko's "nice, good, ole, big, fat, Black Mammy," Langston Hughes and Arna Bontemps describe Popo and Fifina's parents in this way when we first meet them at the beginning of *Popo and Fifina:* Papa Jean was a "big, powerful black man with the back torn out of his shirt" who wore a "broad turned-up straw hat and a pair of soiled white trousers," and "like all peasants of Haiti, he was barefooted." Mamma Anna, "was also barefooted, and she wore a simple peasant dress and a bright peasant headcloth of red and green. She was a strong woman with high glossy cheek bones. She followed her husband step for step in the dusty road" (Hughes and Bontemps 2). The contrasts between these approaches to portraying Black children are clear.

Arna Bontemps and Langston Hughes play a significant role in the history of African American children's literature—so much so that scholar Violet J. Harris has called Bontemps the "father" of African American children's literature (548), while Kate Capshaw Smith extends that designation also to Hughes (229-71). Most American students have probably read or recited Langston Hughes's poetry sometime in our educational journeys, but probably fewer know Bontemps's work or are aware of the incredible body of literature that the two produced both individually and collaboratively for children and Young Adults during their productive careers.

The 43-year-long friendship and professional collaboration that developed between Langston Hughes and Arna Bontemps began late in 1924 during the height of the Harlem Renaissance when writer Countee Cullen, friend of both Hughes and Bontemps, introduced them to one another in New York. According to Charles H. Nichols, who compiled and edited a fraction of the 2,500 letters the authors exchanged between 1925 and 1967, it is easy to see why they became fast friends. They had much in common: "the firmness of their commitment to African and Afro-American culture throughout the world, the creation of a vital and productive art among Negroes [and] the effort to fulfill the splendid promise of an often-despised minority." Nichols continued: "This mission drew them into a lasting bond of mutual interests and deep affection" (1). Both artists were born in 1902—Hughes on February 1 in Joplin, Missouri; Bontemps on October 13 in Alexandria, Louisiana—and they resembled one another "in color, height, hair texture and in their invariably deferential manner" to such an extent that people often assumed they were brothers (though each "insisted jokingly he was slimmer than the other") (8). In fact, Bontemps mused that when he first arrived in New York and journeyed to Countee Cullen's parents' house bearing a letter of introduction, Cullen's father opened the door, saw Bontemps standing there and "yelled to his son, 'It's Langston Hughes!'" (K.C. Jones 60).

While both Hughes and Bontemps felt a steadfast devotion to the working class and the poor throughout their careers, they were born into middle-class, mixed-race families to fathers who sharply scorned the Black folk tradition and Black vernacular speech. Bontemps's father was a bricklayer and itinerant musician and his mother a schoolteacher, and when Bontemps was three years old, the family moved from Louisiana to California when "two drunk white men threatened him for just being Black in their presence" (James 91, K.C. Jones 26). According to

Charles L. James, Bontemps "was fascinated by his bloodline—a gumbo mix of French, African, Native American and British—in part because of his appearance, about which total strangers would often query him" (93). Jacqueline C. Jones notes that before Arna turned 15, Paul shipped him off to a predominantly White Seventh-Day Adventist boarding school, and

> …before he left, Paul admonished him, 'Now don't go up there acting colored.' Instantly, Arna realized the appalling self-hatred embedded in that remark. When he later reflected on it, he challenged the very idea: 'How dare anyone, parent, schoolteacher, or merely literary critic, tell me not to act *colored*?' (27)

Bontemps's father also made a concerted effort—even through the move from Louisiana to California—to prevent Arna from associating with his Uncle Buddy, whom Jacqueline Jones characterizes as a "tale-telling, hard-drinking charmer" (26). Uncle Buddy embraced both "being colored" and telling Arna colorful ghost stories and slave-and-master stories in the African American and French Creole traditions—dialect included (26). Uncle Buddy also encouraged Arna to write, while his father saw no need for Arna to spend so much time reading books since he planned for him to become a bricklayer like himself. Most of Bontemps's relatives, in fact, considered too much reading and studying unhealthy for a boy. According to Kirkland C. Jones, "Even during Arna's early boyhood…both parents had decided to restrict the number of books their son could check out of the library at one time" (48).

Likewise, despite being Black himself, Hughes's father, James, hated Black people and moved to Mexico to put some distance between them and himself. According to Arnold Rampersad, Hughes's biographer, in one of James's infrequent letters to Langston, he wrote of Black people: "I have no faith in him; never did have, and never will. The ignorant uncultured Mexican Indian has got more sense than the American negro does—college bred or otherwise" (298-99). James Hughes withdrew all forms of financial support from Langston when his son decided to become a poet and to write about the very people James despised: common Black people. After Hughes began to experience some writing success, his father wrote to him to say that he had read his book *Not without Laughter* and also reads *Crisis* magazine "only to keep up with the doings of you African monkeys'" (Rampersad 208).

In his discussion of the conflicts surrounding race that both Hughes and Bontemps had with their families, Nichols notes that "each of the men bore a special, marginal relationship to the Black middle class. Hughes's work sometimes met with their censure. And Arna Bontemps moved deftly among a three-layered society—the Black masses, the Creole society of Louisiana, and the larger white world" (Nichols 4). In addition, Hughes and Bontemps were also both teachers: for a time, Hughes taught at the Lab School in Chicago, and Bontemps taught at Oakwood College in Alabama as well as at Harlem Academy prior to becoming the Fisk University librarian (Bontemps and Hughes, *Pasteboard Bandit* introduction). Both were persecuted for liberal or leftist views at some point during their careers: Bontemps, for instance, resigned from his teaching position at Oakwood College after only three years in part because the school's Seventh-Day Adventist administration ordered Bontemps to burn his personal library (K.C. Jones 7) and considered the title of his first novel, *God Sends Sunday* (1931), blasphemous (Bishop and McNair, 110). Hughes, likewise, was "denounced (erroneously) as a communist in the U.S. Senate" in 1948 (Johnson, xiv).

Despite being the center of such controversies throughout their writing careers, they remained gentle men committed to social change accomplished not through violence or aggression but through their art in its multiplicity of forms. In the introduction to *The Pasteboard Bandit* (1997), Alex Bontemps, son of Arna, comments on the relationship between Hughes and his father:

> "They had different contacts and different interests, so at a professional level they were very helpful to one another. But also, their temperaments were almost made for one another. My father

was a very patient and very genuinely affable person, and so was Langston. There was no ego, never any tension, and I think that's why they bonded and held together for so long." (Bontemps and Hughes 7)

Furthermore, both Hughes and Bontemps began to write while they were still very young and determined early in their lives to pursue careers in writing, despite lack of family support for this profession. And though most Hughes scholars often omit this fact in Hughes's biographical details, Hughes published his very first pieces of writing in a publication for children, *The Brownie's Book Magazine*—for "Children of the Sun"—published by the editors of *Crisis* magazine from 1920 to 1921.

Popo and Fifina broke new ground in children's literature both in terms of its publication and its content. As Kate Capshaw Smith explains in *Children's Literature of the Harlem Renaissance*, the children's literature industry in the 1920s was nearly as segregated as American society itself. Rarely were Black children's authors able to cross racial lines and publish with mainstream publishing houses. Carter G. Woodson's Associate Publishers published books by African American writers who targeted children, and many of these were educational works intended for the classroom about important figures in Black history. Macmillan published *Popo and Fifina: Children of Haiti* (1932), the first collaboration of Hughes and Bontemps. Macmillan was a major New York publishing house and the very first, according to Rudine Sims Bishop, to establish a separate children's department, which occurred in 1919 (Bishop 23). Violet J. Harris suggests that the publication of *Popo and Fifina*, along with Bontemps's "16 other novels, biographies, poetry anthologies, histories and folktales—represents the acceptance of African American children's literature among White publishers and readers and the continued expansion of literature for African American children" (548). Oxford University Press reissued *Popo and Fifina* in 1993 as a title in the Iona and Peter Opie Library, making it more widely available to contemporary readers. Most of the other children's

(*opposite*) Cover of *Popo and Fifina*, illustration by E. Simms Campbell, 1932.

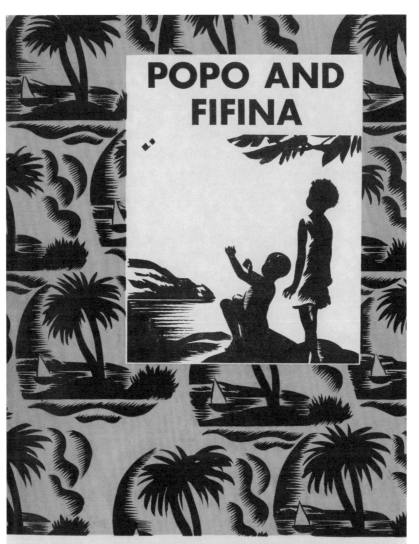

POPO AND FIFINA

BY ARNA BONTEMPS AND LANGSTON HUGHES

literature that Hughes and Bontemps wrote they placed with Morrow; Knopf; Lippincott; Harper; Doubleday; Dodd, Mead; Franklin Watts; and Houghton Mifflin (Boston)—many of which are still around today, even if they've been bought out by larger publishers. Not only were most of these publishers in the mainstream economically, but they also had substantial trade divisions that gave these Black writers literary exposure that went beyond the classroom textbook market—the market that Carter G. Woodson's Associated Publishers primarily served. Both Hughes and Bontemps remained keenly aware of the economics involved in post-Depression publishing and, according to Kate Capshaw Smith, also remained "sensitive to the formidable presence of White children in their reading audience" (233). Furthermore, Bishop notes that "for about a decade and a half after *Popo and Fifina*, [Bontemps] was virtually the only African-American writer being published by what he called the 'front line' publishers of children's books" (Bishop "Parallel Cultures" n.p.). Hence, in writing and publishing intentionally for a mixed-race audience of all American children and not just for Black children, Hughes and Bontemps sought to erase color lines that had previously restricted how and where Black children's authors could publish.

The content of *Popo and Fifina* also made it stand out. Setting the story in Haiti was an intentional choice on the part of its authors—both because of the racial climate in the U.S. at the time and because of events in Haiti's past that the authors admired and wanted to highlight. During the time of the book's 1932 publication, Black and White relations throughout the U.S.—especially in the South and in the North, where many southerners had migrated—were strained. The Scottsboro Boys' trial took place in 1931, in which nine African American young men ranging in age from 13–19 were accused of raping a White woman on a train in Alabama. "The men were convicted by all-White juries, and all but the youngest defendant were sentenced to death." The case was overturned in 1937, but only in 2013 were the last two of the Scottsboro Boys officially pardoned by Alabama's parole board (Associated Press). The Ku Klux Klan had over 4 million members nationwide in its heyday in the 1920s ("Ku Klux Klan"), and despite the negative impact that the Great Depression had on their numbers, lynchings of Blacks were common during this time. One hundred and twenty three African Americans were lynched between 1930 and 1940—a substantial decrease from the decade prior when 357 Blacks were lynched ("Lynching Statistics"). And Jim Crow Laws kept Black citizens out of places the White citizenry didn't want them to go. Setting this story in the United States in a climate in which White readers were much more attuned to reading texts such as E. W. Kemble's *A Coon Alphabet*, *Little Black Sambo*, and *Epaminondas* that made Black children the butt of jokes and the recipients of violence intended as entertainment for young White readers would have set Hughes and Bontemps up for severe criticism or worse. Publishers would also likely have rejected the manuscript for publication. Instead, the authors set it in Haiti, an all-Black society where Hughes had spent three months in 1931. According to Arnold Rampersad in his introduction to *Popo and Fifina*, rather than spending time only with the literati and the elite in the class-based society of Cap-Haïtien or Cape Haiti, Hughes "made it his business to get to know as many people as possible," including the peasants. Rampersad continues:

> He observed the women washing their clothes in the streams and men playing cards in the town. He played games with their children. He made friends with fishermen, who took him out in their boats. He talked to vendors in the marketplace, and he was allowed to attend some of the religious ceremonies, accompanied by drumming, that most foreigners never saw. (Hughes and Bontemps, *Popo*, viii)

Hughes's travels to Haiti in 1931 made such a deep impression on him that it provided writing material for a number of texts for both children and adults. He fell in love with contemporary Haiti, but he was mesmerized by what he knew of the history of Haiti and what Black people had accomplished there in 1804. According to *One World Nation Online*, under French colonial rule, 800,000 Africans were brought to the island as slaves, which accounted for a full third of the Atlantic Slave Trade,

Popo and Fifina
by E. Simms Campbell,
1932.

but conditions on the coffee and sugar plantations were so harsh that
the slave population completely turned over every twenty years. "After
300 years of colonial rule, the new nation of Haiti was declared an independent republic. It was only the second nation in the Americas to gain
its independence and the first modern state governed by people of African descent" ("History of Haiti"). Hughes admired these accomplishments of the Haitian people, having come from a nation where Blacks
still had to enter through the back door of many eating establishments
and drink from "Coloreds only" water fountains. Both the past accomplishments of Blacks in Haiti and the fact that Toussaint Louverture, a
well-educated former slave who had studied the military strategies of

Julius Caesar, had led them to victory impressed Hughes and Bontemps so much that Louverture actually makes an appearance in Bontemps's unpublished children's novel "Tom Tom Treasures," penned in 1938 and housed at the Beinecke Rare Book and Manuscript Library at Yale University. Hence, Hughes and Bontemps had made a strategic choice to set *Popo and Fifina* in Haiti. Given this rather cumbersome process of composing stories together from a distance, it is important to look at how this collaboration worked.

Kate Capshaw Smith and I agree that Bontemps was the "work horse" of the pair. While Hughes traveled all over Europe, Africa, the Caribbean, and other locales abroad, collecting fascinating stories Bontemps stayed at home and got much of the tough work done. Hughes would come back home and fill Bontemps's ear with tales of his adventures, which Bontemps would draft into stories that they would work together to finish. Bishop commented: "*Popo and Fifina* drew on two sources: Hughes's experience during a three-month visit to Haiti and Bontemps' first-hand knowledge of children." As Bontemps remarked in an interview with Lee Bennett Hopkins, "Langston had the story and told it to me. I had the children! So we worked together" (Bishop, 46). Both authors struggled financially throughout their lives, but Hughes remained a bachelor, while Bontemps eventually had six very good reasons to stay home and write for children; their names were Joan, Poppy, Constance, Camille, Paul, and Arna Alexander (nicknamed Alex). Augusta Baker, the first Black Children's Services Director within the New York Public Library system, created a list titled *Books about Negro Life for Children* that she initially published in 1946. This list also served as the catalogue for the James Weldon Johnson Memorial Collection of children's literature in the Countee Cullen Regional Branch of the New York Public Library in Harlem, which Baker established in the 1940s. Baker revised this booklet numerous times as publishers began to recognize the need for Black children's books and published more of them. *Popo and Fifina* was among her recommended titles in the earliest edition of the booklet, as were Arna Bontemps's 1945 *We Have*

Tomorrow, which featured biographies of 12 African Americans, and the 1948 *Story of the Negro*, which also won the Jane Addams Children's Book Award and a Newbery Honor. Baker encouraged and mentored many writers—both Black and White—and wielded a great deal of influence with publishers of children's books, given that she, like Oprah with her Book Club, could influence the life or death of a book by praising or condemning it. Baker was not a theorist but rather a librarian, a critic and a storyteller who trained many storytellers and held high standards for Black children's books. The remainder of this essay employs the criteria Baker developed for *Books about Negro Life and Children* in 1946 to examine *Popo and Fifina*. These initial criteria were simple: language, illustrations, and theme.

Baker noted: "the most important point is to eliminate books which describe Negroes in terms of derision…another language consideration is the use of heavy dialect" (*Books about Negro Life* 81). Hughes and Bontemps wrote this novel in standard English although both were quite capable of writing in dialect, as evidenced in several of the poems in Hughes's 1932 *The Dream Keeper and Other Poems* and Bontemps's 1934 *You Can't Pet a Possum*. In "The Black Experience in Books for Children: An Essay" that introduced Baker's 1971 list of the same name, she noted: "Dialect is too difficult for the child to read and understand, and since it is often not authentic, such usage is misleading. The use of regional vernacular is acceptable, but dialect should be used with great care" (144). This is the way that Hughes and Bontemps both use dialect in their writing for children, and though both of them spoke standard English, they regularly spent time with African Americans who did not (some of whom were family members like Bontemps's Uncle Buddy). Setting the story in Haiti could have given these writers license to try to replicate the creole languages spoken in Haiti. But because children's books about Black children were full of dialect already, writing in standard English was, in and of itself, an act of resistance. Furthermore, these authors spent their lives writing what they knew, and neither would have written in a dialect with which they were not intimately familiar.

Hughes and Bontemps avoid derision in *Popo and Fifina* by offering intricate details about the lives and culture of these Haitian children. The family is poorer than probably most Americans were who would have read the book initially, regardless of race, but the novel makes clear their strength and the values that underlie how Mama Anna and Papa Jean raise their children. Rudine Sims Bishop calls the family "money-poor but love-rich" (Bishop, "Books from Parallel Cultures" n.p.).

For instance, near the end of the book, Popo has an encounter with a little goat that, in the hands of writers like E. W. Kemble or the McLoughlin Brothers, would certainly have been an opportunity to illustrate the child's stupidity and might have even led to his destruction. Under the craftsmanship of Hughes and Bontemps, however, it becomes a teachable moment that also enables Papa Jean to empathize with his son. Popo encounters a small goat standing in the rain one day and thinks: "He looked very poor, very helpless there in the heavy downpour all by himself. Popo wondered what he could do to help the poor creature. "'Look at that poor goat,' he said to Marcel [his cousin who is apprenticing with him]. 'I wish I could help him.'" Marcel tells him that thousands of goats live in their town—more goats, in fact, than people. "Would you like to help them all?" Marcel asks. Popo chides his cousin for making fun of him and says the goat looks pitiful.

"That shed over there is his house," Fifina said. "Why don't you make him go inside?"

He ran to the goat and tried to push him toward the shed. But the goat was blinded by the rain and did not seem to understand that Popo was trying to help him. Suddenly, the confused creature turned around abruptly and butted Popo in the stomach. It was not a very hard butt, but it caught Popo off balance; and over he went into a mud puddle.

When Popo pulled himself out of the mud, he heard loud laughter. He was surprised and frightened but not hurt.

"That goat doesn't know what's good for him," he said sadly.

"That's the trouble with most goats, Popo," Papa Jean said. "They don't know what's good for them." (97-98)

This passage gives a sense of the family dynamics. Popo's sister puts him up to this ludicrous idea of helping a goat get out of the rain, and Marcel teases him about it. Whether Fifina makes her suggestion as a way of goading Popo into doing something she knows will not work so that she and Marcel can tease him, or whether she genuinely thinks Popo can help the goat is not at all clear. And the text does not say *whose* loud laughter rings in Popo's ears when he climbs out of the mud, but in the end, Papa Jean consoles Popo by commiserating with him about the stupidity of goats rather than Popo's own. Surely Popo will know better next time. Letting children learn from their own mistakes so that they will indeed know better next time constitutes a theme that runs throughout *Popo and Fifina*; this is, in fact, the method that Mama Anna and Papa Jean employ most in their child-rearing practices. Instead of preaching to the children or wagging fingers at them, they let events unfold and encourage them to figure out what lessons to take from their daily comings, goings, and mishaps, then they talk about it with them. In this way, the balance of power shifts from the parents to being more evenly shared between parents and children. And the sharing of power is a fine way to show that unlike Epaminondas, Popo and Fifina are smart and growing in the knowledge of how to live well, work hard, and look out for others.

In addition to evaluating children's books for language usage and the treatment of children, Augusta Baker also considered illustrations critically important. African American children's literature scholar Rudine Sims Bishop characterizes this as a "quiet book" but also writes:

> It is noteworthy, however, for its poetic style and for its sympathetic and realistic portrayal of the everyday life of the ordinary folk of Haiti in the early 1930s. It is noteworthy, too, as an example of the work of a highly regarded African-American artist, E. Simms Campbell, who became an illustrator and cartoonist for *Opportunity*, *Esquire*, *The New Yorker*, and several other national publications. ("Parallel Cultures" n.p.)

According to author and blogger Ariel S. Winter, Campbell designed *Esquire*'s mascot and was the first African-American artist to work for a national magazine. He was also the "first African American to have a nationally-syndicated comic strip." Winter considers him the Jackie Robinson of commercial art and cartooning. He designed the artwork for *Popo and Fifina* when he was only 25 years old (Winter).

Popo and the goat by E. Simms Campbell, 1932.

Of illustrations, Augusta Baker wrote:

> The depiction of a black person is exceptionally important in books for children. An artist can portray a black child—black skin, natural hair, and flat features—and make him attractive or make him a stereotype and a caricature. The black child who sees pictures which ridicule his race may be deeply hurt, feel defeated or become resentful and rebellious. The White child who sees the stereotyped presentation of the black person begins to feel superior and to accept this distorted picture of "typed" (Baker, "The Black Experience," 145).

In her 2009 TED Talk, Nigerian writer Chimimanda Adichie refers to this process of stereotyping as "the danger of a single story." Campbell's images in *Popo and Fifina* are sparse enough to make this an illustrated novel rather than a picture book, but they occur frequently enough to give young readers a lively sense of the topography, climate, and simple lifestyle of this Haitian family. The decision to illustrate silhouettes with woodcuts was an excellent one since it shows the essence of the children without the details of facial features or bodies. This also helped Hughes and Bontemps avoid censorship since Popo spends more time in the novel naked than clothed.

Augusta Baker wrote:

As minorities establish their claim to self-hood we will hopefully eradicate the old image of superior man, arrogant Anglo-Saxon man, perfect man. As each group declares its uniqueness, perhaps we can establish with humility our inherent incompleteness as a human species. We are uncommonly common. This might bring us to that ultimate moment of truth when we all—black and white, rich and poor—might say together, "I am you, and you are me; what have we done to each other?" (Baker "The Black Experience," 146)

As detailed earlier in this essay, *Popo and Fifina* was an outlier in children's literary history—an exception in what Violet J. Harris labels the "selective tradition" of the American children's literature canon. As a result, Augusta Baker felt it necessary to spell out what one must ask when considering theme. "Is the black character merely a clown and a buffoon, the object of ridicule, and the butt of humor? Is he a person who is making some worthwhile contribution to the progress of society?" (Baker, "The Black Experience," 145). Baker also noted what she sought to accomplish thematically through her book lists and the James Weldon Johnson Collection:

The whole range of black life is shown in this list representing every class and condition of society, a variety of experiences and all periods of history. Some of the characters are good, some are bad, some brave, some fearful. Together they portray the complexities of life for black people. (Baker, "The Black Experience," 145)

While Bontemps and Hughes did not attempt to accomplish more in *Popo and Fifina* than one book of 100 pages can, they did focus on a sliver of Black life that most American children—Black, White or otherwise—had never seen in their literature, and they did so with respect and with literary excellence.

When the *New York Times* reviewed *Popo and Fifina* on October 23, 1932, the review began:

> Here is a travel book that is a model of its kind. Facts, indeed, the reader acquires, but unconsciously, for what he feels is the atmosphere of the island of Haiti, dusty little roads, that wind along the hills, sun-drenched silences only broken by the droning of insects, and the cry of tropical birds, silver sails on clear green water, sheets of warm, white rain.

While many aspects of this novel are groundbreaking, the book's themes are not. They are really about the daily-ness of being a Black boy and a Black girl in early twentieth century Haiti. Although readers can certainly locate an exposition, a climax, and a denouement if they look, the slopes in the landscape of this plot are gentle and quiet.

I often emphasize with my students in literary discussions not to limit their identification of theme in a novel to a single one, for books can have many. These are some of the themes that whisper to me from between the covers of *Popo and Fifina*:

> Poverty enables families to focus on people instead of things.

> All play and no work can make children useless and lazy.

> Hand-crafted gifts are the best gifts of all, and a little boy has the right to be proud of what he has made with his own hands if he has done his best. (The same holds true for a little girl.)

> Parents must talk to one another daily and agree about how to raise their children . . . and parents must agree about this.

> › Families that take time to play together enjoy life more.

> › Hard work builds character—this is true for adults and children alike.

> › When you get something good, share.

> › Whether you are an adult or a child, always remain teachable.

> › Wealth comes from having the opportunity to learn at the elbow of a master craftsman or craftswoman.

> › Whether you have little or much and whether you are a child or an adult, take care of your family in the best way you can, for they are your best resource.

I would like to end with one final passage from the book that I think best illustrates the authors' respect for children and their determination to honor people of African descent through this novel. In this passage, Papa Jean has just apprenticed Popo to his brother, Uncle Jacques, who teaches Popo and his same-aged cousin, Marcel, the art of wood-carving. This is really the first time in his life that Popo has had such focused work that is his own. When Popo and Marcel ask Old Man Durand, the senior craftsman who works in Uncle Jacques' shop and will mentor the boys, how one manages to think of different furniture designs every day, he tells them that this is a difficult question to answer. When the children persist, he tells them: "Well, boys, it's like this: you have to put yourself into the design." They think he is teasing them. "That's a riddle," they chide. "How can a boy put himself into a design?"

> "Ah, it's a riddle indeed, but I'm not teasing you. If I walk down by the beach on my way to the shop in the morning and see the tiny boats putting out to sea, that makes a picture in my mind. If I see a hungry beggar, that leaves a picture too. Some pictures make me glad to be living. Some make me weep inside. Some make my heart sad. And when I'm glad to be living, trees and birds and leaves look one bright color to me. When I weep inside, they look different.

Well, I don't think about this when I sit down to make my design, I just sing or whistle a tune and carve away with my knife or chisel. But what I am inside makes the design. The design is a picture of the way I feel. It sounds strange, but it is just like that. The design is me. I put my sad feeling and my glad feeling into the design. It's just like making a song."

"It's wonderful," Popo said.

"It sounds just like old folks, but I like it," Marcel said.

"And when people look at your design," old man Durand went on, "when people see the picture, they will see trees and boats and flowers and animals and such things, but they will feel as you felt when you made the design. That's the fine part. That is really the only way that people can ever know how other people feel."

"There is nothing in the world like making designs!"

"Nothing is finer," old man Durand said. (Hughes, *Popo* 70-74)

Uncle Jacques agrees and promises Popo that he can start making a tray of his own the very next day, the prospect of which thrills Popo. The story ends: "Popo was so excited and happy that he could not speak again. To-morrow he would make a tray, a beautiful tray with a design on it. And there would be nothing but happiness in that design" (74).

WORKS CITED

Associated Press. "Ala. Board Approves Pardons for 'Scottsboro Boys.'" *BET News*. BET, 21 Nov. 2013. Web. 14 Jan. 2016.

Adichie, Chimimanda. *Danger of a Single Story*. TED Talk. TED Talk, July 2009. Web. 09 March 2016.

Anderson, Tiffany M.B. "'Ten Little Niggers': The Making of a Black Man's Consciousness." *Folklore Forum* (1 May 2009). Web. 9 March 2016.

Baker, Augusta. "The Black Experience in Children's Books: An Introductory Essay." *Bulletin of the New York Public Library* 75.3 (1971): 143-46. Print.

---. *Books about Negro Life for Children*. New York: New York Public Library, 1949. Print.

Bishop, Rudine Sims. "Books from Parallel Cultures: 'Let our Rejoicing Rise.'" *Horn Book Magazine* 70.5 (1994): 562-568. *Academic Search Complete*. Web. 14 January 2016.

---. *Free within Ourselves: The Development of African American Children's Literature.* Westport: Greenwood Press, 2007. Print.

Bishop, Rudine Sims, and Jonda McNair. "A Centennial Salute to Arna Bontemps, Langston Hughes, and Lorenz Graham." *The New Advocate* 15.2 (2002): 109-119. Print.

Bontemps, Arna and Langston Hughes. *The Pasteboard Bandit.* New York: Oxford University Press, 1997. Print.

Bontemps, Arna and Langston Hughes. *Popo and Fifina: Children of Haiti.* New York: Macmillan, 1993. Print.

Bontemps, Arna. *Sad-faced Boy.* Boston: Houghton Mifflin, 1937. Print.

Bryant, Sara Cone. *Epaminondas and His Auntie.* Illus. Inez Hogan. Boston: Houghton Mifflin, 1938. Print.

Capshaw Smith, Katharine. *Children's Literature of the Harlem Renaissance.* Bloomington: Indiana University Press, 2004. Print.

Gondor, Emery I. *Ten Little Colored Boys.* New York: Howell, Soskin, 1942. Print.

Harris, Violet J. "African American Children's Literature: The First One Hundred Years." *The Journal of Negro Education.* 59.4 (1990): 540-555.

"History of Haiti." *One World–Nations Online.* Nations Online Project, n.d. Web. 28 February 2014.

Hunt, Blanche Seale. *Stories of Little Brown Koko.* Illus. Dorothy Wagstaff. Chicago: American, 1940.

"Lantern Slide: Ten Little Niggers, circa 1900s." Museum Victoria Collections. Museum Victoria, n.d. Web. 24 Feb. 2014.

James, Charles L. "Bontemps's Creole Heritage." *Syracuse University Surface Library Associates: Courier 30* (1995): 91-115. Web. 14 Jan. 2016.

Johnson, Dianne, ed. *The Collected Works of Langston Hughes: Volume eleven: Works for Children and Young Adults: Poetry, Fiction, and Other Writing.* Columbia: University of Missouri Press, 2003.

Jones, Jacqueline C. "Arna Bontemps (1902–1973)." *African American Authors, 1745–1945: A Bio-Bibliographical Critical Sourcebook.* Ed. Emmanuel S. Neslon. Westport: Greenwood Press, 2000. 36-43. Print.

Jones, Kirkland C. *Renaissance Man from Louisiana: A Biography of Arna Wendell Bontemps.* Westport: Greenwood Press, 1992. Print.

Kemble, E. W. *A Coon Alphabet.* New York: R. H. Russell, 1898. Print.

"Ku Klux Klan." *History.com.* A & E Networks, 2009. Web. 1 March 2014.

"Lynching Statistics by Year." Archives at Tuskegee Institute. Web. 27 Feb. 2014.

Nichols, C.H., ed. *Arna Bontemps-Langston Hughes Letters, 1925–1967*. New York: Dodd, Mead & Company, 1980. Print.

Rampersad, Arnold. *The Life of Langston Hughes: Volume 1: 1902-1941, I, Too, Sing America*. New York: Oxford University Press, 1986. Print.

Rev. of *Popo and Fifina: Children of Haiti*, by Arna Bontemps and Langston Hughes. *New York Times*. October 23, 1932. Web. 14 Jan. 2016.

Salley, Colleen. *Epossumondas*. Illus. Jane Stevens. San Diego: Harcourt, 2002. Print.

The Ten Little Niggers. London: Birn Brothers, 18--. Print.

The Ten Little Niggers. New York: McLoughlin Brothers, 1875. Print.

---. New York: McLoughlin Brothers, 1894. Print.

Twain, Mark. *Adventures of Huckleberry Finn*. Illus. E.W. Kemble. New York: Charles L. Webster and Co., 1884. Print.

Winter, Ariel S. "Langston Hughes and Arna Bontemps: Popo and Fifina." *We Too Were Children, Mr. Barrie*. Blogspot, 5 Oct. 2010. Web. 2 March 2014.

JILL CAMPBELL

Taming Llamas
Campe's *New Robinson Crusoe*, Political Economy, and Children's Literature

A wayward animal drifts into Karl Marx's famous invocation of *Robinson Crusoe* in *Das Kapital* to lend his recollections of that novel a note of fanciful eccentricity: in a setting removed from social forms of production and commodity exchange, Marx recounts, Crusoe, with "needs to satisfy," must "perform useful labours of various kinds: he must make tools, knock together furniture, tame llamas, fish, hunt, and so on."[1] The diffident rapidity of Marx's litany of Crusoe's varied labors is deliberate: he is interested in the indifference for Crusoe among "the diversity of his productive functions," as Crusoe "knows that they are only different forms of activity of one and the same Robinson," and in the resulting "simple and transparent" relationship "between Robinson and these objects that form his self-created wealth" (169-70).[2] Marx departs from the circumstances of Crusoe's narrative when he passes over Crusoe's dependence on the many goods he is able to salvage from the ship, themselves the products of advanced forms of social production, including the firearms that allow him not only to hunt for meat but also to dominate the cannibals who arrive on his island and thus to win the fealty of a human companion, Friday. If Marx has altered Crusoe's economic situation by omitting from his island the iron tools, guns, gunpowder, grindstone, clothing, corn-seed, canvas, and Bible that Crusoe transports there from the foundered ship, in a concerted effort over several days, he also adds to Crusoe's island-setting a

(*opposite*) Portrait of Robinson Crusoe by John Bewick, *The New Robinson Crusoe*, London, 1778.

creature that Defoe's protagonist never saw: llamas to be "tamed." How did those llamas get to Crusoe's island, in Marx's rapid survey of Crusoe's activities as *homo economicus* in isolation?

In turning to *Robinson Crusoe*, Marx signals that he chooses Crusoe's situation to illustrate his point about commodity exchange because of its established popularity with political economists. "As political economists are fond of Robinsonades . . . ," he says by way of transition (169). Indeed, Daniel Defoe's *Robinson Crusoe* (1719) has a long history as the source of a crucial paradigm for economic theorists of every stripe. But Marx's brief discussion of *Robinson Crusoe* in *Das Kapital*, written when he was in his late 40s and living in London, shows the lasting influence of his childhood reading in Germany as well as his adult engagement with the writings of political economists: the llamas he recalls on Crusoe's island have their origin in Joachim Heinrich Campe's *Robinson der Jüngere* (1779), where they play a complex and important role in the narrative and figure memorably in illustrations. In Defoe's novel, it is of course goats and not llamas that Crusoe encounters and eventually tames.

In fact, when Marx alludes to political economists' fondness for "Robinsonades," he passingly acknowledges that what he refers to is a whole class of books, a tradition in which Campe's book played a key role, and not simply *Robinson Crusoe* itself. Defoe's novel spawned so many imitations that a generic name was invented to refer to them by type; "Robinsonades" for young people form a particularly numerous and influential sub-group within the type. Campe's book is the first in a vast and cosmopolitan lineage of works for children inspired by Robinson Crusoe that circulated in Europe, North America, and beyond, often moving quickly in translations among German, French, and English, and in some cases into Latin, Swedish, Dutch, Spanish, and Tagalog as well.[3] This lineage includes such enduringly popular works as Johann Wyss's *Der schweizerische Robinson* (1812, translated into French and then English as *Swiss Family Robinson*, 1814–18), followed by Frederick Marryat's *Masterman Ready; or, the Wreck of the*

Pacific (1841), R.M. Ballantyne's *The Coral Island* (1858), and William Golding's polemical rebuttal to *Coral Island*, *Lord of the Flies* (1954), a book still read by most American schoolchildren and many others around the world. It is Campe's late eighteenth-century reworking of Robinson Crusoe in particular, however, that formed the intellectual bridge between narrative fiction and the articulation of political-economic theory in Marx's masterpiece.

Inspired by Rousseau's recommendation of Robinson Crusoe as the only book that young people should read because of its emphasis on direct encounters with the natural world, Campe created a frame-narrative in which a father tells the story of Crusoe to his children, using its episodes as the basis for instruction on subjects as various as geography, zoology, history, moral responsibility, compassion, carpentry, and umbrella-making.[4] A prominent educator and progressive thinker, Campe had served as a tutor and mentor to Alexander von Humboldt, whose career as a naturalist and explorer of South America reflects Campe's early influence; Campe would go on to write a number of books for children, including a trilogy on the Spanish conquest of the Americas. When he adapted Defoe's novel for children, among the many topics of instruction he incorporates, Campe returns particularly insistently to the essential advantages of social means of production, which Crusoe, laboring in solitude, must do without.

The shaping of Marx's account by his childhood reading of Campe's Robinsonade, whether or not he also read Defoe's *Robinson Crusoe* as an adult, appears in the general emphases of his rapid summary of Crusoe's story. Tool-making, for instance, named first in Marx's list of Crusoe's activities, looms much larger in Campe's story than in Defoe's: naturally, it is more urgent for Campe's Crusoe, who brings nothing to the island but the clothes in which he washes ashore and so must laboriously fashion basic tools from oyster shells, rocks, sticks, fish bones, and plant-fiber cords. Campe's alteration of Defoe's story in this respect is programmatic; he emphasizes in his Preface that this alteration is important to the didactic purposes of his adaptation of

Defoe's book. The preface to the 1778 English translation, *The New Robinson Crusoe; An Instructive and Entertaining History*, cites this part of Campe's own preface:

> 'The Old Robinson Crusoe,' says Mr. Campe, in his Preface to the original of this work, 'independent of its other defects, is erroneous in one particular sufficient to destroy every advantage that this History might produce, which is, that Robinson Crusoe is provided with all sorts of European tools and instruments necessary to procure him many of those conveniencies that belong to society. Thus the opportunity is lost of affording the young reader a lively sense both of the wants of man in a state of solitude, and the multiplied happiness of a social life; another important reason why I thought proper to depart from the old History of Robinson Crusoe.'[5]

Thus, as Campe goes on to explain, he has divided the time of his "New Robinson Crusoe" on the island into three periods, a first in which "he is all alone and destitute of any European tool or instrument whatsoever" (vols. I-II), a second in which he gains a single companion (vol. III), and a third in which the shipwreck of a European vessel provides him with "tools and most other articles necessary in common life" (vol. IV [19-20]). The mediating father-instructor in the frame-narrative provided by Campe, Mr. Billingsley, underlines and explicates the advantages of the social means of production as he recounts Crusoe's different experiences in each phase of the story as thus systematically reshaped. In this way Campe himself, in adapting Defoe's imaginative narrative for the instruction of children, moved it toward the lessons in political economy to which Marx responds.

Marx's reference to an exotic animal featured by Campe and entirely absent from Defoe's original is thus only the most striking genetic marker of his account's descent from Campe's book, which also inflects the account's basic lineaments and force. As it happens, that telltale animal, with its provenance in the *New* Robinson Crusoe's island, stands at the crux of Campe's own treatment of several matters essential to political economy: the definition of Crusoe's basic physical "needs"; the depiction of Crusoe's most difficult challenges for survival in the absence of socially-produced European tools; and the understanding offered, via Mr. Billingsley's dialogue with his children, of relations between European colonizers and other peoples.

Written sixty years after Defoe's novel, in a time of widespread political and intellectual ferment and by a leading Enlightenment thinker, *The New Robinson Crusoe* tackles political questions explicitly and with a more systematically progressive agenda than its original. For instance, while a Providential logic of punishment for guilt might be implied by the catastrophes encountered by Crusoe on two of his slave-trading voyages (first his own ironic enslavement by the Turkish pirates who board his "*Guiney* trader," and later the shipwreck that leaves him marooned in solitude for many years), Defoe's Crusoe never makes this causal logic explicit; instead, he details the significant profits he eventually reaps from both adventures, though after much suffering. Campe, on the other hand, reshapes the later episode in which Crusoe watches a European ship founder off the shore of his island, leaving no survivors, by specifying that Crusoe learns from papers found on the ship that it "was bound for Barbadoes, and had a hundred slaves aboard." Mr. Billingsley's narration of this discovery leads into a discussion with his children of the horrors and injustice of chattel slavery, and the explicit hope that it will be abolished:

> *Mr. Bill.* . . . . The lot of such a *slave* (for so these unfortunate people are called by their purchasers) is truly wretched, nor can we wonder that many have even preferred death to it.
>
> *Rich[ard].* It is not well done to use human beings in that manner.
>
> *Mr. Bill.* Certainly it is very unjust; and we have hopes that in time this iniquitous traffic of slaves will be abolished. (IV.52)

Over and over again, the enlightened Mr. Billingsley impresses upon his children that members of other races and cultures are fellow human beings, though they may lack the crucial advantages of Christian teachings, of enlightened morality, and of European goods and industrial modes of production. In the sustained case of Crusoe's relationship with Friday, Campe follows Defoe closely in many aspects of Crusoe's rescue and befriending of a native man, but he systematically revises Defoe's treatment of Friday to render him a more equal companion and partner to Crusoe in "mutual assistance" (III.91). In their first exchange, Campe's Friday indicates his subjection to his rescuer with the same bodily gestures that Defoe's Friday employs; but Campe's Crusoe quickly deflects this obeisance, raising the native from the ground with a friendly hand, for "our hero . . . knew that he had more occasion for a friend than a slave" (III.35). Unsurprisingly, as a linguist, Campe also diverges sharply from Defoe's improbable treatment of the process of Friday's acquisition of the English language, instead detailing the two men's initial exchange of words in their native tongues, Crusoe's slow, systematic instruction of Friday in English words, and the men's gradual gaining of mutual understanding and respect. As he proceeds to narrate their life together, Mr. Billingsley comments, "Whatever superiority Robinson might have over Friday with respect to understanding and industry, the latter, in his turn, was possessed of much skill and dexterity, to which his master had hitherto been a stranger, but which, however, were of infinite service to them" (III.131). It is Friday who teaches Crusoe a method for making fire, which he has never been able to achieve alone, so that he can reliably prepare food in a "civilized" fashion thanks to Friday's knowledge and skills. Following the shipwreck that brings them a stock of European goods, Friday even repays his first great debt to Crusoe by saving Crusoe's life when the men are swept into the sea on their last trip back from the foundered ship (IV.57-58). In this episode, as Friday becomes Crusoe's "saviour" in turn, he demonstrates not only his nobly-savage "faithful[ness]" to his white companion and his superior skill in swimming and diving, but also his mastery and timely application of techniques of mouth-to-mouth resuscitation, a cutting-edge medical procedure in 1779 (IV.57-58).[6] In Campe's retelling, the third phase of Crusoe's stay on the island, in which he finally gains the benefit of access to salvaged European goods, would have ended abortively with his death if it weren't for the effective aid of his non-European companion.

Even as Defoe's *Robinson Crusoe* proved a foundational myth for the great enterprise of nineteenth-century imperialism, the meaning of its original telling for English and European imperial aspirations remains inchoate, incipient, and ambiguous.[7] Campe's recasting of it, on the other hand, engages explicitly and polemically, though ambivalently, with the moral complexities of European imperialism. In fact, in the year following his completion of *Robinson der Jüngere*, Campe went on to publish a three-volume work for young people about the European discovery and conquest of the Americas, in which he combines admiring treatment of the heroism of New World explorers with an indictment of European imperialists' violence, greed, and destruction of native cultures.[8] Even in *Robinson der Jüngere/The New Robinson Crusoe*, with its inset narrative based on a famous novel rather than on historical events, the children's father leads them to discuss the questionable morality of real-world imperialist conquest, suggesting his grave doubts about Spanish imperialism and particularly that carried out by Pizarro (the most iniquitous of the explorers in Campe's historical trilogy). Despite the distinctiveness of Campe's methods and particular agenda in writing for children, the occasion he creates for discussion of such weighty matters within *The New Robinson Crusoe* shares much with other late eighteenth-century writers of juvenile literature from across the political spectrum: he gets to the subject of European imperialism in the New World via his protagonist's encounter with a vulnerable animal, a young llama.

> *Mr. Bill....* These animals, walking on without suspicion, and probably having never been disturbed by any living creature, passed by, free from the least dread of danger, close to the tree where Robinson

stood in ambuscade; and one of the smallest of them coming within his reach, he gave it so effectual a stroke on the nape of the neck, that he laid it dead in a moment.

Harriet. O fy! how could he do so? The poor little sheep!

Mrs. Bill. And why should he not, Harriet? (I.135-36)

Non-human animals figure prominently in a great number of children's books from the eighteenth and nineteenth centuries, as in the present day, and the proper nature of relations between humans and non-human animals is frequently one of the urgent issues that presents itself for immediate consideration in those works with a didactic aim. Within the first pages of Anna Laetitia Barbauld's popular and widely influential *Lessons for Children* (1778–79), for example, little Charles and his mother, whose dialogue makes up the text of the work, turn to discussing why Charles is superior to Puss (she cannot speak or understand words, much less read) but also why Puss and other animals must be treated well by human children and adults. Not much farther into the book, Charles and Mama lament the death of a bird and the cruelty of those who kill animals or rob nests; soon thereafter, however, they celebrate the good meal that a bird felled by a hunter will provide. As Andrew O'Malley suggests, "from helping poor animals [Charles] eventually makes a seamless transition to performing small acts of charity for the poor children he encounters."9 Mary Wollstonecraft's *Original Stories from Real Life* (1788–96) also takes up the alternatives of cruelty or tenderness to animals in its very first chapter, as a wise mentor, Mrs. Mason, begins her tuition of two motherless and neglected girls. In the book's second chapter, she makes explicit the developmental importance of children's proper treatment of animals that O'Malley notes at work in Barbauld's *Lessons*: "It is only to animals that children *can* do good," she explains to her two charges;

> …men are their superiors. When I was a child…I always made it my study and delight to feed all the dumb family.…This employment humanized my heart; while, like wax, it took every impression;

and Providence has since made me an instrument of good—I have been useful to my fellow-creatures. I, who never wantonly trod on an insect, or disregarded the plaint of the speechless beast, can now give bread to the hungry, physic to the sick, comfort to the afflicted...[10]

The stirring certitude and cohesion of Mrs. Mason's message about kindness to all creatures, animal and man, do not prevent complexity from quickly entering her enunciation of principles for the treatment of animals, as also of uneducated or errant humans. Although she surprises the girls on their first walk together by stepping off the footpath into wet grass to avoid treading on insects and snails, she refers in passing to the need that sometimes arises to destroy insects "to preserve my garden from desolation," as she will later impress on them the discrimination required in exercising benevolence to the poor.

Significantly, in the exchange quoted above about Robinson's felling of a small llama with a single stroke, it is Mrs. rather than Mr. Billingsley who immediately challenges little Harriet's sentimental objection to the young animal's death: "O fy! how could he do so? The poor little sheep!" The children's mother, guardian of right feeling and domestic care, and not just their rational and worldly father, is clear that animals rightly die to benefit humankind: "He [Robinson] had occasion for the flesh of this animal for his food and nourishment; and dost thou not know that God hath permitted us to make use of animals whenever we have the like occasion[?]" (I.136). Mr. Billingsley and Harriet's older brothers quickly second Mrs. Billingsley's position, amplifying her justification of Crusoe's killing of the llama in an eager volley of points. They move briskly from declaring a distinction between harming a living creature "without necessity, or to torture it" (which is "cruelty") and doing so "to draw all advantage possible from them" (which is "not forbidden"); to asserting how advantageous it is to many animals themselves, who might otherwise starve or grow infirm, to be cared for by humans, though for the end-purpose of slaughter; to dispelling any fear that animals' slaughtering causes them suffering, since "they are not sensible beforehand

J. Bewick. del. & Sc.t

that they are going to be killed" (I.136-37). This rapid family review of reasoned arguments in defense of killing and consuming animals is oddly dissonant, though, with Mr. Billingsley's characterization of the appetitive, impulsive passion with which Crusoe responds to his first sight of grazing animals on the island: "Robinson, seeing these lamas approach, felt a violent desire to eat some roast meat, which he had not tasted for so long a time" and instantly "thought, therefore, of killing one" (I.135). Moreover, through Campe's characteristic interweaving of narration of the Crusoe story with instructive excurses, Crusoe's "violent" desire for meat and his killing of an unsuspecting, peaceable animal appear in tight juxtaposition with a discussion of Spanish imperialists' greedy domination of Peru's indigenous people.

This juxtaposition is occasioned by Campe's replacement of the goats on Crusoe's island with Andean llamas—that notable revision that makes Marx's debt to Campe most visible. Campe presumably chose to populate Crusoe's island with an animal native to South America rather than with the more familiar goat in order to increase the geographic and zoological interest of his narrative. Although Alexander Selkirk, on whom Defoe's Crusoe is partly modelled, did find goats on Juan Fernandez Island where he was marooned for four years—and even, according to the account by Woodes Rogers, did dress himself in their skins, to iconic effect—those goats were not native to the island, as Campe seems to have known, but instead brought there by Spanish explorers in 1575.[11] In the final volume of *The New Robinson Crusoe* Campe makes goats' imported status on Crusoe's island unambiguously clear when he includes a goat on the ship that is wrecked off the island's shore, making it one of the distinctively European goods that Robinson and Friday glean from the wreck, and even dramatizing Friday's unfamiliarity with the species by depicting his horror at meeting the horned goat aboard. Although also not native to the Caribbean, where Campe's Crusoe is marooned, the exotic species of the llama in Campe's retelling serves to signal the distant southern location of Crusoe's island, to occasion the Billingsley children's inquiry about an animal they do not know, and to

(*opposite*) Crusoe killing a llama, by John Bewick, *The New Robinson Crusoe*, London, 1778.

tie Robinson's individual exploration of his island and his appetite for meat to national imperialist enterprise.[12]

On a walk around the island at dinnertime, Mr. Billingsley recounts, Crusoe sat down under a tree "to regale himself heartily, when, all at once, a noise, at a distance, threw him again into a terrible fright."

> He looked round, with terror in his countenance, and, at length, perceived a whole troop of -------
>
> *Edw[ard].* Oh la! savages, I suppose.
>
> *Geo[rge].* Or else lions and tigers.
>
> *Mr. Bill.* Neither one nor the other; but a troop of wild animals, which have some resemblance to our sheep, except that on their back they bear a small bunch like that of a camel. As to their size, they were very little larger than a sheep. If you would wish to know what these animals were, and how they were called, I will tell you.
>
> *Rich[ard].* Oh! yes, papa, if you please. (I.133-34)

Having incited his children's curiosity through suspense, Mr. Billingsley proceeds to offer a ready encyclopedia entry on the llama, moving seamlessly from a (comically inaccurate) lesson in zoology to one in history and comparative cultures, and then returning abruptly to Robinson's sudden craving for roasted meat. "They are called lamas," he responds to Richard's eager interest, and "their country is properly that part of America which belongs to the Spaniards, and is called Peru."

> There, before the discovery of that extensive country by Francis Pizarro and Almagro, the Peruvians had tamed this animal, and were accustomed to load it, and use it for a beast of burthen, as we do horses and mules. Of its wool they made stuffs for cloathing.
>
> *Rich.* Then the people of Peru were not so savage as the other Americans.
>
> *Mr. Bill.* Not by a great deal. They lived in houses properly built; as did also the Mexicans (here in North America); they had built magnificent temples, and were governed by kings.

Geo. Is it not from this country that the Spaniards draw all that gold and silver for which they go every year to America, in their galleons, as you have told us.

Mr. Bill. The same.---Robinson, seeing these lamas approach, felt a violent desire to eat some roast meat, which he had not tasted for so long a time. He thought, therefore, of killing one of these lamas . . . . (I.134-35)

The possible threat to Crusoe of dangerous "savages" is clearly on the Billingsley children's minds as they listen to their father's story: little Edward jumps in excitedly to complete his father's phrase "a whole troop of---" with the word "savages." When the source of the noise that terrifies Crusoe turns out instead to be "wild animals," Mr. Billingsley's explanation soon links discussion of an unfamiliar zoological species back to that of an unfamiliar people whose savagery is understood to be in question. It is in fact the indigenous Peruvians' relation to the animals of the region that first raises questions about Europeans' self-interested premise that they must be "savage": when Mr. Billingsley reports that before the arrival of European explorers, the Peruvians had tamed llamas and made use of them both as beasts of burden ("as we do horses and mules") and as a source of "wool" for clothes, Richard ventures that the Peruvians must not be "so savage," then, "as the other Americans." As Roxann Wheeler has shown in her account of *Robinson Crusoe*, eighteenth-century articulations of race and colonial relations did not depend as heavily as we might expect on distinctions of skin color, but rather mobilized a shifting array of polarities, including, notably, an opposition between the "naked" savage and the man who wears his own civilized status in the form of proper clothes.[13] Arriving at an account of the peoples encountered by the conquistadors via a lesson in Peruvian animals, Mr. Billingsley highlights that some of those people were not only clothed but clothed in materials requiring sustained, systematic forms of social production: domestication of wild animals, shearing of their fleece, spinning of that fleece into "wool" (associated by both Germans and the English with their own husbandry of sheep), weaving techniques, and so on. Mr. Billingsley quickly adds "properly built" houses, "magnificent temples," and governance by kings to the evidence for a settled and organized culture that these processes entail. Such cultures perhaps should not be lightly overturned by outsiders. And if they are, perhaps the motives of their conquerors should be examined, little George's train of thought implies: "Is it not from this country that the Spaniards draw all that gold and silver for which they go every year to America, in their galleons as you have told us[?]" he inquires. His father answers only "The same" before abruptly returning to the narrative scene that has occasioned this rich, unsettling excursus on Andean animals and colonial relations; he picks up that narrative with Crusoe's "violent desire" for "roast meat" and his consequent impulse to kill.

Campe embeds a kind of "recapitulation thesis" in his organization of Crusoe's story into three parts, whereby the marooned individual's passage from solitary labor, to simple cooperative endeavors with a partner, to indirect cooperation with distant others through the employment of tools recapitulates societies' progression among these basic developmental stages. In volume I of *The New Robinson Crusoe* when Crusoe fells a young llama in a single blow, prompting lively discussion both of proper relations between humans and non-human animals and of colonial interactions between European and non-European peoples, Crusoe is positioned at an earlier, more primitive point on a timeline of political-economic development than the indigenous Peruvians who, Mr. Billingsley tells the children, long ago tamed the same creatures. A person's European origin does not guarantee a higher or even equivalent level of economic and cultural achievement than those of other peoples, Campe's story makes clear. Killing an animal on the spot with a hand-made hatchet to satisfy an appetite for roast meat (and then, as it turns out, being unable to roast it for lack of a method of making fire [I.142-46]) does not depend on the complex and sustained social and economic structures entailed in domesticating animals to serve in various processes of production.

(*opposite*) Crusoe with tame llama, by John Bewick, *The New Robinson Crusoe*, London, 1778.

92

On a small ontogenic scale, Campe's Crusoe himself progresses to that next step after the passage of more time on his island; at the beginning of volume II of the novel, it occurs to Crusoe that he might tame a llama, both for companionship and for the assistance it can give him in his labors—a thought, Mr. Billingsley says, "which by far surpassed, in cleverness, all that he had hitherto conceived" (II.11). Significantly, while the second and third stages of Crusoe's life on the island as laid out in Campe's preface each corresponds to one volume of the work, the first stage, in which "he is all alone and destitute of any European tool or instrument whatsoever," is split into two volumes. The development that differentiates Crusoe's ways of life in volume I and in volume II is his successful domestication of the llamas whom he regarded only as a source of meat upon first encountering them, to little Harriet's horror. Though not human companions, once tamed by him, the llamas on Crusoe's island fundamentally alter both his psychological and his economic situation there, as the volume divisions of *The New Robinson Crusoe* suggest.

Campe's emphasis on the defining nature of the relationship between marooned humans and the animals with which they share their exile persists in the Robinsonades that follow in the wake of his adaptation of *Robinson Crusoe* for children. This relation features large, for instance, in *Swiss Family Robinson*, where the father and his boys successively encounter and domesticate so many animals from so many climes that their family compound is transformed into a fantastically crowded zoological garden. It would even provide a central affective term in a twentieth-century children's book rarely classified as a Robinsonade but that nonetheless shares much with that genre, Antoine de Saint-Exupéry's *The Little Prince* (1943–45).

> "I am looking for friends. What does that mean—'tame'?"
> "It is an act too often neglected," said the fox. "It means to establish ties."
> "'To establish ties'?"

"Just that," said the fox. "To me, you are still nothing more than a little boy who is just like a hundred thousand other little boys.... To you I am nothing more than a fox like a hundred thousand other foxes. But if you tame me, then we shall need each other. To me, you will be unique in all the world. To you, I shall be unique in all the world..."[14]

Under the credo of "taming," the seemingly specialized activity of the domestication of animals—or the mutual domestication of animal and human child or man—becomes a paradigm for the broad processes of individuation, meaning-making, and the formation of ties between creature and creature, and between creature and the world, in which children are urged to join. Whereas Saint-Exupéry employs the language of taming to philosophical ends, in his Robinsonade for young people, Campe made "taming llamas" the crux for questions of political economy that would linger long in one nineteenth-century reader's mind.

1 *Capital*, vol. I, transl. Ben Fowkes (NY: Penguin Books, 1976), from Chapter 1.4, "The Fetishism of the Commodity and Its Secret," pages 169-70. Under the supervision of Frederick Engels, the first English translation of *Das Capital* incorporated significant divergences from Marx's original, including in the passage I have quoted. There, Engels corrected Marx's faulty recollection of the fauna on Crusoe's island, replacing the wayward llamas with goats. See *Capital*, transl. from the third German edition by Samuel Moore and Edward Aveling, ed. Frederick Engels (NY: Modern Library, 1906), page 88. I am grateful to Andrew Lanham, whose outstanding essay on geographic incongruities in *Robinson Crusoe* first drew this error in Marx's reference to my attention.

In the German original the passage reads: "Da die politische Ökonomie Robinsonaden liebt, erscheine zuerst Robinson auf seiner Insel. Bescheiden, wie er von Haus aus ist, hat er doch verschiedenartige Bedürfnisse zu befriedigen und muß daher nützliche Arbeiten verschiedener Art verrichten, Werkzeuge machen, Möbel fabrizieren, Lama zähmen, fischen, jagen usw" (*Das Kapital*, vol. I. *Werke*, Vol. 23 [Berlin: Dietz Verlag, 1956]).

2 Citing Fowkes's translation, I here substitute "Robinsonades" for his translation of Robinsonaden as "Robinson Crusoe stories," given the pertinence of the specific generic term to this essay. See Teresa Michals, *Books for Children, Books for Adults:*

Age and the Novel from Defoe to James (NY: Cambridge UP, 2010), for a detailed and illuminating discussion of the important role played by versions of a Crusoe paradigm in both classical and neo-classical economics.

3   See Ramon Guillermo's fascinating study of the role of nineteenth-century translations of Campe's *Robinson der Jüngere* in transmitting European notions of political economy into Tagalog and Malay ("Themes of Invention, Help, and Will: Joachim Campe's *Robinson der Jüngere* in Tagalog and Bahasa Melayu Translations," *Southeast Asian Studies* 3 [2014]). Guillermo briefly notes Marx's reference to the llamas that appear in Campe's work rather than to goats; cautioning that it would "be rash to conclude" that Marx had read Campe's version rather than Defoe's, he concludes that "it may therefore be the case that Marx was familiar with both versions."

4   In *Emilius and Sophia: or, a New System of Education*, trans. William Kenrick (1762), excerpted in the Norton Critical Edition of *Robinson Crusoe*, 2nd ed., ed. Michael Shinagel (NY: W. W. Norton & Co., 1994), 262-64.

5   Joachim Heinrich Campe, *The New Robinson Crusoe; An Instructive and Entertaining History, for the Use of Children of Both Sexes. Translated from the French. Embellished with Thirty-two beautiful Cuts*, in four volumes (London: John Stockdale, 1788), I.18-19.

6   The efforts of the English physicians William Hawes and Thomas Cogan to promote techniques of artificial respiration led to the founding of the Royal Humane Society in 1774. On controversies surrounding these new techniques, see Carolyn Williams, "'Inhumanly Brought Back to Life and Misery': Mary Wollstonecraft, Frankenstein, and the Royal Humane Society," *Women's Writing* 8 (2001): 213-37.

7   Martin Green comments: "The book's meaning—what values it promotes, what energies it stimulates—is perhaps as variable as any other story's. It was, for its first 100 or 150 years, taken to be a profoundly democratic book, and a defiance of such imperiality as Spain's. But now we are bound to see it as profoundly imperialist, both in Robinson's relations to Friday, and in the stimulus it gave young Englishmen to go out and join in the adventure of the British Empire" ("The Robinson Crusoe Story," in *Imperialism and Juvenile Literature*, ed. Jeffrey Richards [NY: Manchester UP, 1989], 35-36). Many readers, James Joyce and Toni Morrison among them, have seen Defoe's novel as more integrally involved in imperialist ideology than does Green.

8   The work appeared in 1781-82 as *Die Entdekkung von Amerika: ein angenehmes und nützliches Lesebuch für Kinder und junge Leute*, with one volume each devoted to Columbus, Cortez, and Pizarro. The first volume was published in English in 1818 under the title *Columbus, or the Discovery of America; as Related by a Father to his Children, and Designed for the Instruction of Youth*. It offered a largely heroic portrait of Columbus but was followed by two volumes which emphasize Cortez's and Pizarro's imperialist crimes.

9   Andrew O'Malley, *The Making of the Modern Child: Children's Literature and Childhood in the Late Eighteenth Century* (NY: Routledge, 2003), p. 57.

10 *Original Stories from Real Life; With Conversations, Calculated to Regulate the Affections, and Form the Mind to Truth and Goodness* ("a New Edition" [London: J. Johnson, 1796], 12-16), in *The Works of Mary Wollstonecraft*, ed. Janet Todd and Marilyn Butler, vol. IV (NY: New York UP, 1989), 372-73.

11 See David H. Caldwell and Daisuke Takahashi, "Finding Robinson Crusoe," *Post-Medieval Archaeology* 41 (2008): 270-304. A summary of their findings appears in Marco Evers, "Trapped on a Pacific Island: Scientists Research the Real Robinson Crusoe," *Spiegel Online International*, Feb 6, 2009 (consulted June 8, 2015).

12 The llama thrives in cold, high-altitude conditions, as in the Andes, and so would adapt poorly to the hot climate and sea-level altitudes of Caribbean islands.

13 Roxann Wheeler, *The Complexion of Race: Categories of Difference in Eighteenth-Century British Culture* (Philadephia: U of Pennsylvania P, 2000).

14 *The Little Prince* (NY: Reynal & Hitchcock, 1943), page 66; ellipses at the close of the quotation in the original.

JOANN CONRAD

"Typically Norwegian"
The d'Aulaires' Imaginary Homeland

In mid-twentieth-century America a significant number of picture-book illustrators were newly arrived European immigrants.[1] Although the names of artists such as Feodor Rojankovksy, Gustaf Tenggren, H.A. Rey, Esphyr Slobodkina, and Tibor Gergely may not be that well known, their work is, due the volume of images these artists produced not only in children's picturebooks, but also in an array of new visual media that included advertising, animation, and magazine illustration. Their illustrations were thus incorporated into mainstream popular culture even as the general American sentiment was persistently isolationist, anti-immigrant, and anti-Semitic.[2] Seeking to assimilate in varying degrees, their work, as well as the construction of their own personal stories as new Americans were effected through a series of ideological operations with both nostalgic and conservative undercurrents which reaffirmed dominant assimilationist, patriotic, and Americanist discourses. That is, as these artists adapted their art to the American scene, so too did they construct their own narratives of arrival and assimilation. But even as they shared a common immigrant experience, they also were emigrating *from* different places of origin in Europe. American expectations had these artists possessing innate "Old Country" sensibilities rooted in "traditional culture," and yet the variety of ways in which this "Old Country" was to be rendered was informed by and embedded in the modern nation-building discourses specific to each country, all of which deployed "tradition" in tactical ways. That these immigrant artists were trained in many of the capitals of Europe placed them within

(*opposite*) Detail of endpaper, *Ola*, 1932.

99

these discourses, and their art must be seen within that context, rather than as a kind of ethnographic rendition of reality. Somewhat typical of this pattern is the husband-wife team of Ingri and Edgar Parin d'Aulaire, who interwove their own story as immigrant artists into their work in children's picturebooks which consisted, roughly in equal measure, of books with a Norwegian theme and those with American themes.

As characters in their own story, the d'Aulaires' personal and family histories were shaped to conform to an existing script—all part of the publishing world's promotional and advertising strategy—in which the lines between fantasy and reality, ideology and history were intentionally blurred and inverted. Characters in their children's books also conform to several standard formulas: American Pioneers, Heroes and Discoverers;[3] (Norwegian) Folklore characters—*East of the Sun and West of the Moon* (1938), *Leif the Lucky* (1941),[4] and *Trolls* (1972);[5] and "picturebook ethnographies"[6] of Norway—*Ola* (1932), *Ola and Blakken and Line, Sine, Trine* (1933), *Children of the Northlights* (1935), and to some extent *Wings for Per* (1944). The Norway presented in these books, however, is a place of the imagination, drawing on an already-in-place visual vocabulary of modern Norwegian nation-building, but also conforming to the nostalgic expectations of the "Old World" in American audiences which affirmed America's sense of its place in the world.

IMMIGRANTS FROM THE OLD WORLD

Along with those of many other émigré artists, the d'Aulaires' story is emphatically one of immigration and assimilation; coming to the land of "limitless opportunity" in which they pulled themselves up by their bootstraps through grit and determination. Edgar's 1940 Caldecott Medal acceptance speech echoes this sentiment. Imagining themselves as twentieth-century pioneers, Edgar remembers arriving in "the country where everything we had in us could be used to its full extent, and where we could fulfill our full measures as human beings and help in building up the world."[7] Thus it was only in America that their full potential could be realized. The couple's individual histories and dissimilar backgrounds were made to fit into this standardized and redemptive narrative, necessitating the reconfiguration and sometimes elimination of many aspects of their lives prior to coming to the United States.[8] Editorial adjustments and cuts to their biographies were also necessary to distinguish America (of the present and the future) from the "Old Country," effecting an exaggerated break with the past.

The Old World provides a perfect contrast for the land of opportunity into which the artists immigrated, and is part of the larger narrative of America—one into which these immigrant artists' lives are interpellated. Their stories follow a standard format which begins with a brief description of the artist's early childhood and quickly shifts to the moment of arrival in America, excluding any serious investigation into their adult experiences prior to emigration. In the case of the d'Aulaires, emphasis was shifted away from Edgar's cosmopolitan childhood towards Ingri's Norwegian background, which was exoticised, infantilized, and mired in the past. Ingri's family is said to "trace back to the Vikings" and her big, noisy, happy family is settled in the Norwegian countryside, although Ingri's family lived in Kongsberg, at one time the second-largest city in Norway, where her father was the director of the Kongsberg Silver Mines.

Part of the d'Aulaires' story can be explained by analyzing their unique publishing history. The couple, in contrast to almost all their fellow illustrators, only worked with children's books, and did not work in advertising (Ingri noted that Edgar "refused steadfastly to paint potato salads to make the mouths of advertising agents water").[9] They also produced far fewer books than most illustrators of the time, in part because of their preferred method—stone lithography. In fact, together they produced a total of only 27 picturebooks between 1931 and 1976,[10] all published by Doubleday and Viking, and most under the editorship of the influential May Massee.[11] Massee and similar "minders"[12] of the children's publishing world such as the powerful Anne Carroll Moore of the New York Public Library's Children's Division and Bertha Mahoney of *The Horn Book* were largely responsible for shaping the d'Aulaires' personal narrative—a fiction that influenced their work and readers' responses to it. Massee attributes the d'Aulaires' inspiration to Ingri's childhood and also to the land and lore of an imaginary Norway: "the roots of the creative work of the d'Aulaire's [sic] are deep in the landscape and folklore of Norway, originally inspired by Ingri's background and her living memory of a happy childhood."[13]

In order to effect this fiction, however, Edgar's story was sacrificed. The cursory treatment of his own story and the subsequent overemphasis of his "adopted" Norwegian family belies a long involvement with the arts both on the part of Edgar's parents and of Edgar himself in the 27 years *before* marrying Ingri and going to Norway. Edgar was born in Munich in 1898 to Gino Parin (1876–1944), and Ella Auler Parin (1875–1962). Gino, born Federico Guglielmo Jehuda Pollack in Trieste (then part of the Austro-Hungarian Empire), was a Jewish-Italian artist, trained in Munich. He was part of the significant Jewish-Italian art world of the period, and was influenced by Symbolism as well as the Viennese Secessionists—both movements informed by Freudian theory and psychoanalysis.[14] During World War I, Gino returned to Trieste, which in 1919 became part of Italy. In 1938, Italy began to impose racial laws, and despite having Swiss citizenship, Gino was arrested and died in the Bergen-Belsen concentration camp in 1944. Ella Auler Parin was born and died in St. Louis, Missouri. She had German[15] and American roots (from settlers in Texas and New Orleans), albeit not the America of the founding fathers or Buffalo Bill and the Wild West, but rather, the complicated and diverse America of the trans-Mississippi—more German, French and Native American than Anglo. In the mid-1890s she moved to Paris for her own artistic aspirations,[16] married Gino, took Swiss citizenship and started a family in Munich. Ella and Gino divorced in 1904 when Edgar was six years old, and he and his three-year-old sister moved with their mother to Paris. Ella returned to St. Louis in 1922, having lived mainly as a single mother in Europe for nearly 20 years. Edgar spent much of his formative years in pre-World War I Paris, the hub of the avant-garde, and it is clear from the few pieces of Ella's artwork in the d'Aulaire Papers at the Beinecke Library that Ella, too, was influenced by both Art Nouveau and Symbolism. This inward-looking, psychoanalytically informed art milieu was thus one in which young Edgar found himself through his mother and his father. The effect is apparent in Edgar's early work.

The elision of this information from the d'Aulaires' story speaks to the ideological imperatives of the time. In the logic of mid-century America, divorce—let alone free-spirited women who took off by themselves to pursue careers—were anathema to existing "family values." In addition, anti-Semitism was still prevalent. Edgar's non-normative, broken family needed (narrative) rehabilitation, and it came in the form of Ingri's large, boisterous, happy Norwegian family. In the process of this rehabilitation, Edgar's sister, Maria Aspasia Parin, Gino's Jewish identity, and Edgar's early life as a working artist in Munich were all omitted from official biographies of the couple. Ella's American roots were also de-emphasized (in some articles she's referred to as Parisian!), because in order to re-imagine Ingri and Edgar as "American pioneers" it was first necessary to make them immigrants with no family scaffolding in the U.S.[17] Real life seems to have mirrored this erasure of Ella, for while Ingri, Edgar and, later, their two sons maintained contact with the Mortensons, Ingri's family in Norway, visiting almost yearly, Ella was not incorporated into this new family structure, and significantly, she kept the surname Parin until her death. Ella's life in St. Louis from 1922 to her death, which overlapped with the d'Aulaires' life in Connecticut is also never mentioned in official biographies, perhaps because she played no part in the life of the reconstructed d'Aulaires.

SUPERNATURAL NORWAY[18]

The break effected with the past by the construction of an "Old World" that is explicitly linked to childhood and to the realm of magic and superstition and which is juxtaposed with the "New World" of America, which represents the more-developed, adult, rational world of progress and opportunity, fits clearly into the developmental model, but it is also turned back on itself and reified in subsequent understandings of Norwegian land and lore. That the wild, uninhabited landscape of Norway with its untamed Nature is by now the unquestioned source not only of the distinctive characters of Norwegian lore (trolls), but also of a distinctly dark and brooding mood that inheres in that lore is a commonplace in all descriptions of Norwegian Folklore. A recent review of the 2015 Taschen re-issue of George Dasent's *East of the Sun and West of the Moon*,[19] a selection of 15 tales translated mostly from Asbjørnsen and Moe's classic *Norske Folkeeventyr* [Norwegian Folktales] and illustrated by Kay Nielsen repeats the by-now common understanding that the "trolls, ogres, and witches" are clearly based in "Norse pagan mythology" and thus "distinctly Scandinavian," and emerge from a land of "snow, ice, and brittleness" which has "determined the character of these legends"[sic].[20] This is an ironic claim, given that none of the stories featured have any references to snow or ice nor to any recognizable Norse mythology, and all are versions of wide-spread international tale types.[21] This "common knowledge" that Norway's empty landscape is the "natural" breeding ground for supernatural creatures and lore is reiterated in the introductions to many of the d'Aulaires' books. In their 1932 book *Ola*, the d'Aulaires describe Norway as "…the strangest country in the world. It is so crowded with mountains, forests, huge trolls, redcapped gnomes, and alluring Hulder-maidens that only a few human people have room to live there." Similarly, their introduction to their 1938 edition of *East of the Sun and West of the Moon*[22] claims that "[b]etween the little houses and huts that lie scattered across the hilly and rocky land of Norway, there are wide stretches of deep forests and blue mountains. For days you can wander about without meeting another human being, and all unaware you step into a strange fairy-tale world."[23] And in *Trolls*: "In the old days, when only narrow, twisting paths wound their way through the moss-grown mountains of Norway, few human beings ever set foot there. The mountains belonged to the trolls, who were as old and moss-grown as the mountains themselves."[24] In fact, all of the d'Aulaires' "Nordic-themed" books—

Ola (1932), *Ola and Blakken, and Line, Sine, Trine* (1933), *Children of the Northlights* (1935), *East of the Sun and West of the Moon* (1938),[25] *Leif the Lucky* (1941), and much later *Norse Gods and Giants* (1967) and *Trolls* (1972)[26] seem to verify and fulfill expectations of a Nordic natural wonderland that is penetrated by magical and supernatural forces, and that these beliefs have persisted from the distant past. But these naturalized connections belie a much more recent history involving the complicated processes of Norwegian nation and identity formation in texts and images, the translation and dissemination of these cultural productions, now decoupled from Norwegian nationalist imperatives and logics, and American political, social and pedagogical discourses into which these were inserted, often through cultural mediators such as editors like Massee. That is, rather than emerging out of a supernatural *Nature*, the landscape is the product of its narrative construction, a product of *Culture*.

Colored lithograph after black-and-white image that appears in *Ola, 1932*: "In this country there is a forest, in winter a very strange forest. For under the heavy burden of snow the trees turn into a crowd of solemn creatures."[27]

The relationship between folklore and Norwegian nation building is well-attested.[28] The Norwegian folktales that circulate today, including specifically those in d'Aulaires' *East of the Sun and West of the Moon*[29] and more generally in their 1972 collection *Trolls*, can be traced to the seminal folklore collections of Per Christen Asbjørnsen and Jørgen Moe, whose materials were first serialized in weekly newspapers in the early 1840s, compiled in the 1841-44 *Norske Folkeeventyr* [Norwegian Folktales], and expanded in the subsequent *Norske Folkeeventyr: Ny Samling* in 1871. Asbjørnsen also published his own separate collection: *Norske Huldre-Eventyr og Folkesagn* I-II (1845–48), which was also expanded in a second collection.[30] Not only were their books reprinted often, but individual tales were also excerpted and included in magazines and textbooks for several generations as part of the nation-building effort. As with the Grimms' *Kinder- und Hausmärchen*, Asbjørnsen and Moe's hundreds of stories were reduced to a standardized canon, and stories from the collaborative *Norske Folkeeventyr* [*NF*], which tend for the most part to be international tale types most specifically recognized as Fairy Tales, were mixed with those from Asbjørnsen's solo efforts, which contained most of the "strange" stories associated with Norway—the legends of trolls, *Huldrefolk*, and other supernatural beings. In the context of the pre-modern countryside of the as-yet-to-become independent Norway, it is perhaps Asbjørnsen's legends that best capture the discursive nature of narratives about day-to-day encounters with inexplicable phenomena, while the most popularly circulated Fairy Tales from *NF* tend to coalesce around what folklorist Ruth Bottigheimer refers to as "rise tales"—tales of unpromising youths who, through luck and a bit of magical intervention, achieve wealth by marrying up, reflecting, perhaps the aspirations of a population just recently moving into the middle class.[31] These abridged and recombined tales from Asbjørnsen and Moe then became quintessential "Norske Eventyr"—Norwegian tales, claimed as common heritage—even though the pair's collected material is almost exclusively from the southern parts of Norway. These stories circulated without illustrations for almost 40 years. With subsequent illustrated volumes, most particularly with the introduction of the work of Erik Werenskiold in 1879 and Theodor Kittelsen in 1883, the hitherto ambiguous and imagined relationship between the natural and supernatural realms became visualized, literalized, and instilled in popular memory.[32] It is Kittelsen's work in particular that plays with reality's ambiguities and captures the dangers that are present at the borders of the known. Kittelsen gave form to the now famous and typical Norwegian trolls and provided the template for other famous (Swedish) illustrators of trolls and gnomes—John Bauer and Gustaf Tenggren. These would have been the illustrations that Ingri Mortenson grew up looking at, and it is impossible to deny the influence of these illustrations on the work of the d'Aulaires more than two generations later.[33]

In the introduction to their *East of the Sun and West of the Moon*, the d'Aulaires describe Kittelsen's earlier illustrations as "so subtly Norwegian, that only Norwegians can truly understand them," and conclude that they must "translate" the illustrations so that non-Norwegians might understand them, while remaining true to the original meaning.[34] Similarly, in an interview in 1936 with the Norwegian newspaper *Morgenbladet*, Ingri describes an essential and naturalized sense of *Norskhet* [Norwegianness] that inheres in both the tales and their earlier illustrations, which, in her words are "too Norwegian" for American audiences without mediation.[35] Edgar, a non-native introduced to Norway as an adult, thus works to complement Ingri's native understanding because, unaffected by the previous material, he can approach it as if "with the eyes of a child," thus approximating the interpretive needs of an uninitiated audience. Thus, seamlessly, Edgar's point of view is configured as an asset in that it both mimics the perspective of American audiences, supposedly unaware of the Norwegian material, *as well as* that of the implied child reader. But, by the 1930s any suggestion that American audiences might be unaware of the folklore of Norway is hard to support. Despite Edgar's emphatic assertions that he would avoid the Norwegian illustrations so as not to be influenced by them,[36] by the 1930s it is too late, and all representations are informed by the general nostalgia implicated in identity-formation.

By the 1930s Norway was a modern nation-state, and the trappings of nation-building had become the basis of nation-hood. Folklore (and in the case of Norway this is explicitly the work of Asbjørnsen and Moe illustrated by Werenskiold and Kittelsen) had become institutionalized, with folklore both linked to childhood (and thus the future), while also explicitly nostalgic (the past of the imagination). Whereas Kittelsen's trolls had existed in an uneasy in-between and ambiguous terrain—outside the realm of reason, emergent from Nature, slippery and dangerous, the d'Aulaires' trolls were part of a larger movement in which trolls and other supernatural creatures in nature were "domesticated" and rationalized—no longer dangerous, but playful, harmless, and even cuddly—the stuff of children's toys and books.[37] Through the processes of mass publication, public education, and the emergence of industries targeting not only children but peddling nostalgia to the new middle class, the ambiguity of the Kittelsen's trolls was lost. Trolls now literally fill the landscape at every shop, on every card rack, at every amusement park, and so have become ordinary and harmless. Trolls are now not only an aspect of the Norwegian landscape but of the Norwegian psyche,[38] and one need only remember the ceremonies at the 1994 Lillehammer Olympics to see the clear linkage of trolls with something essentially Norwegian.

While the d'Aulaires saw it necessary to "translate" the illustrations, no such requirement applied to the texts themselves, as their own recycling of George Dasent's English translations of Asbjørnsen and Moe's tales in their *East of the Sun and West of the Moon* attests. In fact, Dasent's translations of over 108 of the tales in two volumes of *NF* (1859 and 1874) have been the basis for most of the English collections in circulation, including the d'Aulaires', and the particular reduction and selection of a few well-circulating tales from this large corpus is also part of the story of what shaped American expectations of Norwegian folklore. It is important to note that although almost all of the English tales in circulation to this day derive from Dasent's original translation (although now uncredited), the illustrations vary from book to book. Most American collections did not use the famous Norwegian illustrations, preferring to experiment with new, more colorful ones. The most significant, famous, and replicated is Dasent's 1914 collection *East of the Sun and West of the Moon*, illustrated by the Danish-born Kay Nielsen, whose style fits clearly into the English "Golden Age" of illustrators such as Arthur Rackham. It is these illustrations, so distinct from the earlier Norwegian ones, that are ironically most often associated with the Norwegian tales in America today, and it is on the basis of Nielsen's illustrations that tales continue to be characterized as "weird." It is also clear that May Massee's editorial decisions about the d'Aulaires' book were based on already-in-place American expectations of the Norwegian landscape that was shaped by this earlier Dasent/Nielsen collection. In a letter dated Dec. 29, 1937, Massee wrote to Ingri "last night *all of a sudden it occurred to me* that we ought to call the book 'East of the Sun and West of the Moon' (emphasis added), despite the fact that there is only partial overlap between the 15 tales in the Dasent/Nielsen collection and the 21 tales in the d'Aulaires'.

That editors shape the look and feel of books, and guide the authors based on their own ideologically laden backgrounds is a back story normally omitted, and yet it clearly influenced the resulting texts. As if deriving her descriptions directly *from* the d'Aulaires' images, Massee stated in 1935 that Norway, "with its fascinating pine forests whose trees need only a proper amount of snow to turn into 'a crowd of solemn creatures'—trolls, perhaps...is a country where reality quickly meets fantasy and merges into it; a beautiful land, perfect for a sensitive child. It is all Ingri's by inheritance and living, but it became Edgar's through his close association with Ingri's family."[39] Massee's description of the magical Nature of Norway and her assertion that this was Ingri's inheritance by birth now echo with the common knowledge about Norwegian folklore, reiterated by subsequent folklore collections, that it is based in rural life, "surrounded by great forests and high mountains…where folk still saw the *nisse* and captured the sea-serpent , and swore that it was true."[40] Patricia Connolly, of Doubleday, focused on this topic in a letter she wrote to the d'Aulaires in 1970 in response to their proposal for the book, *Trolls*. In praising the idea for the book, she reflects on her own childhood and effuses:

> There is something about old, long-settled Europe, so that even when one is alone in the middle of nowhere—and of course I am thinking of England in particular—yet, one is aware of a particular feeling. There is more there in the grass and fields and trees and woods…I've had that feeling in so many places there—but not here. It is as though the earlier inhabitants are all piled up close and deep like dead leaves. And it is a feeling American children don't really know about; but I think you can get it to them in Trolls. The way that in twilight a bump on a hill can suddenly turn into a man stealthily setting snares. How a man can suddenly freeze into a dead tree when you get close. The constant movement between things that seem to be there, and aren't. And things that are there, and seem to be something else.[41]

Connolly reiterates the belief that the supernatural inheres in the Old-World landscape, a belief that American children lack, and this naturalized association of Nature and Norwegian Folklore (generalized to the broader "Scandinavian" Folklore) is by now axiomatic. Across decades the idea of Norway has been preserved in amber as a kind of rural and natural world inhabited by supernatural beings and quaint villagers.

OLA—TYPICAL NORWEGIAN

The adapted-for-American-audiences "Nordic-themed" books by the d'Aulaires fit into what Nathalie op de Beeck has called "picturebook ethnography"—popular fare in U.S. children's book publishing in the mid-twentieth century. In the midst of social anxieties about immigration and assimilation of racial, ethnic, and religious groups, these picturebook ethnographies addressed cultural difference at a significant remove, their subjects located at a spatial and temporal distance. As op de Beeck observes, "[American] Picturebooks were part of a mainstream culture that often assumed fixed social boundaries based on ethnic and racial stereotypes"[42] and provided a "visual shorthand for signs of cultural difference."[43] As such, they were ideologically laden texts that introduced young readers into a system of signification whose historical roots had been obscured. Rather than representing immigrant stories, the picturebooks of this period tended to "limit potential immigrants to countries of origin"[44] thus reaffirming social divisions and conventionalizing stereotypes while purporting to represent cultural diversity. In these picturebooks of strange and exotic lands, children were represented in the ethnographic present, living in pre-industrial rural settings in quaint houses and wearing "national dress" in their day-to-day lives. On this didactic slippery slope, books *for* children were also *about* children, representing an entire country or region almost exclusively with child characters. In a state of arrested development, the region itself was thus infantilized, its inhabitants children, living in correspondingly un-developed lands. This semiotic system can be further broken down into stories about children from Europe—the Old Country—and picturebook ethnographies of the non-white and colonized—the "global South" and Asia. It is within the first category that the d'Aulaires' *Ola* falls, whereas their *Children of the Northlights* falls into the second.

The template had been established earlier by Maud and Miska Petersham, the author-illustrator pair who were also May Massee's clients. Their *Miki* (1929) is the story of their own son, who goes on an imaginary trip to an equally imaginary old Hungary (from whence Miska had emigrated). In a review in *The Three Owls*, Hammett Owen applauds *Miki* for presenting "everyday life in a picturebook country,"[45] obviously conflating fiction with ethnography. D'Aulaires' *Ola*, following three years later, is the story of a little Norwegian boy who goes on a trip through the Norwegian countryside. May Massee clearly takes this story as ethnographic in nature: "The pictures reveal not only how Ola's house looks inside and out and Ola's good times, but also how the natural world looks to the children and how the folk and fairy tales grew directly out of this appearance."[46] But this celebration of Old World quaintness with its colorful countryside and infantilized and pre-industrial inhabitants has been mediated through a "modernist filter"[47] which renders any kind of direct "ethnographic" reading impossible.

Norwegian nationalism emerged out of the Norwegian independence movement. In the process of Norwegian nation-building, the ideological work necessary to arrive at a common sense of nation-hood depended on the integration and incorporation of identities that were seen to have emerged out of a common "land, language, and lore,"[48] and the cultural producers of this distinct identity looked to the medieval past and to the rural areas for inspiration. Justifying independence through evoking a "Golden Age" that preceded Danish Rule, an urban, bourgeois intelligentsia looked to the Middle Ages and the spread of Christianity to claim a "genealogical continuity with early medieval Viking chiefs."[49] Similarly Norwegian free farmers—*bonde*—were seen as further historical justification for an independent Norway, metaphorically rooting independence itself in the soil. In addition to folktale collections (both from the rural folk and survivals from an earlier time), other "traditional" items of material culture were deployed and reimagined as a common heritage. These material and visual items were, in contrast to written texts, immediately apprehended, and often, in the case of food, clothing, and shelter, were literally incorporated and embodied, disallowing cognitive/critical distance between the user and the sign. In this enterprise, children were brought into an ideological framework by the heavy use of visual imagery, which linked them to a larger national destiny in seemingly ordinary acts.

The association of specific identity markers in the land was made often and early in the case of Norway. A post card image from 1905, the year that Norway achieved nation-statehood, is typical: surrounding a free-floating map of Norway (not attached to any surrounding

Doubleday, Doran and Company, Incorporated
Garden City   1932   New York

End page and title page
of *Ola.*

states) is an array of images that attest to Norway's cultural markers—
a Stave church, not only an indigenous form but a *survival* from
medieval Christianity; Nidaros Cathedral; a raised, sod-roof farm house;
a woman clad in traditional, pre-industrial clothing; Viking ships and
sail-powered fishing vessels along the north coast; eagles; migratory
geese; great expanses of nature; and, in the far north, two Lapp reindeer
herders and their herd.[50] Thirty years later, *Ola* emphatically replicates
these cultural markers situating them in the land, but also within the
context of modern, institutionalized forms of identity formation—
education. The double-spread title page of *Ola* connects geography with
the past by the placement of "runic" figures around the page margins,
and by the reference at the bottom of the map to the homestead of Leif
Ericson. On the title page, a seated Ola reads an open book along with
his new friends who surround him, all dressed in "traditional" clothes. A

preliminary watercolor mock-up of this page, with "NORWAY" spread across Ola's book, makes the connection between the map, the book, and the subject clear. Additional markers on the map plot Ola's eventual itinerary through the landscape—"Birds Here," and "Lapps here," but in this apparently innocent gesture, the Lapps (Sami) are singled out as different, and in fact part of nature. It is worth noting that the location of both the birds and the Lapps is identical in both the 1932 and the 1905 maps.

Ola is, in fact, a "laundry list" of identity markers: skis, Northern Lights, Midnight Sun, cod and cod liver oil, eider down, Stave churches, "traditional" farm houses, and the distinctive regional dress—the *bunad*. This "laundry list" approach is underscored in the end papers of *Ola* with their nostalgic display of rural handicrafts alongside the Norwegian flag, which seems to give the reader a "true glimpse of the varied life in Norway."[51] The conceit of the book is that Ola's trip through the landscape is not only that it represents what is essential to the Norwegian identity, but that the book itself provides a basic geography lesson on that land and its people.

These "geography lessons" effected through a child's magical journey through the landscape have precedent in Norway, most famously in Selma Lagerlof's 1906 *Nils Holgerssons underbara resa genom Sverige* (*The Wonderful Adventures of Nils*, which was translated from Swedish into Norwegian in 1927), but more importantly in the mandatory schoolbooks, *Lesebok for Folkskolen*, which were distributed in millions of copies from the 1890s through 1950. In these schoolbooks, the twin projects of mass literacy and nationalism converged in the "Rundt Norge" chapters, which featured lessons in regional landscapes, frequently including the archetypal (if exotic) Lofoten fisheries and the reindeer-herding Sami (Lapps) of Finnmark—the very places visited by Ola in his travels. Regional distinctiveness thus became the national, collective identity through standardized education, which was then projected to American readers as typical. *Ola* is the result of two, distinct conceptual moves: the normalization of the dominance of south Norwegian cultural forms as

common heritage; and the use of identity markers for nation-building in the Norwegian context, which were then extracted from that context and placed into American racial and social discourses in which identity formation is transformed into the reification of otherness.

Ola is introduced five pages into the book, only after a description of the land and (magical) landscape. Ola is blond and blue-eyed, with a face "rosy from much fresh air"—shaped by Nature. He gets up from his sled bed with elaborate carvings, which vaguely evoke the *Saga*, dresses in a distinctive regional costume, a Setesdal *bunad*, and exits from an old door ornamented with "quaint paintings." "Quaint" here has to be read in the context of the implied American reader, as the two images on the door are outside of Norwegian tradition: The "Crocodille" (neither crocodile nor *krokodille*, and hardly an indigenous species) would be better placed in a sixteenth or seventeenth century *Wunderkammer* of a rich merchant of central Europe; and the *havfrue*, sketched as a comely and alluring mermaid, does not often appear in Norwegian Folklore.[52]

Ola and his sisters. Detail of endpaper in *Ola and Blakken, and Line, Sine, Trine*, 1933.

115

In the American construction of the Old World, it is a generic "quaintness" that is being signified. After putting on his skis, another sign of Norwegian distinctiveness, Ola skis across the next four pages until he falls into a group of *bunad*-clad girls who take him to their hamlet, where a traditional wedding is taking place. This wedding provides the opportunity for the full array of Norwegian markers—everyone is wearing *bunad*, the two-story, sod-roof houses are the classic Telemark style (also shown on the 1905 map), and the wedding takes place in a Stave Church, which, in *Ola*, is modeled on the Borgund Stave Church. The choice of the Borgund church is intentional and inevitable. It is not a church near Ingri's home region, nor, on the basis of Ola's Setesdal *bunad*, is it near his. Instead, it is one of the iconic Stave churches, one of the oldest and best preserved, and its image has been reproduced and circulated in the construction of a Norwegian identity, one which the d'Aulaires reproduce. The d'Aulaires have created a fantasy Norway, constructed out of the tropes of nationhood, now reconfigured to represent the Old Country. The most significant of these sign of Norwegianness is the *bunad*.

Norwegian anthropologist Thomas Hylland Eriksen defines the *bunad* as a "particular kind of [Norwegian] festive dress" (275). The term itself—*klædebunad*—was introduced by Hulda Garborg in 1903 on the eve of Norwegian independence (1905) in an effort to create national, distinctive costumes that were based on regional, rural, traditional forms. Although the *bunad* evokes a pre-industrial, rural, handicraft-based economy, in its modern, nationalist-inspired incarnation it is a product of industrial production, and (urban) consumerism. *Bunad* wearing is thus a modern phenomenon that is symbolically linked to the pre-modern and the rural as constitutive of Norwegian identity (as are folktales). Ever since they were introduced, the trend in *bunad* wearing has increased.[53] Ingri's hometown of Kongsberg is in Buskerud, which has its own regional *bunad*, but rather than draw inspiration from that, Ola and the friends he meets (Siri and Turi, etc.)

all wear the formal Setesdal *bunad* as do Ola and his sisters Line, Sine, and Trina in *Ola and Blakken*, and the selection of this particular *bunad* is again intentional and self-conscious. Recognizable and iconic, the Setesdal *bunad* comes from "one of the few areas in [Norway] where there has been an unbroken tradition of folk costume,"[55] thus it is both "authentic," in its unbroken traditionality, and, when re-signified in the context of Norwegian nationalism, typical. Not a *bunad* from Ingri's home region, it most likely was nonetheless part of Ingri's visual world growing up because she had seen its image in countless illustrations. The role of publishing—especially the role of illustration—in effecting this common, national heritage cannot be underestimated. Mid-twentieth-century Norway witnessed a proliferation of illustrated postcards and

Christmas Card by Milly Heegaard, 1942, two children wearing Setesdal *Bunads*.[57]

magazines whose subject matter is often *bunad*-wearing Norwegian children. These images, many by women illustrators,[56] circulated in "throw-away" mass-produced paper products—Christmas cards and gifts, gift tags, greeting cards as well as picture—and text books, saturating the visual field, and, in the process, normalizing those images.

A well-inscribed motif in the celebration of unity in diversity is the image of a ring of children, each wearing a miniaturized and regionally distinct *bunad*, holding hands and singing allegiance to Norway.[58] For cards that depict individual children, however, it is the Setesdal *bunad*,[59] and the Sami *gakti* [Sami for *bunad*], which are the most common. But whereas the Setesdal *bunad* indexes a shared, common heritage, the Sami *gakti* marks difference—that which is distinct from Norwegian—highlighting it by the juxtaposition. Significantly, in *Ola* there are three distinct kinds of dress: the Setesdal *bunad* of Ola and his Norwegian friends, the Sami *gakti*, and the fishing gear of the Lofoten fishing industry, thus northern Norway serves as the exotic foil to the normalized south.

TODAY'S PERSPECTIVE

The imaginary landscapes of the d'Aulaires reflect a very specific period in the U.S. with a time-bound understanding of what constituted the American identity and Norwegian culture. For any critical approach to their work to have value, it is important to put their books in context. The d'Aulaires resisted new technologies and were hesitant to work in a fast-paced commercial realm. Their work is remarkably consistent in its look, and this is some indication as to how insular they were to the changes that were occurring both in the art world and in society at large over the many decades they were producing books. Read today, their work can seem dated in appearance, and, like so many children's books from the mid-twentieth century (however beloved at the time), their books are out of touch with both the revisited historical record and social issues. Their American biography series is out of print except for their circulation through the Beautiful Feet Press, which specializes in the home-school market. *Ola* was published in Norwegian in 1951 by Mittet, as was *Ola og Blakken* in 1933, but they had very poor reception and low distribution. *Lappe Lasse og Lappe Lise*, the Norwegian translation of *Children of the Northlights*, was also released in 1935 to slightly better response, perhaps because it mirrored contemporary Norwegian representations of the Sami decades prior to their own indigenous movement, but none of the d'Aulaires' works has any place in the Norwegian memory. Several of their Nordic-themed books — *Ola*, *Leif the Lucky*, *East of the Sun and West of the Moon*, and *Children of the Northlights* — are being republished by the University of Minnesota Press, likely due to their appeal to adults of Scandinavian heritage — an exercise in nostalgia for that generation of Americans raised on these images.

1 Holmgren, Beth. "Émigré-zation: Russian Artists and American Children's Picture Books," in *Kazaam! Splat! Ploof!: The American Impact on European Popular Culture since 1945*, eds. Sabrina P. Ramet and Gordana P. Crnković. New York and Oxford: Rowman and Littlefield, 2003: 219-233. Quote on pg 220.

2 In the 1930s a high percentage of those immigrating/fleeing were Jewish. Of the handful of artists named in this paragraph, three out of the five were Jewish.

3 Almost all of these deal with the discovery and settling of America, and American heroes—not the focus here.

4 *Leif the Lucky*, published in 1941, precedes the discovery of L'Anse aux Meadows in Newfoundland as the probable location of Leif Erikson's settlement by almost 20 years. The discovery was the work of two Norwegians, Helge and Anne Stine Ingstad, beginning in 1960, and provided material evidence for what had been, until then, information from the *Saga*. *Leif the Lucky* is thus in the category of folklore, although it is also one of Westward exploration, like several other of the d'Aulaires' books.

5 Intentionally not included here is the d'Aulaires' *Norse Gods and Giants* (1967). Although this might reasonably be assumed to be in the category of Norwegian folklore, especially since that connection is made in contemporary book reviews, along with statements about Ingri's being of Viking stock, this book is more along the lines of a "condensed-for-children omnibus" and more similar to the d'Aulaires' *Book of Greek Myths* (1962). From Edgar d'Aulaire's notes in the Beinecke Library, it is clear that *Norse Gods and Giants* was heavily researched, and his notes include source material on the Edda and on folklore, mythology and religion from the likes of Max Müller, Sophus Bugge, Wilhelm Mannhardt, Jan de Vries, Edward Tylor, Andrew Lang, James Frazer, Axel Olrik, and Carl von Sydow.

6 op de Beeck, Nathalie. *Suspended Animation*. Minneapolis: Univ. of Minn. P., 2010.

7 Edgar's Caldecott Medal acceptance speech, reproduced in *The Horn Book*, July–August 1946: 252.

8 This narrative process began immediately in the popular press. See, for example, Elizabeth Sacartoff's "Freedom for the Artist Pays Rich Dividends," *PM* 4 May, 1941: 56-7, and "Exiled Artists from Paris Hope to Make New Start Here," *PM* 22 June, 1941: 54. The leftist *PM* was more enthusiastic and embracing of both immigrants and modernist art than mainstream, but the redemptive promise of the U.S. is consistent and unchallenged. Nonetheless, there is much evidence that paints a different picture—one of financial precarity, anti-Semitism, and the pain of separation from family and homeland.

9 Edgar Parin and Ingri D'Aulaire Papers, Beinecke Rare Book & Manuscript Library, Box 148.

10 Edgar illustrated a few other books, authored by others.

11 Massee worked from 1922–1933 with Doubleday, and until 1960 with Viking. This was the period in which the d'Aulaires produced most of their work. In the 60s and 70s they produced only four books total, three of those the "compendium" type collections, and one a re-issue of the 1933 *Ola and Blakken, and Line, Sine, Trine.*

12 See Marcus, Leonard. *Minders of Make-Believe*. New York: Houghton Mifflin, 2008.

13 May Massee, proof, D'Aulaire Papers, Box 148.

14 Mann, Vivian. *Gardens and Ghettos: The Art of Jewish Life in Italy*. Berkeley: UC Press, 1989.

15 Auler is a German name. D'Aulaire, often mispresented as Ella's "maiden name" is a made-up, French-sounding adaptation of Auler, used professionally by Ella to perhaps better fit in with the art world of Paris. In contrast to Edgar, however, she did not keep up its use, and used Ella Parin as her name once back in St. Louis for the next 43 years.

16 Box 204 in the collection included Ella Parin's Paris notebooks, clearly influenced by Art Nouveau and Symbolism.

17 Stories of Edgar's grandfather later were deployed when the d'Aulaires began writing their American heroes books to give legitimacy to the European immigrant couple's claim on American history.

18 The remainder of this essay focuses on the books I refer to as the "Nordic-themed" books. Those dealing with American heroes are also based on, and constitutive of an imaginary world, but these are both beyond the current scope and are also covered elsewhere. See, for example, Chapter 6 in Gary D. Schmidt's *Making Americans: Children's Literature from 1930 to 1960*. Iowa City: Univ. of Iowa Press, 2013; and also Leonard Marcus, "Life Drawings: Some Notes on Children's Picture Book Biographies," *The Lion and the Unicorn*, Vol 4.1, Summer 1980: 15-31.

19 Asbjørnsen, Peter Christen, Jørgen Engebretsen Moe, Noel Daniel, Kay Rasmus Nielsen, and George Webbe Dasent. *East of the Sun and West of the Moon: Old Tales from the North*. Cologne: Taschen, 2015.

20 http://www.theparisreview.org/blog/2015/12/03/east-of-the-sun-and-west-of-the-moon/. This is particularly ironic, since the one story selected in the review to indicate how "weird" this Norwegian material is, the story "Prince Lindorm," is not from Asbjørnsen and Moe at all but from a Danish collection: Svend Grundtvig's, "Kong Lindorm," in *Gamle danske Minder i Folkemunde* (Copenhagen: C.G. Eversens Forlag, 1854), no. 216: 172-80.

21 Uther, Hans-Jörg. *The Types of International Folktales: A Classification and Bibliography*. Based on the system of Antti Aarne and Stith Thompson. FF Communications no. 284–286. Helsinki: Suomalainen Tiedeakatemia, 2004.

22 This collection, featuring 21 stories from Asbjørnsen and Moe, is significantly different from the 1914 illustrated collection of the same name (with 15 stories), although both are based on the translations by Dasent (who also compiled his own *East of the Sun and West of the Moon and other Norse Tales*, in 1917, which contained 37 tales). The title of the book, actually a title of one of the tales within the collection, was suggested to the d'Aulaires by May Massee, in a letter dated Dec. 29, 1937 (d'Aulaire Papers, Beinecke Library).

23 D'Aulaire, Ingri and Edgar Parin. *East of the Sun and West of the Moon*. New York: Viking, 1938: 6.

24 D'Aulaire, Ingri and Edgar Parin. *D'Aulaires' Trolls*. Garden City, New York: Doubleday, 1972: 4.

25 Not a picturebook but a reprinting of a selection of 21 tales from Asbjørnsen and Moe accompanied by 22 etchings and lithographs.

26 It is significant that with the exception of the last two, the larger-format, omnibus-type collections, none of these Nordic-themed books had large runs or significant appeal. The 1938 *East of the Sun and West of the Moon* had, for example, an initial run of 2100 copies and was out of print by 1940. *Ola*, *Ola and Blakken*, and *Children of the North Lights* [Nor.: *Lappe Lasse og Lappe Lise*] were translated into Norwegian and published by Mittet Forlag, but they did not sell well (correspondences with author) and only had one printing. Furthermore, the Norwegian *Ola* was only published in 1951, well after the first English version in 1932.

27 Compare with Theodor Kittelsen. "Nyttårsløyer," 1903. Watercolor and pencil on paper. 44x67 cm. Private coll.

28 See, for example, Hult, Marte Hvam. *Framing a National Narrative: The Legend Collections of Peter Christen Asbjørnsen*. Detroit: Wayne State UP, 2003.

29 The d'Aulaires' *East of the Sun and West of the Moon* was based on *Popular Tales from the Norse*, Georg Dasent's 1904 translation of 59 tales from Asbjørnsen and Moe.

30 Asbjørnsen, Peter Christen. *Norske Huldre-Eventyr og Folkesagn: Anden Samling*. Christiania. P.J. Steensballes Forlag, 3rd ed., 1870.

31 Bottigheimer, Ruth. *Fairy Tales: a New History*. Albany, N.Y.: State Univ. of N.Y. Press, 2009.

32 See Conrad, JoAnn. ""This is what Trolls really look like": the folklore that is Norway," in *News from Other Worlds: Studies in Nordic Folklore, Mythology and Culture*, eds. M. Kaplan and T. Tangherlini. Berkeley: North Pinehurst Press. 2012: 290-316. It is ironic that whereas Kittelsen's illustrations are inherently ambiguous and question the very notions of reality, they have become the literalization and materialization of the supernatural in subsequent distribution.

33　See Conrad, JoAnn. "Tracking the Ogre—the Sami Stallo," *Ural-Altaische Jahrbücher* N.F. 16, 1999/2000:56-75—on the striking similarity between Kittelsen's illustration of the story of "Askeladden who had an eating match with the Troll" and that by the d'Aulaires in their book *Troll* (1972).

34　d'Aulaires. *East of the Sun and West of the Moon*: 6.

35　"kunstnerparet med de festige billedboker," *Morgenbladet* (1936). This interview with Ingri and Edgar was when they returned to Oslo in 1936 to begin work on the book. (Box 210, d'Aulaire Papers).

36　Bolo (pseud.). "Stor amerikansk utgave av Asbjørnsen og Moes eventyr" n.d. but ca. 1937.

37　John Lindow points out in his book *Trolls* that the Swedish yearly magazine *Bland Tomtar och Troll* is an example of this domestication, linking, in the title, the trolls of the wilderness with the domestic gnomes. Lindow, John. *Trolls: An Unnatural History*. London: Reaktion Books, 2014.

38　See the Paris Review blog cited in Note 20.

39　Massee, May. "Ingri and Edgar Parin D'Aulaire: a Sketch." *The Horn Book*, vol xi, September–October 1935, no. 5: 269.

40　Shaw, Pat. "The Norwegian Folk Tales and Their Illustrators," in *Norwegian Folktales: Selected from the Collection of Peter Christen Asbjørnsen and Jørgen Moe*. New York: Pantheon, 1960: 5.

41　Letter from Patricia Connolly to "Mrs. and Mrs. E.P. D'Aulaire," November 16, 1970, d'Aulaire Papers.

42　op de Beeck. *Suspended Animation*: 54.

43　Ibid.: 56.

44　Ibid.: 59.

45　Hammett Owen, Helen. *The Three Owls, Third Book*: 441. Barbara Bader, notes the irony of a "picture book country" appearing in a picture book in *American Picturebooks from Noah's Ark to the Beast Within*. New York: Macmillan. 1976: 39.

46　Mahoney, Bertha E. and Margueritte M. Mitchell. "Ingri and Edgar Parin d'Aulaire" [note, in the article all letters are caps except for "and"], *The Horn Book*, July-August 1940: 259.

47　op de Beeck: 63-64.

48　Abrahams, Roger D. "Phantoms of Romantic Nationalism in Folkloristics." *The Journal of American Folklore*, 106, no. 419 (1993): 3-37.

49 Eriksen, T.H. *Ethnicity and Nationalism: Anthropological Perspectives*, 2nd ed. London: Pluto Press, 2002: 68-69. This same genealogical continuity with the Vikings is also imputed to Ingri by her book publishers—literalizing the symbolic connection.

50 Gamledags Postkort, series no. 1222, ca. 1905. On pg. 324, Fig. 77, Conrad, Jo Ann. "Contested terrain land, language, and lore in contemporary Sami politics." Thesis (Ph. D. in Folklore/Cultural Studies)—University of California, Berkley, Spring 1999. http://catalog.hathitrust.org/api/volumes/oclc/81845954.html

51 Inside flap of dust cover of *Ola*, written by the d'Aulaires.

52 *Store Norske Leksikon*. https://snl.no/havfru. There are some recorded migratory legends, all collected from the far north, in the Digital Samling av Eventyr og Sagn, at www2.hf.uio.no. The title for these is, however, "Sjøvetter varsler storm" [the Sea spirit warns of a storm], a completely different narrative tradition.

53 Eriksen, T.H. "Traditionalism and Neoliberalism: The Norwegian Folk Dress in the 21st Century," in *Properties of Culture—Culture as Property: Pathways to Reform in Post-Soviet Siberia*, ed. Erich Kasten. Berlin: Dietrich Reimer Verlag, 2004: 267-286.

54 It is important to note that in the remake of *Ola and Blakken* in 1976, which was re-named *The Terrible Troll Bird*, there are very few changes. The style of the illustrations is a bit modernized, however, significantly in the new book, although it is still Ola of the earlier books, Ola now wears a pair of slacks and a shirt—no *bunad*, although his sisters and mother still wear *bunads*.

55 Haugen, Bjørn Sverre Hol: «Kvinne- og mannsbunad fra Setesdal». I: *Norsk bunadleksikon*, b. 2, s. 162-169. (Oslo), Damm 2006.

56 Women illustrators such as Milly Heegaard, Anne Eline Coucheron, Jenny Nyström, and Elbjørg Øien Moum were extremely productive illustrators, their images mass produced. Although their role and that of these commercial art forms have been under-examined, it is arguable that they contributed to the construction of a visual sphere that served to re-educate consumers on what Norwegian looked like.

57 Image from Norsk Folkemuseum.

58 See, for example, *ABC* (Samisk) by Margarethe Wiig, Tanum, 1951:4.

59 See, for example, this 1942 Christmas postcard http://digitaltmuseum.no/011 013419184?query=postkort&name=Stjerner&pos=2#&gid=1&pid=1 by postcard artist Milly Heegaard. In many other illustrations, children, holding hands in a ring are featured wearing all the various regional bunads, celebrating a kind of unity in diversity. These always include a Sami child wearing a Sami *gakti* (*bunad*), although Norwegian Sami policy was blatantly assimilationist, not pluralist. http://digitalt museum.no/011013419124.

KATIE TRUMPENER

Nature in the Kitchen
Animals, Children, and Mothers in Robert McCloskey's *Blueberries for Sal*

In Memory of My Mother, Mary Dorris Trumpener (1932–2014)

In *Blueberries for Sal*, the identical front and back endpapers in the original printing (Viking, 1948) are key (although some present-day reprints do not reproduce it). A mother and her daughter stand in a rural kitchen, making blueberry jam from the berries they gathered together on Blueberry Hill. The kitchen is old-fashioned, heated by a big cast-iron pot-belly stove. It is still late summer, the kitchen window propped open, geraniums basking in the sunlight, and on the hillsides beyond, dense, tough backwoods vegetation (coniferous trees, able to weather Maine's winters). The wall calendar shows August; the clock shows four o'clock.

Everything has its proper place in this kitchen: containers of coffee, oats, and sugar stand on the counter, plates lined up in the cupboard. (A shopping list, too, hangs on the wall; in winter, when the snow is high, it will seem a long journey to the store.) At the kitchen table, the mother is pouring jam—berries still whole and visible inside their sugary mass—into canning jars. Another pot is still steaming on the stove, boiling more jam jars, or more jam to fill them. Three jars are already filled and sealed; a fourth is almost full, three more stand at the ready.

The aproned mother looks calm and confident as she fills each jar. Her close-fitting sweater hangs neatly, her hair hangs smoothly down the sides of her face, she smiles as she concentrates on aiming the

(opposite) detail, *Blueberries for Sal,* 1948.

stream of molten jam into the open jar. No sweaty brow, mussed hair, jam-stained clothing, nothing burning; she has made this jam before and knows what she is doing.

Sal should perhaps be watching closely, to see how it's done. But she's not, not yet. Instead, she's playing with the rubber jar seals. Sal is standing on a tall high bow-backed Windsor chair (the solid, locally-made, saddle-seated wooden chairs used in New England since the eighteenth century). The wooden kitchen table next to her has its flyleaves out, to accommodate the jam-making. A package of rubber rings is spilling onto the tabletop, and Sal has gotten a long series of them running, bangle-like, up and down her arm and hands, with several more dangling on a long kitchen spoon, making an improvised mobile.

Sal herself dangles. She wears Mary Janes, a short-sleeved sweater, a slightly droopy pair of overalls—yet here, as throughout the book, the overalls don't stay on her shoulders as intended. Instead, as she bends one wrist to balance the jam rings, her right strap has slid down her shoulder so that her arm balances it too. Like her mother, she concentrates intently on what she is doing. Ignoring her slipping strap, her straw-like, cow-licked hair, her sagging pants, she is utterly absorbed in her own experiment.

Her mother condones her efforts. It is she who has dressed Sal in overalls that morning, combed Sal's hair, and watched it get messy again, brought Sal berry-picking, and pulled Sal, on her chair, up to the kitchen table, to watch the jam-making without interfering too much. How will this disheveled girl ever become a competent homemaker like her mother, shapely and soignée, able to drive the family car up the mountain and boil jam with quiet confidence? Sal's mother is calm and above all, patient. Sal does not yet have to undertake womanly duties, or, as yet, wear female dress. It is enough that she is along, looking on, occasionally understanding what her mother is doing.

Mother and daughter went up the mountain in the same spirit. Only in the tale's epilogue, the endpapers, are mother and daughter shown inside, in the kitchen. Throughout the main story, they are outside, on terrain familiar but still wild. Maine's climate is only for the hardy. The

bears of Blueberry Hill need to fatten up for the winter ahead, when they hibernate, tucked into the hills. The humans, too, need to pick what's edible on Maine's mountains before the snow. Canning the blueberries to preserve them, transforming the raw into the cooked, the transient into the storable, they turn nature into culture, into human cuisine.[1]

Yet Robert McCloskey's book also develops a tight equivalence between bear and human foraging, human and ursine families. Their stories are symmetrical: the bears come up one side of the mountain, humans up the other, on the same afternoon—both searching for blueberries. The adults know that winter is coming. Their young are too inexperienced to understand what lies ahead; for them, foraging still seems a game. While Sal's mother accumulates hundreds of berries, Sal gives herself over to eating in the moment, retaining only three berries in her pail.

Bears and humans—at least adults old enough to know—are wary of one another, potentially in competition or in conflict. Cubs and toddlers do not yet know enough to be afraid. Their worlds, so far, are not defined by threat or scarcity, but by their familiar surroundings, anchored and guarded by their mothers.

Yet because they are not alert, cub and girl lose their invisible tethering, straying too far and becoming separated from their respective mothers, then erroneously attached to each other's, as each mismatched pair makes their way through a blueberry patch. The cub, reliant on

Kitchen scene, *Blueberries for Sal*, 1948.

127

Sal and the Mother bear, *Blueberries for Sal*, 1948.

sound, is genuinely startled to find a human mother before him. Sal can see perfectly well that the bear's mother is not her own, yet ambles along anyway behind her. And even when the bear mother addresses her cub, urging him to eat all he can hold, Sal is not frightened by her growl. Instead she blithely throws three berries into her pail: *kuplink*, *kuplank*, *kuplunk*. Startled at the sound, the bear mother looks around to discover a human child trailing behind her. On the other side of the mountain, Sal's mother is equally startled to find a cub, not Sal, trailing behind her.

Yet although perturbed to see even a small member of the other species, neither panics. Meanwhile, as Sal hunts for her mother, she mistakes the sounds of a mother eagle and her children for her own mother; the cub, listening for his mother, initially mistakes the sound of a mother partridge and her children. Luckily, the mother-child pairs of bears and humans soon find each other too, and each pair, just as peacefully as they have come, goes back down its side of the mountain: bears presumably to their cave, where they will eventually spend the winter sleeping, mother and daughter back to the kitchen.

⁂

Ever since Aesop, literature has drawn on the animal kingdom and interactions between species to derive lessons about human behavior. Since the Middle Ages, bestiaries have shown adults and children the animal kingdom's diversity, characteristic appearances and reported behaviors. During the eighteenth century, dedicated books for children began inviting them to observe and contemplate animal lives. First, children were asked to differentiate their own behavior from that of their animal counterparts. "Let dogs delight to bark and bite, / for God has made them so," Isaac Watts exhorts in his *Divine and Moral Songs: Attempted in Easy Language for the Use of Children* (1715):

> Let bears and lions growl and fight,
> For tis their nature, too.
>
> But children, you should never let
> Such angry passions rise:
> Your little hands were never made
> To tear each other's eyes.

In contrast, Sarah Trimmer's *Fabulous Histories, or the History of the Robins: Designed for the Instruction of Children, Respecting Their Treatment of Animals* (1786) made its robins themselves into talking characters and focused closely on bird-human interactions, pleading for moral behavior in both species, and for human guardianship over more vulnerable species. This humanizing of animals to ensure their humane treatment informed later best-sellers like Anna Sewell's *Black Beauty* (1877) and Marshall Saunders' *Beautiful Joe* (1893). By the mid-nineteenth century, indeed, children's hymnals reprinted Watts's song next to hymns preaching against cruelty to animals.[2]

The turn of the twentieth century saw a return to animal fables, comical bestiaries, and comic cautionary tales (Rudyard Kipling's 1902 *Just So Stories*; Hilaire Belloc's 1896 *Bad Child's Book of Beasts*; Beatrix Potter's 1902 *The Tale of Peter Rabbit*).[3] Naturalist stories like Ernest Thompson Seton's 1898 *Wild Animals I Have Known* made pioneering efforts to emphasize the wildness, animality, and unknowability of other species.[4] Children's literature continued to take an observational interest in the habits and habitats of wild and domesticated animals; Potter, indeed, brought a naturalist's visual sensibility even to the comic animal cautionary tale.

Yet the predominant strain in children's literature anthropomorphized, humanized and with it, often sentimentalized animals. This turn was sparked in part by the American and German fad for "teddy bears," following a real-life incident neither sentimental nor humane. During a 1902 Mississippi bear hunt, President Theodore (Teddy) Roosevelt, the famous Rough Rider and war hero, refused the unsportsmanlike suggestion that he shoot a bear cub his attendants had already captured and trussed. Roosevelt believed the bear must be killed to put it out of its post-capture misery; he objected only to the idea of taking trophy credit for a bear already subdued. A 1902 satirical political cartoon about the incident depicted the tethered cub as cute—and the "teddy bear" was born, that diminutive, soft, huggable cloth animal who remained a fixture for the next century. The teddy bear obsession spawned not only popular music (John Walter Bratton's 1907 "The Teddy Bears' Picnic") but classic children's bear stories (from A.A. Milne's 1926 *Winnie the Pooh* to Michael Bond's 1959–2014 Paddington Bear series).

Teddy bears at once humanized wild animals, making them cuddly, and celebrated the emotional bonds (and analogs) between children and animals. Popular children's books explored these emotional bonds not only to foster sympathy for the animals themselves, but as a way to describe children's own coming-of-age or ground human losses and grief in terms of animal loyalties and instincts.[5]

Many more children's stories collapsed the boundaries between the human and animal worlds, introducing animals with human names, speech, or social habits. Kenneth Grahame's Mr. Toad (*Wind in the Willows*, 1908) drives a motorcar, Winnie-the-Pooh has friends stop in for tea, just as Walt Disney's animated Mickey Mouse pilots a steamboat in *Steamboat Willie* (1928) and George Herriman's cartoon cat-and-mouse Krazy Kat and Ignatz (1913–1944) pursue one another with hurled bricks or declarations of affection.

Yet animals also occupy an uneasy relationship to human culture. In Jean de Brunhoff's *The Story of Babar* (1931), Babar is orphaned after hunters shoot his mother. And although he is adopted by humans, donning human clothes and riding the department store elevator, he still weeps at night for his mother. The duck family in McCloskey's *Make Way for Ducklings* (1941), the dog Muffin in Margaret Wise Brown's *Noisy Book* series (1939–47), Chester Cricket, Tucker Mouse, and Harry

Cat in George Selden's *The Cricket in Times Square* (1960) struggle to adapt themselves to the traffic, noises, and lights of the human city. And in E. B. White's *Stuart Little* (1945), a talking mouse born into a human family struggles to adapt himself to the scale of an uncomprehending human world.

Arguably, such books become particularly uncanny when animals talk, narrate, or—as in White's *Charlotte's Web* (1952)—write. Yet these tales' ability to offer fables about human attitudes and social bonds depends crucially on their ability to suggest that animals think, feel, and express themselves in quasi-human terms.

Picture books are structurally less reliant on language; addressed at once to young readers, parents reading aloud, and listeners too young to read (and in some cases not or barely able to speak yet), they must communicate through visual as much as verbal means. The animal protagonists of H. A. Rey's *Curious George* (1941) and Gene Zion and Margaret Bloy's *Harry the Dirty Dog* (1956) don't speak in human words.[6] Instead, their body language and facial expressions—and their interactions with their human "families"—bear the tales' meaning. Following Aesop and Watts, Rey, Zion, and Bloy use animal misdeeds to help children understand adult norms of conduct. Harry relishes his contact with the city's dirtiest places. But his filthy coat stops his own family from recognizing him; even his best and most familiar "tricks" fail to identify him. Finally, he for the first time seeks out the bathtub, and relishes the soap that turns him back into their familiar and beloved pet. George's curious explorations of human technology and spaces likewise get him into repeated trouble—but he is relieved to be rescued and re-domesticated by the Man with the Yellow Hat, his initial captor in the African jungle. A knowledge of human language may not be important; instead it is the voluntary acceptance of domestication and human rules of comportment which reestablish the bond—and social contract—between people and domestic animals.[7]

As Lisa Rowe Fraustino points out, picture books centered on mother-child bonds, domesticity, and feeding are particularly insistent in upholding the "ideology" of familial ties, enshrining human motherhood as instinctual, its self-sacrifices part of the natural order.[8] This seems particularly evident—and particularly questionable—when the picture book nominally concerns an animal family. *Blueberries for Sal* conveys "the message that mothering and feeding are a natural pairing." (69). And the animal mothers in Beatrix Potter's *The Tale of Peter Rabbit* (1902) and Margaret Wise Brown and Clement Hurd's *The Runaway Bunny* (1942) wear human costumes, proffer human food, and adopt the social role of human mothers: Peter Rabbit's mother tries to control her children's behavior by giving or withholding food; the Runaway's mother forestalls her bunny's bids for autonomy, tying her very identity to his utter dependence. Both books end in subterranean, live-in rabbit kitchens, where baby animals eat and sleep near their mothers.

Faustino's argument potentially illuminates why the mother mallard in McCloskey's *Make Way for Ducklings* seems so central to animal family life. Male and female mallard may search, as equals, for the optimal place to build a nest, yet it is Mrs. Mallard who vetoes potentially dangerous nesting sites, already thinking of the welfare of her young, and Mr. Mallard who eventually leaves her with the newborns, while he flies off to explore. Mrs. Mallard is happy to stay behind. "'Don't you worry…I know all about bringing up children.' And she did."[9] Eventually, undaunted by human traffic, she calmly moves her ducklings to join her husband at the edge of Boston's Public Garden. Naturally ordained gender roles, *Make Way for Ducklings* suggests, give even new parents an instinctive sense of how to raise their young—and their confidence helps cement the social contract between urban animals and the humans they live among.

Yet *Blueberries for Sal* offers a more complex vision of human and animal nature, as of species coexistence. In rural Maine, animals and humans lives occasionally unfold in proximity or in parallel, yet follow fundamentally different logics. Bear families, like human ones, forage, communicate, care for one another, anticipate colder weather. But their physical, psychic and emotional metabolisms differ fundamentally.[10]

Blueberries is likewise interested, within the human species, in the radical differences between adult and toddler sensibilities. Yet the

(*opposite*) Kitchen scene, *One Morning in Maine*, 1952.

15

child, somehow, will grow into the adult, Sal become her mother. In *Blueberries*, as in *One Morning in Maine* (1952) and *Time of Wonder* (1957), McCloskey used his own wife, his daughter Sal, and (in the second and third book) his younger daughter Jane as models, using their real names for his characters; all three books thus seem autobiographical. In *One Morning*, Jane is still a toddler, but Sal is now a young girl. Sal still moves awkwardly and asks naïve questions, but at times—reminding her younger sister to brush her teeth—she tries out adult, even maternal roles. Meanwhile her hair and profile are now strongly reminiscent of her mother—who herself appears somewhat older while still beautiful, kind, sedate.

Readers familiar with *Blueberries* will note the passage of time since the first book, and the shift of roles. *One Morning*'s title places its action, like *Blueberries*, on a particular day in Maine. Yet the story juxtaposes this particularity to a wide-ranging meditation on temporality and change. Sal has a loose tooth. In the kitchen (a different kitchen than in *Blueberries*, centered on a different stove, but still containing the same table and chairs), her mother reassures her by reframing her imminent tooth loss as a rite of passage: "Today you've become a big girl."[11] Sal suddenly senses the interplay between growth and loss. And as she spends the morning clam-hunting with her father (McCloskey draws himself substantially into this narrative), Sal formulates new questions about life-cycles and the animal kingdom.

In *Blueberries*, Sal is herself still half-animal, feral in the way of young children. But under her mother's care and eye, she is in the process of becoming human. Even her occasional forays into nature don't reverse this process, because her mother remains close by—and because daily life in the kitchen, where she watches her mother's actions and plays with the physical world, is far more formative. In *One Morning*, Sal, now older, acts in her turn as a parental admonisher, and hypothesizes about animal behavior from the distance of the human.

In *Time of Wonder*, the girls, older still but recognizable at moments by their faces, distinctive profiles, hair and physique, use the final day at

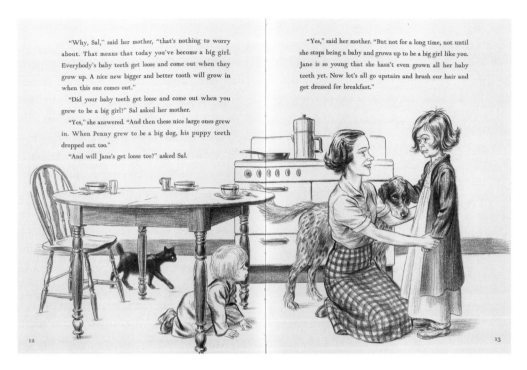

"Why, Sal," said her mother, "that's nothing to worry about. That means that today you've become a big girl. Everybody's baby teeth get loose and come out when they grow up. A nice new bigger and better tooth will grow in when this one comes out."

"Did your baby teeth get loose and come out when you grew to be a big girl?" Sal asked her mother.

"Yes," she answered. "And then these nice large ones grew in. When Penny grew to be a big dog, his puppy teeth dropped out too."

"And will Jane's get loose too?" asked Sal.

"Yes," said her mother. "But not for a long time, not until she stops being a baby and grows up to be a big girl like you. Jane is so young that she hasn't even grown all her baby teeth yet. Now let's all go upstairs and brush our hair and get dressed for breakfast."

their Maine summerhouse to meditate on time and nature. "It is time to reset the clock from the rise and fall of the tide, to the come and go of the school bus."[12] This moment of transition initiates a sense of wonder: at a hurricane, at bird movement, at a shell cache buried in a tree root by Indian children who lived there "before the coming of white men" (page 56).

The trilogy, then, moves from Sal on the cusp between animal and human existence, to Sal beginning to observe natural processes from a stance outside them (even as she begins to help socialize her younger sister), to the girls wondering about bigger questions, the way the natural world fits together. Along with these shifts of scale, from a particular kitchen and a particular mountain to a whole Maine island (and by implication, the whole of nature and human history), McCloskey's illustration style shifts between the second and third

Kitchen scene,
One Morning in Maine,
1952.

135

The children at the toppled tree, *Time of Wonder*, 1957.

volume: from blue-black line drawings to a blurring, quasi-impressionistic use of color, even as a child's struggle for language, reason, experience and understanding give way, over time, to lyrical, quasi-mystical wonderings about nature and human epochs.

"In the beginning," Virginia Woolf writes memorably in *The Waves*, "there was the nursery."[13] In Sal's beginning was the kitchen, the first flare of consciousness and remembered memory, centered on her mother. But gradually, Sal realizes, she is anchored equally in time, in natural time, bear time, blueberry time, human time, geological time, in a seasonal, diurnal world, and in layers of human history. Her first, intimate world is anchored by a pot-belly stove, the taste of blueberries, the weekly shopping list, the sound of her mother at work. But there is also her own play in that kitchen, the beginning of her own dangling into the world of wonder.

1   Claude Levi-Strauss, *The Raw and the Cooked*, Trans. John and Doreen Weightman. New York: Harper and Row, 1969.

2   In Thos. O. Summers, *Hymns for Schools and Families, Specially Designed for Children of the Church* (Nashville: Southern Methodist Publishing House, 1859), Watts's hymn, Nr. 318, is followed directly by 319: "Sweet it is to see a child / Tender, merciful and mild: / Ever ready to perform / Acts of kindness to a worm...."

3   See also Horacio Quiroga, *Cuentos de la selva* (1918); André Hellé's *Drôle de Bêtes* (1911); and E. Boyd Smith's *The Story of Noah's Arc* (1905).

4   See for instance Jack London's *The Call of the Wild* (1908), a line continued for instance by Farley Mowatt's *Owls in the Family* (1961)—and arguably also by Diana Wynne Jones's fantasy story *Dogsbody* (1975).

5   For animal-centered coming-of-age stories, see for instance Alfred Olivant, *Owd Bob: The Grey Dog of Kenmuir* (1898); Marjorie Kinnan Rawlings, *The Yearling* (1938); Mary

O'Hara, *My Friend Flicka* (1941); Fred Gipson's *Ole Yeller* (1956); Sterling North's *Rascal* (1963). For animal-centered stories of loss and restitution, see Eleanor Atkinson, *Greyfriars Bobby* (1912); Felix Salten, *Bambi, A Life in the Woods* (1923); Eric Knight, *Lassie Come-Home* (1940); Sheila Burnham, *The Long Journey* (1961).

6   Yet see also Ingri and Edgar Parin d'Aulaire's *Foxie, the Singing Dog* (1949) and Susan Meddaugh's *Martha Speaks* (1992), in which animals unexpectedly come into voice.

7   On voluntary captivity, also Leonard Marcus, "Picture Book Animals: How Natural a History?," *The Lion and the Unicorn* 7/8 (1983–84), 127-139, esp. pp. 121-23.

8   Lisa Rowe Fraustino, "The Apple of Her Eye: The Mothering Ideology Fed by Best-Selling Trade Picture Books," in Kara Keeling and Scott T. Pollard, eds., *Critical Approaches to Food in Children's Literature*. New York: Routledge, 2009, pp. 57-72.

9   Robert McCloskey, *Make Way for Ducklings*. New York: Viking Press, 1941, n.p.

10 Despite its overly symmetrical and slightly sentimental ending, Leonard Marcus concludes, *Blueberries* "is managed with such understatement, simplicity, and matter-of-factness that the very uneventfulness of the tale assumes tremendous dignity, a dignity behind which lies a deep respect for the natural world." "Picture," 136.

11 Robert McCloskey, *One Morning in Maine*, New York: Viking, 1952, p.16.

12 Robert McCloskey, *Time of Wonder*. New York: Penguin, 1989, p. 60.

13 Virginia Woolf, *The Waves*, 1931; London: Granada, 1981, p. 162.

PÁDRAIC WHYTE

A Place in the Canon
Padraic Colum's Newbery Books and the Development of American Children's Literature

The Betsy Beinecke Shirley Collection of American Children's Literature is a rich and varied resource that allows readers to better understand the history and development of writing for children in the U.S. The status of the collection within contemporary culture is complex, as the exclusion or inclusion of items affects the perceived cultural value placed on a book, an object, the papers of an author, and so on. The very fact that an item is held within the collection suggests that it is important, that it is worthy of preservation and research; therefore the collection participates in the canon-formation of American children's literature. Drawing upon this theme of canon-formation and a history of literature for children in the U.S., I wish to explore the institutions and mechanisms of canon-formation at the beginning of the twentieth century and to examine the status of the writing of Irish-American author Padraic Colum (1881–1972), a significant figure in the development of American children's literature, whose work can be found in the Shirley Collection.

The first three decades of the twentieth century saw major developments in the writing, illustrating, publishing, and promoting of children's literature in the United States, a period that "catapulted American children's literature from mere recognition to literary and commercial success in its own right."[1] With the professionalization of

(*opposite*) "The Argo" from *The Golden Fleece or the Heroes who Lived before Achilles*, illustrated by Willy Pogány, 1921.

librarianship, the establishment of children's sections in libraries, the creation of children's departments in publishing houses, the popularization of children's stories in mainstream newspapers, and the demand for high-quality books for children of all ages, this period can be characterized as a golden age of American children's literature. Significant developments that can be read as contributing to the process of canon-formation include the establishment in 1918, by Anne Carroll Moore, of *The Bookman*, one of the first substantial serial publications dedicated to the criticism of children's literature in the U.S.; the awarding of the first John Newbery Medal for the Most Distinguished Contribution to American Literature for Children in 1922; and the founding of *The Horn Book Magazine* by Bertha E. Mahony in 1924. During this period the work of Padraic Colum, who had recently moved from Ireland to the U.S., was championed by "arguably the most powerful and formative influence on books for children in the twentieth century," Anne Carroll Moore.[2] Contemporary critics viewed Colum "as a leader among those who were producing... literature for children"[3] and histories of American children's literature argued that his books "foreshadowed the future" and had "an important influence on children's books in the years ahead."[4] Colum published twenty-six works for children, and three were cited as Newbery Honor Books: *The Golden Fleece and the Heroes who Lived before Achilles* (1921), *The Voyagers: Being Legends and Romances of Atlantic Discovery* (1925), and *The Big Tree of Bunlahy: Stories of My Own Countryside* (1933).[5]

Colum was not the only Irish writer of children's books who was popular in the U.S. at that time. During the early years of *The Horn Book*'s publication, roughly forty-eight items on Irish authors appeared between 1924 and 1937.[6] There was a suggestion that the Irish had a unique approach to storytelling and many critics, including Anne Carroll Moore, supported and promoted work from Irish authors and writers with a connection to Ireland, such as Anne Casserly, Lady Gregory, Eleanor Hull, Seumas McManus, James Stephens, and Ella

Young. However, Colum's works stood apart and were instrumental in elevating the status of Irish literature in America. As Aedín Clements notes, "American perceptions of the Irish, and of Irish literature, had changed by the 1920s, and it is apparent from the reviewing literature that the regard for Irish literature was influenced by Colum's writing."[7] It is evident that Colum was highly regarded by his contemporaries and his skill as a writer was recognised at various points throughout the twentieth century: In 1961 he was awarded the Regina Medal for his "distinguished contribution to the field of children's literature" from the American Catholic Library Association, and in the 1980s the Children's Literature Association included Colum's *The Children's Homer* (1918) and *The Golden Fleece* in their list of sixty-three "Touchstone" titles—a project that explored the potential of developing a canon of children's literature and resulted in the *Touchstones* series, a three-volume compilation of criticism of sixty-three titles, edited by Perry Nodelman. Despite such success, Colum's work has received limited discussion in more recent children's literature criticism. An analysis of his Newbery Honor Books and a focus on the American context of his publications reveal the valuable contribution that Colum made to the development of American children's literature of the period, the influence of American experience on his writing for children, and the complexity of the author's own relationships with both Ireland and America.

Born in County Longford, Ireland, in 1881, Padraic Colum played a central role in the Irish Cultural Revival of the early twentieth century and was one of the founding members of the Abbey Theatre. He also collected and wrote folk songs, the most famous being "She Moved through the Fair". Colum left Ireland in 1914, returning on occasion, but eventually settling in the U.S. and becoming an American citizen in 1945. Along with his wife Mary, he taught at Columbia University. A poet, author, and playwright, Colum remains best remembered for his outstanding contribution to children's literature. His writing for children in the U.S. in fact preceded his arrival in Pittsburgh, as his first children's book, *A Boy in Eirinn*, "was written in Ireland in 1913, according to a plan drawn up in America" and was directed toward an implied American readership.[8] During the early days of his time in the U.S., in order to keep his connection with Ireland and the Irish language, Colum began translating an Irish folk story which eventually found its way into the *New York Tribune* and caught the attention of the prolific illustrator Willy Pogâny. The Hungarian artist suggested that Colum write a book that Pogâny would illustrate, and so *The King of Ireland's Son* was published in 1916. The book was well received and was to mark the beginning of Colum's success in writing for children in America. Colum wrote children's stories for newspapers such as the *New York Tribune*, received a major contract with Macmillan publishers, and was subsequently commissioned by the Hawai'ian legislature to write up Hawai'i's myths and legends as children's stories. Pogâny continued to work with Colum on many books for children, including *The Golden Fleece and the Heroes who Lived before Achilles* which, in 1922, became Colum's first Newbery Honor Book.

THE GOLDEN FLEECE AND THE HEROES WHO LIVED BEFORE ACHILLES (1921)

In 1921, Frederic G. Melcher proposed at the American Library Association Conference that a prize be awarded each year to an outstanding children's text, and thus The Newbery Award, the first children's book award in the world, was established. The winner of the Newbery Medal in 1922, the inaugural year of the award, was Hendrik Willem Van Loon for his *The Story of Mankind*, an account of the history of the Western world. Books from Padraic Colum, Chares Boardman Hawes, Bernard Marshall, William Bowen, and Cornelia Meigs were placed in a runner-up category and later cited (retroactively) as Newbery Honor Books. While the Newbery Award has received much praise, as well as criticism, its impact on the development of American children's literature cannot be denied. For Colum to have three books cited as Newbery Honor Books (the most by any Irish author), within this awards program that undoubtedly contributed to the formation of a canon of American children's literature, is a significant achievement. Colum's versions of Greek myths, *The Children's Homer* (1918) and *The Golden Fleece*, were also the only books on classical myths to be included in Perry Nodelman's *Touchstones* publication. In her critical essay on *The Children's Homer* in *Touchstones*, Yancy Barton writes that "Colum achieves a simplicity and quality of style that preserves the same authenticity of Homer as do the best adult translations,"[9] while Nancy Huse, in her entry on *The Golden Fleece*, argues that unique "to Colum is the wholeness of his version"[10] echoing Lionel Trilling's 1956 analysis of Colum's Greek myths as remarkably complete and accurate.[11] In comparison to the writings of authors such as Edith Hamilton, Nathaniel Hawthorne, Roger Green, and H.A. Guerber, Colum's versions of Greek myths incorporate fresh storytelling techniques, innovative use of narrative voice, an intimacy between narrator and narratee, and space for the exploration of female experience.

In *The Golden Fleece*, Colum draws upon a traditional storytelling technique and places the story of Jason as a frame narrative before effortlessly weaving a significant number of Greek myths into this structure. With an omniscient narrator, the role of storyteller is transferred to various characters as the tale progresses. For example, Orpheus is placed on the ship with the Argonauts and sings the story of the origins of the world and the birth of Zeus; tales of Zeus, Heracles, Pandora, Perseus, and many others are revealed to the reader. Adopting this technique, the author ensures that the implied child reader is never overwhelmed by the vastness and detail of Greek mythology because the story of Jason and his Argonauts functions as an anchor narrative. An intimacy is constructed as the implied child reader is encouraged to position him/herself as an Argonaut narratee, listening intently to the tales being told. As was the case with *The Children's Homer*, Colum uses a poetic language and rhythm throughout, interspersing archaism and lavish words into expertly constructed sentences to build a vivid world of heroic adventures, as is evident in his references to Polydeuces who was "like that star whose beams are lovely at evening-tide."[12] Throughout, Colum foregrounds the oral pattern of storytelling, an approach that offers a welcome relief from some of the more conservative writing for children from the period. Within the context of American children's literature, the use of such a framing device was not entirely new, as Nathaniel Hawthorne had adopted such an approach in his famous retellings of Greek myths in *A Wonder-Book for Boys and Girls* (1851). Gillian Avery, noting the importance of Hawthorne's Greek tales, argues that "what Perrault did for [fairytales], so Nathaniel Hawthorne did for Greek myths."[13] However, his use of character-narrator Eustace Bright to frame the narratives ultimately distances the reader from the action of heroes in the myths rather than creating a sense of intimacy and immediacy, as is the case with Colum's versions.

Lionel Trilling viewed Hawthorne's text as condescending in comparison to Colum's and, indeed, it was for this approach to writing for children, which featured throughout all of his works, that Colum received much praise.[14] His material was celebrated for not "writing down" to an implied child reader. In his 1927 essay "Story Telling, New and Old," Colum revealed his belief that

> …the story-teller must have respect for the child's mind and the child's conception of the world, knowing it for a complete mind and a complete conception. If a story-teller have that respect he need not be childish in his language in telling stories to children.[15]

Colum believed that poetry and music form patterns of speech for the reader that can be held in memory[16] and it is this technique that is used throughout *The Golden Fleece*—setting it apart from previous retellings of Greek myths for American children. It is not simply the use of language or multiple character narrators that impressed critics, but also the emphasis on giving voice to female experience. This was the focus of Nancy Huse's essay in *Touchstones*. She argues that "Colum's narrative—unlike many contemporary retellings of the myths—includes female experience as essential to the human story he tells."[17] Although these tales are ultimately framed and limited by patriarchal narratives, the text may be read as pioneering due to the emphasis on female experience and empowerment as well as the author's ability to talk *to* rather than *at* an implied child reader.

With his Irish myths and legends, his Norse tales in *The Children of Odin* (1921), along with the expert retellings of Greek myth in *The Children of Homer* and *The Golden Fleece*, Colum quickly earned himself the reputation of master-craftsman in the retelling of myths for children. As a result, in 1922 he was commissioned by the Legend and Folklore Commission of the Territory of Hawai'i to write two volumes of myths and legends of Hawai'i for children that would be used in schools throughout the islands. The result was three volumes published by Yale University Press: *At the Gateways of the Day* (1924), *The Bright Islands* (1925), and *Legends of Hawaii* (1937). (Hawai'i had the status of a United States territory at the time; it became a state in 1959.) In an interview with Anne Carroll Moore, Colum positioned these texts as linked to, if not directly part of, American children's literature, arguing that "It would be well for America to realize the heroic ancestry that the adopted child can lay claim to."[18] Without a doubt, the "adopted child" metaphor is extremely problematic and hints at the greater cultural colonialism that was involved in this project. However, that is not to deny that Colum's approach to writing these tales can be understood as well researched and considered; he spent several months on the Hawai'ian islands, gathering folklore and stories from a range of people, and he was fully aware of the complicated nature of writing Polynesian tales within established conventions of Anglo-centric narrative frameworks.[19] However, the essentialising of the islanders is also readily apparent, and the preface of *At the Gateways of the Day* implies a core readership outside Hawai'i rather than within. Nevertheless, it could also be argued that Colum's project has preserved and popularised versions of Hawai'ian myths for American readers.[20]

THE VOYAGERS: BEING LEGENDS AND
ROMANCES OF ATLANTIC DISCOVERY (1925)

At the time that Colum was writing tales of the voyages of Polynesian heroes, he was also engaging with versions of mythical and historical voyages across the Atlantic. *The Voyagers: Being Legends and Romances of Atlantic Discovery*, published in 1925, with pictures by Wilfred Jones, was a Newbery Honor Book in 1926 (while the Newbery Medal went to Arthur Bowie Chrisman for his *Shen of the Sea: Chinese Stories for Children*). In *The Voyagers*, Colum engages directly with U.S. history and signals the vital roles that myth and story play in the European settlement of the American continent. The book opens with a chapter on Prince Henry of Portugal (also known as Henry the Navigator) who built a tower so that he might gaze upon the Atlantic Ocean and imagine the land that lies beyond the horizon. As part of this project,

> …men who had traveled far, or knew histories of those who had traveled far, were brought by the prince to his tower above the Atlantic Ocean in the hope that they would help him towards which he sought—certain knowledge of a land beyond and of ways to come to it.[21]

The stories told by these men serve as the impetus for the so-called "discovery" of America, and thus Colum highlights the central role that imagination and storytelling can play in an age of scientific discovery. The first section of the book features the tale of Atlantis, the Voyage of Maelduin, the Voyages of Saint Brendan, as well as the story of the Children of Eric the Red, all suggesting European knowledge of a land existing across the Atlantic—often represented as a promised land. By grounding the narrative in a specific locale and attaching events to an historical figure, the myths are positioned within linear time (rather than mythical time), a time to which the implied reader is able to relate. As with *The Golden Fleece*, the sophisticated storytelling technique uses a framing narrative to grant coherence to many disparate, yet related, narratives, and through first-person accounts it encourages an implied reader to engage directly with the action of each tale.

The opening story demonstrates the links between oral storytelling, poetry and written accounts:

> It came to Plato from Solon, his ancestor; it was handed down from Solon's time, a tradition that came from father to son for many generations. First it was told by a priest of Egypt to Solon, the wise man of Greece. Solon thought of making a poem about it... [22]

This passage implies that to understand who we are and from where we have come, we need a multitude of diverse forms of story, rather than a single source. This approach gains increased significance as the narrative progresses and myths, historiographies, and journal entries are used to create a coherent and cohesive narrative that moves toward a singular conclusion. The book ends with a story of the naming of the land mass, the final word in bold capitals being "AMERICA." Naming demonstrates that the exertion of control as something that was once vague and elusive—the stuff of stories—is now a concrete reality.

It is significant that Colum devotes a large amount of space in *The Voyagers* to the retelling of Irish myths and legends, documenting the adventures of Maelduin and of Saint Brendan. In positioning Irish myths subsequent to Greek myths, Colum elevates the status of Irish legends and places them on a par with those of Greece. The prolonged focus on Irish myths and legends also creates a sense of an established history between Ireland and America and suggests that Ireland and her stories had a major influence on shaping world events. It also implies that knowledge of Irish narratives is central to granting a fuller insight to and understanding of America. The narrative progresses from mythical accounts to first-person narratives of those connected to real historical events, a literary device that adds legitimacy to the preceding myths. However, the language of these first-person narratives lacks the poetry of the myths and legends, arguably to create a sense of authenticity and credibility. The second section of the book features a journal account from Christopher Columbus's first voyage across the Atlantic before advancing to the stories on the land through revealing journal entries from historical figures such as Captain Barlowe, Captain John Smith, and

One of the ship-boys cried out and pointed to the mountain.

The Voyagers: Being Legends and Histories of Atlantic Discovery, illustrated by Wilfred Jones, 1925.

Ralph Hamar—along with a mention of the experiences of Pocahontas. In his article on "Discoverers, Strange Lands, and Books," Henry Beston recommends a number of texts for young male readers and notes that in Colum's *The Voyagers* there "are romantic quests, the dash of waves, the scream of sea birds in the darkening night, and the far, flaming ramparts of legendary isles—all cunningly made into a tapestry of truth and dream, woven of Mr. Colum's sensitive and distinguished prose."[23] Beston places his discussion of Colum's texts within the context of non-fiction books of the period that engage with voyages, adventure, and discovery, such as Vilhjalmur Stefansson's *My Life with the Eskimo* (1912) and John Buchan's *The Last Secret* (1923), as well as President Theodore Roosevelt's books on Africa and Brazil. Beston thus implies that Colum's book may be closer to fact than fiction.

Constance Lindsay Skinner, in her contemporary review of an abridged 1926 edition of Stefansson's *My Life with the Eskimos*, describes it as "an answer to the modern demand, which is increasing in the juvenile as well as the adult field, for truth as the basis of fancy."[24] And while elements of truth may form the foundation of *The Voyagers*, it is Colum's skill in integrating such truths with popular forms and genres of the period, including the adventure story, that leads to successful storytelling. Adventure stories of the early 1920s include the work of Newbery Medal winners such as: Hugh Lofting's *The Voyages of Dr. Dolittle* (1923 winner), which documents voyages to the Mediterranean and South America; Charles Hawes's *The Dark Frigate* (1924 winner), a historical novel and sea story; and Charles Finger's *Tales from Silver Lands* (1925 winner), which contains folktales from Central and South America. Despite Colum's apparent shift toward historiography as *The Voyagers* progresses, myth and history once again become intertwined in the text as the author includes a story of Ponce de Leon and his search for the Fountain of Youth. It seems apt, therefore, that the title refers to "Legends and Romances" in the 1925 edition, rather than the misleading "Legends and Histories" title given to later printings. While Colum's text encompasses many genres, forms, and sophisticated approaches to storytelling, it could be argued that it results in a simplified account of history. His interweaving of history and myth and his condensing of the journal entries into the same time period, so as to grant a coherent linear narrative of the European settlement of America, is problematic. It erases the accidents, discontinuities, and complexities of historical discourse from the narrative, particularly in relation to Native American experience and the problematising of the settler project. Perhaps it is for these reasons that this text from Colum has received limited attention in comparison to his other Newbery Honor Books.

THE BIG TREE OF BUNLAHY: STORIES OF MY OWN COUNTRYSIDE (1933)

Colum's 1933 book, *The Big Tree of Bunlahy: Stories of My Own Countryside*, illustrated by Jack B. Yeats and published in the United States, was a 1934 Newbery Honor Book, and the last of his books to receive this recognition. Cornelia Meigs won the Newbery Medal that year for her historical novel *Invincible Louisa*, a biography of Louisa May Alcott, while Honor books included Agnes Hewes's *Glory of the Seas*, a historical novel set in 1850s America, Elsie Singmaster's *Swords of Steel*, set before and during the American Civil War, and other historical novels from Erik Berry, Ann Kyle, and Caroline Snedeker. It is evident that Colum was writing during a period when biographies and historical novels for children were popular, or at least deemed worthy of attention by the Newbery committee. Indeed, *The Big Tree of Bunlahy* has elements of both biography and history, as the subtitle indicates; this is an autobiography of sorts—weaving together myth, folklore, and Irish history, as well as the author's own personal history.

The popularity of Irish myths, legends, and folktales was part of a growing interest in folklore and folktales in America during the first part of the twentieth century. However, Ruth Hill Viguers notes that in comparison to other children's literature published in the U.S. at the time, Colum's works stand apart and that "in addition to their freshness and the authenticity of their folk sources, they are marked by the very special genius of Mr. Colum, which makes them sing."[25] Similarly, in her review of *The Big Tree of Bunlahy* in *The Horn Book* in January 1934, Bertha E. Mahony refers to the book as "wonderfully varied," describing it as a permanent "treasure" and a "splendid collection of stories to read not once but many times."[26] While the Irish tales are designed to appeal to an implied American child reader, at the heart of this text is Colum's meditation on his legacy as an Irish storyteller. If Colum's success arose out of his initial experience as an immigrant, translating passages of Irish folklore that led to the publication of *The King of Ireland's Son*, then *The Big Tree of Bunlahy*, is a reflection, almost twenty years later, on his relationship with Irish and American culture.

The Big Tree of Bunlahy is made up of a number of subtly interconnected stories. As with *The Golden Fleece* and *The Voyagers*, the tales are anchored by the fact that they are told under the Big Tree of Bunlahy by various storytellers. The frame narrative is that of an adult narrator recalling his childhood memories, and the volume is granted a coherence by this single narrator who recounts the tales he heard under the tree when he was a child, with the space between stories filled with accounts of events of his childhood or musings on the lives and characteristics of the storytellers. This structure provides rhythm for the reader akin to music or poetry. Each space between the stories offers the reader an opportunity to reflect upon what has been read, or speculate about what is to come. The town of Bunlahy is a real place, located in County Longford in Ireland, where Colum spent much of his

childhood listening to traditional storytellers. The same year that *The Big Tree of Bunlahy* received a Newbery Honor Book citation, Colum wrote an essay called "Storytelling in Ireland" for *The Horn Book* where he outlined the origins of his storytelling techniques: "I recognize that the earliest strata were laid down by an elderly relative of mine. She told very vividly fragments of folklore that were unusually poetical." He continues, explaining the optimum environment for storytelling: "The best time is night and the best light is the one which leaves some shadows around, I favor a candle or a candle helped out by the light of a fire on the hearth."[27] It is therefore significant that the narrator of the text opens with an account of himself as a child arriving in to the town of Bunlahy, and that "it was to get two candles that I came; I had two eggs to pay for the candles."[28] The expedition to purchase candles, which are equated with food and sustenance, results in his hearing stories under

"Here was the old Clockmender, seated under the Big Tree, with Patch the Nailer and Martin the Weaver beside him. I came over, and I was there when the Clockmender told the story," *The Big Tree of Bunlahy: Stories of my own Countryside*, illustrated by Jack B. Yeats, 1933.

the tree, stories of light and shadow. The myth of Usheen that follows, a hero who travels to the land of eternal youth, Tir na nÓg, only to return to a world where all of his family and friends have died, echoes the themes of youth and loss found throughout the book.

In an interlude between stories, the author/narrator and the character Martin the Weaver discover treasure in the bog, a metaphor for the author's return to place to unearth the stories of his childhood. The sequence implies that if the American reader delves deep enough, great treasures can be found in Irish culture. It is the author's attempt to make sense of his own personal narrative and his relationship with story, myth, and landscape that dominates the text. In this regard, the bog becomes significant, as it is in so much Irish literature. Through this bog episode, Colum justifies the status that he has granted Irish lore and myth when he writes, "A King's treasure and firing for the hearth, I kept saying to myself, thinking how strange it was that peat and rich ornaments should have come out of the same bog."[29] Once again the fireside is invoked, suggesting the optimum environment for the telling of tales. The King's treasure may be read as the stories unearthed in Ireland and the "firing for the hearth" as the mode of storytelling, the fuel to illustrate the story's shadow and light; both emerge from Ireland, and both are necessary for a successful storytelling experience.

While Colum may align himself with the storyteller and the scholar in the book, his work also reveals his self-doubt, an aspect placed at the fore of the final tale, "The Story of the Spaeman," which is told by Patch the Nailer. A Spaeman, it is revealed, is a person who has a second sight of sorts, a magical insight into things that others cannot see. The Spaeman thus becomes synonymous with the storyteller. Patch the Nailer comments, "I think, like the Spaeman, you'll come back to the Big Tree,"[30] thus directly aligning Colum with the Spaeman. At the end of the tale, the Spaeman returns to his home village, but the children do not see a need for such a person: "But the young people who were there asked me what a Spaeman was, and when I told them they laughed and said that they could make discoveries by insight themselves. As is the way with people, they had become more foolish than their fathers."[31] As this is the only story in the book that is told in the first person, it could be argued that the author is alluding to himself as a carrier of culture who has left his home and moved to a place, America, where his insight is valued and rewarded, but on his return home to Ireland, there are few who take notice of his stories. Therefore, a tension exists throughout this work. On the one hand, Colum highlights the importance of storytelling and of listening; he elevates the status of the storyteller as a master craftsperson and highlights how these seemingly insignificant tales from Ireland can engage a reader outside of Ireland. On the other hand, the collection is framed by loss and a sadness that people may no longer be interested in listening to such stories.

CONCLUSION

It is evident from contemporary reviews and accolades, as well as from analyzing Padraic Colum's Newbery Honor Books, that the author was indeed a significant figure in the development of American children's literature in the early part of the twentieth century and that his works were once positioned firmly within a canon of children's literature. However, canons and collections shift and change; they are in a continual process of evolution. While Colum engaged with many of the popular genres of the period, it was his original storytelling techniques, his innovative engagement with U.S. myth and history, and his sophisticated writings on Irish legends and folktales for American children that set him apart from his contemporaries. Though his work was celebrated throughout the twentieth century, his material for children has received limited attention in the last few decades. *The Big Tree of Bunlahy* may be understood as a prophecy of sorts since Colum's books are now not widely available in libraries and there are only a few recent reprints of his work that make them accessible to a child reader. In *The Big Tree*, Colum as narrator, Patch the Nailer, and the mythical hero Usheen all return to a land where they, and their stories, are not known or valued. Despite this, the book ends on a note of hope; Usheen and Patch have found at least one person to hear their tale. The final words in the book are from Patch as he finishes his story, returning to the Big Tree of Bunlahy:

> And came back to where I had started from—
> The Tree That Withstood
> The Big
> Wind—The
> Big Tree of Bunlahy.[32]

Despite the need to seek out these volumes, Colum's stories stand the test of time. They will always be there for anyone willing to listen.

1   Bernice Cullinan and Diane Person (eds.), *The Continuum Encyclopedia of Children's Literature* (New York and London: Continuum, 2003), p. 20.

2   Anne Lundin, *Beyond Library Walls and Ivory Towers: Constructing the Canon of Children's Literature* (New York and London: Routledge, 2004), p. 23.

3   Mary Lamberton Becker, "Back and Forth with Children's Books," in Anne Carroll Moore (ed.), *The Three Owls: Third Book, Cotemporary Criticism of Children's Books, 1927-30* (New York: Coward-Mc Cann, 1931), p. 104.

4   Ruth Hill Viguers, in Cornelia Meigs et al., *A Critical History of Children's Literature* (New York: The Macmillan Company, 1953), p. 432.

5   *The Golden Fleece and the Heroes who Lived before Achilles* (New York: The Macmillan Company, 1921), *The Voyagers: Being Legends and Romances of Atlantic Discovery* (New York: The Macmillan Company, 1925), and *The Big Tree of Bunlahy: Stories of My Own Countryside* (New York: The Macmillan Company, 1933).

6   Aedín Clements, "Padraic Colum, the Horn Book, and the Irish in American children's literature in the early twentieth century," in Mary Shine Thompson (ed.), *Young Irelands* (Dublin: Four Courts Press, 2011), p. 160.

7   Ibid., p. 163.

8   Anne Carroll Moore, *The Three Owls, Vol I* (New York: Macmillan, 1925), p. 104.

9   Yancy Barton, "The Children's Homer: The Myth Reborn" in Perry Nodelman (ed.) *Touchstones: Reflections on the Best in Children's Literature, Volume Two: Fairy Tales, Fables, Myths, Legends, and Poetry* (West Lafayette, Indiana: Children's Literature Association, 1987), p. 55.

10 Nancy Huse, "The Golden Fleece: The Lost Goddesses" in Perry Nodelman (ed.) *Touchstones*, p. 71.

11 In Zack Bowen, *Padraic Colum: A Biographical-critical Introduction* (Carbondale: Southern Illinois University Press, 1970), p. 126.

12 *The Golden Fleece*, p. 45.

13 Gillian Avery, *Behold the Child: American Children and their Books, 1621–1922.* (Baltimore: Johns Hopkins University Press, 1994), p. 26.

14 Quoted in Bowen, p. 126.

15 "Story Telling, New and Old," in Padraic Colum, *The Fountain of Youth* (New York: Macmillan, 1927), p. 200.

16 Ibid., p. 198.

17 Nancy Huse, p. 66.

18 Padraic Colum in Anne Carroll Moore (1925), p. 105 .

19 Ibid., p. 107.

20 His tales received renewed attention in recent years when the Irish Taoiseach (Prime Minister) Enda Kenny presented a first edition of *At the Gateways of the Day* to U.S. President Barack Obama on the occasion of his visit to Ireland in 2011, an event that highlighted Colum's contribution to the development of U.S. literary culture.

21 *The Voyagers*, p. 2.

22 Ibid., p. 7.

23 Henry Beston, "Discoverers, Strange Lands, and Books," in Anne Carroll Moore, *Three Owls: Second Book, Contemporary Criticism of Children's Books* (New York: Coward-Mc Cann, 1928), p. 331.

24 Constance Lindsay Skinner, in Anne Carroll Moore, *Three Owls: Second Book*, p. 50.

25 Viguers, p. 454.

26 Bertha E. Mahony, "Tir-nan-Oge and Tir Tairngire," *Horn Book*, 10.1 (1934) pp. 31-36.

27 Colum, "Storytelling in Ireland," *Horn Book*, 10.3 (1934), pp. 190 and 192.

28 *The Big Tree of Bunlahy*, p. 2.

29 Ibid., p. 114.

30 Ibid., p. 159.

31 Ibid., p. 166.

32 Ibid., p. 166.

Flee the Pleasure that will bite To-morrow. Joh.

Flee the Pleasure that will bite To-morrow. Joh.

Flee the Pleasure that will bite To-morrow. Joh.

Flee the Pleasure that will bite To-morrow. Joh.

Flee the Pleasure that will bite To-morrow. Joh.

Flee the Pleasure that will bite To-morrow. Joh.

Flee the Pleasure that will bite To-morrow. Joh.

Flee the Pleasure that will bite To-morrow. Jo.

Flee the Pleasure that will bite To-morrow. Jo.

Flee the Pleasure that will bite To-morrow. Jo.

Flee the Pleasure that will bite To-morrow. Joh.

John Hancock. 1753.

SANDRA MARKHAM

For the Illustration of the Mind and the Delight of the Eye

Penmanship Copybooks in the Betsy Beinecke Shirley Collection

Betsy Beinecke Shirley's extraordinary collection of American children's literature is widely recognized by scholars for its breadth and depth of work created for American children by authors and illustrators. That is the material that forms the bulk of the collection and is the focus of the majority of the essays in this volume. Less often explored is her wonderful and varied collection of unique works created by children. Betsy Shirley was interested in what children read, certainly, but she was also deeply interested in how American children were educated, and what they produced in the process of that instruction. The student workbooks, embroidered samplers, and songbooks she accumulated are kept with other historical material in the Shirley Collection, where they are supported by school account books, letters, tuition receipts, rewards of merit, and other material, dating from the seventeenth to the twentieth centuries, that document public and private instruction in both formal academic subjects and life lessons. Notable items in the latter category include instructive letters from three founding fathers: John Adams to his grandson George; Benjamin Franklin to his grandson Benjamin; and George Washington to his nephew George. In 1756 and 1757, Nicholas Ray, an American merchant living in London, filled an entire bound volume with letters of advice directed at his nephew Richard Ray Jr. in New York, accompanied by an armchair travelogue of his journeys to the Caribbean, Europe, and Great Britain.

(*opposite*) Page from John Hancock's copybook, 1753.

Works in the collection created by children for adults are as charming as they are diverse. Examples include a colorful 1914 construction paper scrapbook holding Roscoe Hersey's drawing assignments and handicraft projects made at an American school in China, a group of students' absence notes submitted to teachers in Newark, New Jersey, between 1888 and 1906, and Joseph Rappleyea's 1812 arithmetic cyphering book with his whimsical watercolor vignettes of monkeys, birds, and flora sprinkled among the exacting columns of figures. Perhaps most fascinating of all, from both visual and historical perspectives, are penmanship copybooks that children created in fulfillment of pedagogical assignments. These small-scale volumes, in particular those from the eighteenth and early nineteenth centuries, present evidence of practical structured exercises considered by adults to be as valuable for discipline as they were for equipping a student for a life of personal communication and professional employment.[1] For her children's literature collection, Betsy Shirley gathered a number of beautiful examples made by boys and girls, demonstrating the tutelage of writing masters who worked separately from the reading-based curriculum offered in grammar schools. These copybooks show how the writing masters' expertise, which relied on manuals and other books imported from London, helped four students living in two cities during three different decades produce fine specimens of a legible hand fit for business or pleasure. Like the rest of the Shirley Collection, these little unassuming books tell stories, but here the stories are about American children, their teachers, their times, and one important segment of the American system of education in the eighteenth and nineteenth centuries.

From colonial and early republic Boston, the home of the most prominent writing schools in the country in that era, came two distinctive student copybooks, one filled by the Hancock brothers, John (1737–1793) and Ebenezer (1741–1819) in the 1750s, and the other written by Allan Melvill (1782–1832) some thirty years later. Of these three fellows, the first barely needs an introduction, having grown up to become president of the Continental Congress and governor of Massachusetts. Most educated Americans are—or should be—familiar with John Hancock's iconic signature on the engrossed copy of the Declaration of Independence, and from advertisements for the various Boston-based insurance and financial services companies that have used his signature as a logotype for more than a century. Indeed, what would John Hancock think if he could see www.johnhancock.com?

The son of the Reverend John Hancock (1702–1744) and Mary Hawke Thaxter Hancock (1711–1798) of Braintree (now Quincy), Massachusetts, young John was sent after his father's death to live with his uncle Thomas Hancock (1703–1764), a successful importer in Boston; his younger brother Ebenezer remained in Braintree with their widowed mother. Both boys attended the Boston Latin School, John entering in 1745 and graduating in spring 1750 before Ebenezer entered later that year.[2] During their time in grammar school, the brothers would have taken classes at a writing school twice a day, typically at 11 a.m. and 5 p.m.[3] At age fourteen or fifteen, their fellow students of promise would have moved up to Harvard College, while those graduating from the writing schools would have sought positions as clerks or bookkeepers in mercantile establishments or other business offices.[4] Both Hancock brothers went on to study across the river at Harvard, from which John was graduated in 1754 and Ebenezer in 1760.

The small penmanship book in the Shirley Collection holds 36 pages filled by the Hancock boys during their years at the college, in continuation of their study with a writing master while at Boston Latin.[5] John's pages are signed and dated in 1753; Ebenezer's are from 1757 and 1758. They are true writing exercises: letters, numbers, or words were inscribed along the top edges of the sheets by the master, and filled down each page with rows copied by the student who signed his name at the bottom. John Hancock simply signed his name, but his brother Ebenezer signed *Eius Liber* (his book) between his name and the date. Some pages bear full rows of single and joined letters, and others have single-line aphorisms repeated. Although it is not known where the Hancock brothers studied, whether at one of the three Boston writing schools such as the South Writing School run by Abiah Holbrook Jr. (1718–1769) or with a private writing master, it is certain that their instructors used manuals imported from London. The most prominent of these manuals was George Bickham's *The Universal Penman* (issued in parts between 1733 and 1741),[6] but the masters training the Hancocks were likely also using George Fisher's *The Instructor, Or Young Man's Best Companion* (published in more than 30 editions beginning in 1727); its "Duty, Fear, and Love, we owe to God above" appears in John's book and "Every plant and flower, shows to us God's power" was copied by both Hancocks. Abiah Holbrook owned a library of English writing books—by Bickham, John Clark, Robert More Jr., John Seddon, George Shelley, and others—which are now in the Houghton Library at Harvard along with a collection of specimen sheets prepared by his and other students.[7] George Fisher's popular manual was published in Philadelphia by Benjamin Franklin and David Hall as *The American Instructor: or, Young Man's Best Companion* (1748) and by Isaiah Thomas in Worcester, Massachusetts, as *The Instructor: or, American Young Man's Best Companion* (1785).

After completing his college studies, John Hancock entered his uncle's firm, the House of Hancock, and at his uncle's death in 1764 inherited the business, eventually earning great fame and fortune. Ebenezer Hancock was not as accomplished a penman as his older brother, if the Shirley copybook is an indication, and he did not fare as well in life: upon his uncle's death, he received £666 and land in Maine. Ebenezer's attempts at business were not successful, but he was able to be carried through by connections to his older brother, and inherited one-third of his brother's fortune in 1793.[8]

Never having reached the fame of either Hancock, Allan Melvill, is remembered (if at all) for three things: marrying into one of the first families of New York; being the father of author Herman Melville (1819–1891; Allan Melvill's widow added the final "e" after his death in 1832); and suffering a bankruptcy that upended the lives of his wife and eight children. He started off with promise, though, as the son of Major

Thomas Melvill (1751–1832), who participated in the 1773 Boston Tea Party (and kept a vial of tea leaves to prove it) after earning degrees from Boston Latin School, the College of New Jersey (now Princeton University), and St Andrews University, with an honorary degree from Harvard College.[9] The fourth of eleven children of Thomas Melvill and his wife Priscilla Scollay Melvill (1755–1833), Allan Melvill was born in Boston on April 7, 1782.[10] Like the Hancock brothers, he attended a writing school and he left behind five copybooks to show his work. Four of these (dated 1790–1794) are in the Gansevoort-Lansing Collection at New York Public Library[11] and one (from 1793) is in the Betsy Beinecke Shirley Collection. As a group, they display various levels of proficiency and intent of exercise appropriate for a boy aging from eight to twelve years while he was a student at Amherst Academy and at the West Boston Academy. At the second school, Melvill was a student of Oliver Wellington Lane, a now-forgotten man whose decade of achievements in Boston extended beyond his accomplishment in penmanship.

One of a number of writing masters teaching in Boston by that time, Oliver Lane was born in Bedford, Massachusetts, on October 27, 1751, the son of James and Mary Wellington Lane. He attended Harvard College, graduating in 1772, and was granted a Masters of Arts diploma from the college in 1779.[12] Following his military service during the Revolutionary War, Lane taught school in Hampton, New Hampshire, before returning to Boston where he married in 1784 and opened the West Boston Writing School in Staniford Street.[13] Aside from his life as a teacher, Lane was a deacon of the First Universalist Church of Boston and compiler, with George Richards, of a collection of hymns for use in his congregation.[14] Lane's most notable civic achievement, however, was perhaps his part in establishing in April 1791 the first Sunday school in Boston, just a month after one had been founded in Philadelphia by a group of citizens including Benjamin Rush (Universalist), Mathew Carey (Roman Catholic) and the Episcopal Bishop William White. Aimed at teaching poor and working children to read on a day free from employment, Sunday schools had been opened in the 1780s in

England by the Anglican evangelical Robert Raikes (1725–1811) but the movement had a more difficult time taking hold in America.[15]

A notice appeared in Boston newspapers on April 20, 1791, and was reprinted in several papers in the region and along the East Coast within the week: "A SUNDAY SCHOOL, Established by the liberal subscription of a number of patriotick Gentlemen of this Metropolis, was opened on Sunday last. It is under the direction of Mr. Oliver W. Lane, and embraces in its object, those of both sexes, under a certain age, whom habits of industry or other causes, debar from instruction on week-days."[16] The announcement was qualified the next day: "A Sunday School, established by the Proprietors of the DUCK MAN-UFACTORY, and intended for the female children employed therein, was opened on Sunday under the direction of Mr. Oliver W. Lane. The attention to the morals and instruction of those who are prevented from receiving the benefit of instruction on any other day than this, does the Gentlemen who instituted it, infinite honour. Its being confined to the young daughters of industry employed in the Factory, will enable the superintendent to do the fullest justice to the children committed to his care. It is not a general Sunday School, as has been stated in the CENTINEL and CHRONICLE, but its views are restricted as above-mentioned."[17] The Duck Manufactory, a textile mill producing canvas woven from local flax, had opened in early 1789, and supplied sails for many of the ships regularly seen in Boston Harbor.[18]

Allan Melvill's earliest extant penmanship album was begun at Lane's West Boston Academy on October 2, 1790. The eight-year-old student was not shy about identifying its author; on its gray wallpaper front wrapper he lettered in ink "Master Allan Melvill's," on the first page "Allan Melvill's Writing," and inside the back cover "Master Allan Melvill's Writing West Boston School November 22, 1790." The 40 pages inside are largely filled with single letters and words, including "understanding," "improvement," "promise," "money," "fortune," "lost," and "discretion" copied over and over, with short words such as "love" appearing some 78 times—77 of those are copies of the first "love" inscribed at the top of the page by Lane. The second album is signed "Allan Melvill Amherst Academy January 3 1792" on the inside of the front cover of its 32 pages. Amherst Academy was a short-lived school in Amherst, New Hampshire, founded by a group of citizens in February 1791 "to encourage and promote virtue and piety, and a knowledge of the English, Greek, and Latin languages, Mathematicks, Writing, Geography, Logic, Oratory, Rhetoric, and other useful and ornamental branches of literature."[19] Melvill's penmanship work there involved copying words and maxims, such as "Opportunity is presented to all mankind," "Fear accompanies guilt," and "Innumerable annoyances accompany mankind," in small and large round hand, as well as copying out short poems on themes of music, friendship, beauty, painting, spring, and "How to get Riches." Included in the little book is a one-page letter inscribed by Melvill to: "Honoured Parents" which reads: "By these lines I let you know that by your good Care and conduct, I am well settled and pleased with my station; and could not but in Duty return my hearty Thanks in a greatful Acknowledgement of your Love and Care of me. I will endeavor to go through my Business cheerfully and having began well I hope I shall persevere to do so to the end that I may be a Comfort to you hereafter." The following year Allan Melvill returned to Boston to take up again his study with Master Oliver Wellington Lane.

The fourth Melvill copybook bears marbled paper wrappers on which he inscribed "Master Allan Melvill's Writing Book West Boston Academy September 24, 1793," and its 32 pages contain a mix of all exercises described above: words in large and small round hand, and poems on topics of friendship, wit, and spring. An unusual addition is his pictorial composition dedicated to the "Inscription for the Monument of General Montgomery," where he copied out "On the Death of General Montgomery" by Bryan Edwards (1743–1800) to create his own memorial to the Continental Army's Major General Richard Montgomery (1738–1775) and the Battle of Quebec complete with "a brave American officer," his tent, cannon, and flags.[20] Melvill also dedicated one page to a quotation taken from the composition "To the Ingenious Practitioners in the Art of Writing," published in Edward Cocker's *Arts Glory, or, The Pen-man's Treasurie* (1657): "Writing is an Art, neither Mechanical nor liberal yet the Parent and Original of both, not a Science but the way to all Sciences, serving naturally for the Illustration of the Mind and the delight of the Eye." His last copybook, titled "Allan Melvill's Writing Book Begun November the 1st 1794," contains 22 pages of poems in longhand with their titles inscribed at top and his signature at bottom in many fancy scripts including secretary hand. The poem titles span a variety of themes from "Enjoyment" and "Friendship" to "False Greatness" and "The Vanity of Riches," with a nod to Anacreon and "The Antient Poets."

Betsy Shirley's Melvill penmanship copybook fits chronologically in the center of the four albums in the Gansevoort-Lansing Collection, but stands apart from them in style right from the paper wrapper

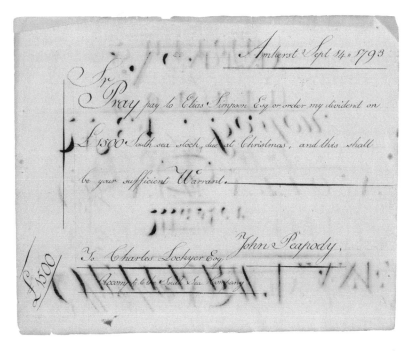

that forms the cover. It features a rare (if not now unique) satirical etching titled "The Macaroni Dray Man," issued by Carington Bowles (1724–1793), a London book, map, and print publisher, which was likely hand-colored by the young student himself. Melvill signed the cover in ink above the plate mark: "Master Allan Melvills Printing Book," and on the final page of the book, added: "Finished this Book At West Boston Academy 19 Day of September 1793." This copybook also differs from the others in content. Its 22 pages were composed so that every right-hand page contains a carefully lettered penmanship sampler with an equally careful simulation of a business invoice on its verso, the latter so careful as to mimic an engraved statement. The first and third pages contain sets of alphabets neatly lettered in upper and lower case Roman and Italic hands, with subsequent pages showing a variety of exercises including lettered names of Massachusetts and American towns (with some demonstrating his use of secretary hand), placard pieces with the

Page from Allan Melvill's copybook, sample invoice, 1793.

legends: "George Washington Esqr, the Political Saviour of America;" "John Adams Esqr, Minister Plenipotentiary to the Court of England;" "Joseph Warren Esqr Who was slain at the Battle of Bunker Hill Seventh of June 1775;" "Elbridge Gerry Esqr one the late Convention for the County of Suffolk;" and similar designs for his master and himself, which demonstrate his accomplishments in controlled display lettering. The nine business statements copied out on the verso pages are invoices for "a knuckle of Veal" and "A Neats Tongue," stationery items including "A Pocket Book with a silver Lock & Key" and "Rheams fine demy paper," promissory notes, and other financial documents. These examples were likely taken from writing manuals, but one in particular gives a hint of Melvill's future career as well as providing a local connection. An invoice for fabrics and trimmings made out to a "Mrs. Sparhawk" could possibly be a reference to the milliner Susannah Sparhawk who arrived in Boston from London in May 1791 and operated a shop in the city until she relocated to New York in November 1793.[21] Another text for a model promissory note signed by "Nahum Neednothing," however, was copied directly from George Fisher's *The Instructor.*

Two of Melvill's fellow students at the West Boston Academy were General William Hyslop Sumner (1780–1861) and the author and antiquarian Lucius Manlius Sargent (1786–1867). Hyslop had once reminisced about the visit of George Washington to Boston in late October 1789, when he and the rest of the boys at the school were lined up in the street: "[They] carried long quills with the feathers on; and, when Washington passed, they paid him a salute by rolling those quills in their hands."[22] A different type of remembrance was published by Sargent's friend John H. Sheppard in a posthumous tribute: "He was then sent to Master Lane's school, in West Boston, which he reached by going up Hancock Street and round by the Beacon monument, on the sides of which were four historic tablets. He says that in 1793 it was 'a lonely spot to travel.' The master was 'harsh;' he did not like him. One mode of his punishment was to make a boy stand on a very narrow log, with scarcely any foothold, with a large chip in his mouth, for an example; yet if any urchin lifted up his eyes to look at him, he was condemned to a similar punishment."[23] Whether Allan Melvill shared the same sentiment or experiences is unknown, but Sargent's story belies the newspaper notice that appeared when Oliver Wellington Lane suddenly died at age 42 on November 8, 1793, leaving behind a wife and six children: "The Civil Community, of which he was a valuable and useful member, will long regret the loss of an excellent Preceptor, whose modes of instruction gained the confidence of the Parent, and won the affections of the child."[24] Later carved in stone in the Old Granary Burying Ground, the legend on his monument described him as one "In whom was United the Real Christian, the Accomplished Gentleman, and Unrivall'd Preceptor."[25]

Allan Melvill did not go to Harvard or any other college; instead he traveled to London and Paris when he finished his school studies. He remained in Paris for nearly two years, and when he returned to Boston he opened an importing business.[26] After a few years and several good business connections, he married well, to Maria Gansevoort of Albany, New York, in 1814, and moved his shop to New York City where he arranged imports of French and Italian fancy goods including umbrellas and parasols, shawls, fabrics, and trimmings. Melvill's economic fortunes prospered initially, but then began to decline until the summer of 1830 when his business collapsed; the family was forced to flee up the Hudson River to Albany to seek the support of the Gansevoort family. Allan Melvill died there in January 1832, deeply in debt, leaving nothing for his wife or their eight children. His boyhood calligraphic wish to "go through my Business cheerfully and having began well I hope I shall persevere to do so to the end that I may be a Comfort to you hereafter" was not to be. Within a year of his death Allan Melvill was joined by both his father and his mother; it is hoped he was able to comfort them in the hereafter.

In terms of quality with quantity, the penmanship standouts in the Shirley Collection are albums owned by Mary Trotter (1797–1827), the orphaned daughter of the eminent Philadelphia cabinetmaker

Hail blushing goddess beauteous Spring,
Who in thy jocund train dost bring,
Loves and graces, smiling Hours,
Balmy breezes, fragrant flowers,
Come with tints of roseate hue,
Nature's faded charms renew.

Mary Trotter.

7th mo. 6th 1832

Daniel Trotter (1747–1800) and his wife Rebecca Conarroe Trotter (1754–1797). The four volumes that preserve her penmanship exercises date from 1810 to 1813 and were made at a Quaker Select School in Philadelphia and at the Westtown School in nearby West Chester, Pennsylvania, attended by Mary, her brothers Nathan (1787–1853) and Thomas (1789–1821), and her sister Rebecca (1791–1815), whose autograph album is also in the Shirley Collection.[27] Mary Trotter's workbooks, with both marbled and plain paper wrappers, contain practice pages of round-hand script ranging from mathematical projections and alphabets in Roman, Italic, Square Text, Old English, German Text, and Set Chancery, to full sheets holding maxims such as "Admonish bad dispositions" and "Benevolence is commendable." She also composed floral-decorated panels enclosing quotations copied from workaday sources including Daniel Fenning's *Universal Spelling-Book* (published in London in multiple editions for decades after 1756, and featuring a Table with handy "Verses upon various Occasions and proper for Writing-Pieces"), literary works by the popular author James Thomson, and more obscure literary pieces such as "An Ode to Spring by Swift's Miss Van Vanhomrigh [From Mr. Sheridan's Life of Dr. Swift]."[28] Mary Trotter's albums offer page after page, and book after book, of a teenaged girl's beautiful calligraphy—different from those created some decades before by the Hancock brothers and Allan Melvill, whose exercises fitted them for lives of public service and business. But the penmanship copybooks by those young boys stand with Mary Trotter's works in mute tribute to a lost art made more exquisite in our time, when the teaching of cursive handwriting is no longer emphasized in formal education. These small volumes remain as exemplars that serve, quite naturally, "for the Illustration of the Mind and the delight of the Eye."

1   E. Jennifer Monaghan, in her studies "Readers Writing: The Curriculum of the Writings Schools of Eighteenth-Century Boston," in *Visible Language* 21, no. 2 (Spring 1987): 167-214, and *Learning to Read and Write in Colonial America* (Amherst: University of Massachusetts Press; Worcester: American Antiquarian Society, 2005),

(*opposite*) Page from workbook by Mary Trotter, 1812.

detail early efforts to train American youth for their futures. Both build upon the scholarship began by Ray Nash in his works *Some Early American Writing Books and Masters* ([Hanover, N.H.], 1943), *American Writing Masters and Copybooks* (Boston: Colonial Society of Massachusetts, 1959), and *American Penmanship, 1800–1850* (Worcester: American Antiquarian Society, 1969).

2 *Catalogue of the Boston Latin Public School Established in 1635* (Boston: Boston Latin School Association, 1886), 64, 71.

3 Ibid, 36.

4 Monaghan, "Readers Writing," 171.

5 Betsy Shirley acquired the Hancock copybook at auction in 1991, prior to which it had descended through five generations of the family of Ebenezer Hancock.

6 P.H. Muir, "The Bickhams and their Universal Penman," in *Library*, 4th ser., 25 (1945): 162-84.

7 Holbrook's collection of copybooks in the Houghton Library were discovered and described by Ray Nash in his article, "A Colonial Writing Master's Collection of English Copybooks," *Harvard Library Bulletin* 14 (1960): 12-19; the writing samples are held in a separate collection, Specimens of Penmanship from Writing Schools in Boston, 1748–1782 (MS Typ 473.22), Houghton Library, Harvard University.

8 *Guide to the Hancock Family Papers*. Baker Library Historical Collections. Harvard Business School.

9 *Catalogue of the Boston Latin Public School*, 78.

10 Jay Leyda, *The Melville Log* (New York: Gordian Press, 1969), xxviii; "Thomas Melvill," *National Cyclopedia of American Biography* (New York: James T. White and Company, 1901), 9:364.

11 Gansevoort-Lansing Collection (MssCol 1109), Box 307, Manuscripts and Archives Division, New York Public Library; the four penmanship copybooks were given to the library in 1930 by Melvill's granddaughter Charlotte Elizabeth Hoadley (1858–1946).

12 Frederick Clifton Pierce, *The Descendants of John Whitney, Who Came from London, England, to Watertown, Massachusetts, in 1635* (Chicago: Press of W.B. Conkey Company, 1895), 32-33.

13 *Reports of the Selectmen and Superintending School Committee of Hampton* (Boston: Tolman and White, 1872), 23. James Hill Fitts, *Lane Genealogies*, vol. 3 (Exeter, N.H.: News-Letter Press, 1902), 87.

14 *Psalms, Hymns, and Spiritual Songs, Selected and Original* (Boston: I. Thomas and E.T. Andrews, 1792).

15 "The Universalist Origin of American Sunday Schools," in *Universalist Quarterly and General Review* 19 (October 1882): 448. The most complete source for biographical material on Oliver Wellington Lane is Albert Matthews, "Early Sunday Schools in Boston," in *Publications of the Colonial Society of Massachusetts, Transactions* 21 (1919): 280-282.

16 *Columbian Centinel*, April 20, 1791, 43.

17 *Herald of Freedom*, April 22, 1791, 3.

18 *Salem Mercury*, January 6, 1789, 3, and June 16, 1789, [3].

19 Daniel F. Secomb, *History of the Town of Amherst, Hillsborough County, New Hampshire* (Concord: Evans, Sleeper & Woodbury, 1883), 322-323. The school closed in 1801 due to a lack of financial support.

20 The poem was published in *The American Museum, or, Universal Magazine* 10 (July 1791).

21 *New-Hampshire Spy*, May 29, 1791, 39; Boston Gazette, November 21, 1791, [3]; *New York Daily Advertiser*, November 22, 1793, [3].

22 Joseph Palmer, *Necrology of Alumni of Harvard College, 1851–52 to 1862–63* (Boston: Printed by J. Wilson and Son, 1864), 390-91.

23 John H. Sheppard, *Reminiscences of Lucius Manlius Sargent* (Boston: David Clapp & Son, 1871), 8.

24 *The Mercury*, November 5, 1793, [3].

25 Thomas Bridgman, *The Pilgrims of Boston and their Descendants* (New York: Appleton; Boston: Phillips, Sampson and Company, 1856), 118.

26 William H. Gilman, *Melville's Early Life and Redburn* (New York: New York University Press, 1951), 7.

27 Elva Tooker, *Nathan Trotter, Philadelphia Merchant, 1787–1853* (Cambridge: Harvard University Press, 1955), 6. Mary Trotter attended Westtown School, also written as "Weston" in her albums, from 1807 to 1810; she was enrolled on October 22, 1807, as girl number 682, age 11, in the school's *Girls Register, 1799–1836*. Esther Duke Archives, Westtown School, West Chester, Pennsylvania.

28 *The New Annual Register of History, Politics, and Literature for the Year 1784* (London: G.G.J. and J. Robinson, 1785), 203.

India: Elephant Riding

R André

LAURA WASOWICZ

Headstrong Travels By Land & Water
The Trans-Atlantic World of the Nineteenth-Century Picture Book

In the 1990s, Betsy Beinecke Shirley, who was already well known for her library of children's literature, enhanced her fine collection with the acquisition of a very significant cache of picture book artwork from the McLoughlin Brothers' business archives. Between its establishment in 1858 and its sale to arch competitor Milton Bradley in 1920, New York-based McLoughlin Brothers dominated the publication of color picture books in the United States. Through their early embrace of mechanized color print technologies including chromolithography and photoengraving, they made picture books affordable to the widest possible consumer market nearly a century before Golden Books were launched in the 1940s. In an era before image-laden books were fully protected under international copyright, McLoughlin was a prolific publisher of American editions of English picture books designed by titan illustrators including Randolph Caldecott, Kate Greenaway, and Walter Crane, churning them out at a fraction of the price of the imported original. Although McLoughlin dominated American children's book publishing between 1870 and 1900, the firm is not well known partly because their business records apparently did not survive. So the history of McLoughlin Brothers must be carefully excavated through examining their published products, which includes thousands of books, games, paper toys, and the artwork that served as the

(*opposite*)
Original illustration for *By Land & Water*, ca. 1888.

173

foundation of the McLoughlin publishing empire. In 1997, a massive treasure trove of drawings, printers' proofs, and "plate house" copy picture books from the McLoughlin business archives was acquired by bookdealer Justin Schiller, who sold it in parcels to parties including the American Antiquarian Society, the Cotsen Children's Library at Princeton University, and Betsy Beinecke Shirley. This material is very important because it reflects both the relationship between publisher and illustrator, and the trans-Atlantic nature of late nineteenth-century picture book publishing. These connections are very apparent in drawings held in the Betsy Beinecke Shirley Collection produced by two popular nineteenth-century artists: Englishman Richard Andre (born William Roger Snow, 1834–1907) and American William Bruton (1854 or 1855–1885).[1] As will be seen in their drawings for McLoughlin Brothers, both were starting to enjoy reputations as "named" artists who earned the freedom to brand their illustrations with their personal style. Both managed to break out of routine illustration jobs for fairy tales to produce books celebrating travel to then-current destinations by children as in Andre's *By Land & Water*, and in Bruton's *Johnny Headstrong's Trip To Coney Island*.

By the 1880s, McLoughlin Bros. had been in the picture book business for twenty years and of its hundreds of titles in its stock, only a very small subset of them had illustrators credited on title pages. A marked exception to this practice were picture books with images created by already well-known artists, such as Thomas Nast, who in 1869 provided illustrations for titles including *The Night before Christmas* and *Yankee Doodle* that quickly became classics. Other exceptions were picture books redrawn by McLoughlin staff artists after English editions of the wildly popular work by Walter Crane, Randolph Caldecott, and Kate Greenaway—done without the burden of artistic copyright royalties; in fact Walter Crane denounced McLoughlin's wholesale "pirating" of his artwork in the periodical press.[2] Most of the illustrations in McLoughlin's vast output were created by the firm's stable of staff artists, who rarely got any recognition in print beyond occasionally getting their monograms reproduced as part of the published illustrations. For these reasons, the cases of the English illustrator Richard Andre and the McLoughlin staff artist William Bruton reflect striking departures from standard McLoughlin business practices.

When Richard Andre corresponded with McLoughlin Brothers about his original drawings for *By Land & Water* in 1887, he was already using his second pseudonym, having embarked on a second career as a book illustrator. Thanks to the excellent sleuthing of illustration historian Thomas E. Blom, we now know that "Richard Andre" was the pseudonym of soldier turned professional illustrator William Roger Snow.[3] Born into a wealthy family in 1834, Snow joined the British army as a young man, and literally traveled around the world during his military career to places including Turkey, Hong Kong, Canada, and Ireland. He dabbled in illustration as a sideline; his first artistic work, a book titled *Sketches of Chinese Life & Character*, was published in 1860.[4] He enjoyed some success as an illustrator, painter, and satirist under his own name until 1872, when his wife Christina obtained a legal separation from him on the grounds of his having taken a mistress. In order to avoid paying his estranged wife the annual support guaranteed under the terms of the separation, he abandoned his army post in 1875 and assumed the alias "Clifford Merton," under which he gained some notoriety as a playwright reworking sensational novels, and as an illustrator of picture books published by the London firm of Dean & Son. As Blom skillfully shows, Merton/Snow's illustration work for Dean included the publication between 1880 and 1881 of the *Pantomime Toy Books*, first and second series—including standard fairy tales like *Cinderella*, *Beauty and the Beast*, and *Aladdin*. These were movable picture books designed with five set scenes and nine "trick changes" (shorter, narrower inset pages that serve to instantly change the scene depicted on the larger pages), accompanied by verses likely also written by Snow/Merton. Dean then issued a simplified and cheaper version of these fairy tales under the series title *Children's Pantomime Toy Books*, one of which, a version of *Bluebeard*, contained an illustration signed, "Andre."[5]

McLoughlin Brothers quickly reissued these *Pantomime* books for the American market; and at least some of those Snow/Merton/Andre's images were redrawn by none other than William Bruton.

Andre likely took on this second pseudonym to distance himself after the finalization of his legal separation from his wife in 1882. Having taken a new mistress, actress Clara Foote, with whom he fathered two children, the newly minted Richard Andre needed to provide for his growing family. Through a stroke of luck, he gained the acquaintance of popular children's author Julia Horatia Ewing, and illustrated several of her titles published by the Society for Promoting Christian Knowledge—quite an irony, considering Snow's/Merton's/Andre's checkered career. After his estranged wife's death in 1885, he married Clara Foote, thus sealing his new emergence as Richard Andre, artist and poet. The drawings for *By Land & Water* and the accompanying letter from Richard Andre to McLoughlin Brothers dated August 2, 1887, held in the Betsy Beinecke Shirley Collection provide rare evidence of Andre's workings as an artist at a key point in his career.[6] Freed from the ongoing threat of legal scandal and having established himself as a popular illustrator in the English children's press, Richard Andre was now a seasoned illustrator working at the top of his game who could confidently enter into a publication arrangement with McLoughlin Brothers.

Andre's design for the front cover imitates an actual book cover; a red leather "spine" is painted down the left-hand side of the drawing. Within this composed frame of the book cover, Andre skillfully depicts a child sailor navigating the waves with a racing horse as his craft, combining the excitement of land and sea travel in one fantastical image. With its almost ominous background of dark clouds and slate gray waves, the design is a potent combination of mystery and humor. Donned in a common sailor's middy blouse and bell bottomed pants (as opposed to a naval captain's regalia), this barefooted sailor seems in total control of his equine "craft." He controls his horse with a ship's wheel, and does not seem to need the nautical weathervane emerging from the horse's mane like a fancy headdress. The sailor has long blond hair freely blowing

in the breeze, both hearkening back to a time several centuries past when men and women wore their hair long, and begging the question to the contemporary viewer as to whether Andre deliberately kept this sailor's look androgynous, allowing for the girls in the reading audience to picture themselves as the pilot of this unusual craft. A fortification is barely visible in the distance, with seagulls flying around it, as if to signal to the viewer that the young sailor is boldly heading away from land and all its humanly constructed structures and comforts. Andre punctuates the fantastical subject of his image with concrete signs identifying the book's title, publisher, and illustrator. The title is lettered in whimsical calligraphy designed by Andre that he also incorporates in the book's text, creating a solid design connection between word and picture. The imprint, "A trip personally conducted by…& Co. London" reflects the probability that Andre floated his picture book project to various London firms before striking a business deal with McLoughlin Brothers. Andre's own name figures prominently in the cover design, inscribed

Original illustration and printed cover of *By Land & Water*, ca. 1888.

Original illustration for back cover of *By Land & Water*, ca. 1888.

on the buoy, and in lettering equal to the size devoted to the imprint, reflecting Andre's intent to place his personal brand on the picture book.

In the published version of the book, the cover design's colors are definitely brightened, with a patch of blue sky prominent diagonally to the right of the young sailor giving a sense of movement to the scene, as well as a more positive cast. The biggest change in the finished design is the lettering of the title; Andre breaks up the title so that "By Land" appears in the upper right corner, and "& Water" literally rests in the ocean—thus making the physical appearance of the title itself more dynamic, and providing an attractive frame for the young sailor on horseback.

Andre's design of the land traveler for the back cover is many ways the flip side of the barefoot, androgynous sailor. This traveler is drawn as an older masculine boy dressed and shod in the most modern attire the late Victorian era had to offer. His hair seems to be cut short (or hidden in his coat to look that way) reflecting the contemporary adult male fashion of the time, and his clothes symbolize both comfort and gentility. He wears a roomy great coat that looks like it could be a precursor to the trench coat worn by soldiers during World War I. Its plaid fabric looks like it could be tweed or a wool blend now known as gabardine that was developed by British clothier Thomas Burberry in the 1870s.[7] Our land traveler wears a matching deerstalker cap designed to protect the wearer's face, neck, and ears from weather elements including sun, rain, wind, and cold. Its most famous wearer was the fictitious detective Sherlock Holmes. Although Arthur Conan Doyle published his first Sherlock Holmes story in 1887, the same year that Andre sent these drawings to McLoughlin Brothers, Doyle did not mention Holmes wearing a closely fitting cap with earflaps until at least 1892.[8] Underneath the young traveler's coat we see a pair of striped grey pants that were popular attire for men in both the United States and England at the time.[9] On his feet are a pair of elegantly fitting dark shoes probably of leather, over which are white spats (likely cloth) providing an extra level of protection from the elements, and announcing the wearer's sophistication and resources to have this extra layer of protection.[10] He sports a brown shoulder bag, an umbrella and walking stick bundled in his left hand, and a black brief case in his right with silver studs and the artist's initials "RA" (perhaps to brand the drawing, and to insinuate that either the traveler is his alter ego, or has at least received a dossier of personal instructions from the well-traveled Andre).

This young traveler is standing literally on top of the world, a globe, leaning forward as though he is eagerly setting forth in a new direction. His right foot is on the polar ice cap of the North Pole; his left leading foot is on what appears to be eastern Siberia. Antarctica, Africa, Europe, and Australia are pictured, with some major cities marked such as Cape Town, Cairo, St. Petersburg, Berlin, Bombay, Sydney. His right foot is placed directly north of London (whose letters are barely visible on the edge of the globe), and he seems to be headed toward the New World, and indeed, the book begins with a picture of children riding in England, and ends with young men and women riding recently invented bicycles in the United States.

As it turns out, these two bold young travelers so elegantly represented on the cover drawings (and ultimately, the cover of the published book) do not carry over as ongoing characters. Andre focuses more on the conveyances of travel than the actual travelers. For example, in the depiction of "Elephant riding" in India, Andre lavishes his detail in depicting the features of the Emperor's elephant and the riding chair it so grandly carries; perhaps reveling in the exotic details that he examined firsthand as a British soldier or studied in the voluminous travel literature available at the time. The riding chair does contain two clearly Caucasian children, a pith-helmeted boy and a girl dressed in frilly white clothes—who bear at least a passing resemblance to the sea and land travelers on the cover, but in the published version of the book their faces are blurred so as to cause them to become more a part of the overall design of the image, placing the focus squarely on the elephant carrying them. Arguably, this illustration is an exception to the rule; many of them contain groups of indistinguishable children, sledding in Canada or riding camels in Egypt. Some pictures in the published book do not have any distinguishable pictures of children, such as those depicting boats sailing off the coast of Gibraltar or a steam-powered train wending its way through the rugged cliffs of Australia. The final picture, "America's Silent Wheel," shows young adults riding bicycles, including an early tandem.

Andre's commentary on the drawings to McLoughlin Brothers reflects this attention to detail regarding the conveyances; he comments about the bicycle drawing: "I assume the pattern in use in America are [sic] exactly similar to English."[11] He also leaves a tantalizing clue in the notes referring to another picture book he had just completed for McLoughlin; he comments on the size of one of his *By Land & Water* drawings, "I hope this will cause no inconvenience. All the other drawings are same size in Santa Claus Book." This brief mention probably refers to his drawings for *Around the World with Santa Claus*, another travel book featuring Santa delivering gifts around the world and poetry printed in Andre's whimsical script. The earliest locatable edition of *Around the World* is from 1891, although McLoughlin issued the images in 1889 in the *Santa Claus Cube Puzzle*, a copy of which is held at the Beinecke Library.[12] Andre's Santa book capitalized on the McLoughlin Santa Claus brand firmly established in 1869 by American cartoonist Thomas Nast's rendition of *The Night before Christmas.* Andre's Santa has the white beard, long hair, and pointed cap, but he resembles more of a bohemian renaissance man in his moccasins, striped stockings, blue pants and red jacket trimmed with ermine, providing a rich contrast to Nast's portrayal of Santa as a rather unkempt elfin man in a fur suit... but that is the subject for another essay. In short, the influential river of talent and ideas in the picture book world ran both ways between London and New York, as Betsy's collection so tellingly testifies.

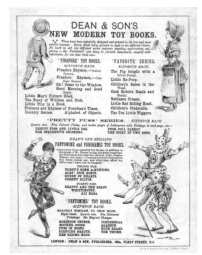

Just as William Snow/Clifford Merton/Richard Andre was hitting his stride as an internationally recognized illustrator, the Brooklyn artist William Bruton used the opportunities afforded him as an illustrator for McLoughlin Bros. to develop his own unique voice. During his short life, William Bruton (1854 or 1855–1885) started working for McLoughlin in about 1878, and his signature can be traced to at least some fifty McLoughlin titles, the bulk of them published between 1882 and 1884.[13] He created cover designs for various picture books, managing to get his initials or "W. Bruton" on the published copy, which was a pretty impressive feat, considering that he was new on the scene, and that artist signatures show up only occasionally in McLoughlin books published at that time, aside from the already well-known artists commissioned by McLoughlin like Thomas Nast, or eventually, Richard Andre. It is in this medium of cover design that William Bruton emerged as a master of eye-catching composition that visually brands a picture book both on the front and the back.

While copying the illustrations for a McLoughlin edition of the *Pantomime Toy Books* originally designed by Richard Andre, Bruton created a back cover design composed of visual icons representing all

(*left*) Original back cover design of Pantomime toy books, ca. 1880.

(*right*) Back cover of *Aladdin*. Dean & Son's Children's Pantomime Toy Books, ca. 1880.

the fairy tales in the series, namely *Aladdin*, *Sleeping Beauty*, *Puss in Boots*, *Cinderella*, and *Blue Beard*, forming a frame around the perimeter of the cover, with four stock pantomime characters dominating the center design, visually reinforcing the series name and its titles, and closing the frame with "McLoughlin Bros., New-York" lettered in elegant outline. This essentially visual approach to picture book advertisement is quite striking, given the fact that from the birth of a literature published exclusively for children in the mid-eighteenth century up until the 1880s, advertisements on the back covers of children's picture books tended to have crowded entries printed in tiny type. Dean & Son, the original London publisher of the *Pantomime* series, did visually brand the series by putting images of Pirouette and two clowns on either side of the series list.[14] Bruton pushed this idea a step further by using visuals from each book to advertise the series, dispensing with a printed list. Perhaps he was responding to the changing consumers of picture books in the United States that would have included immigrants whose first language was not necessarily English, or maybe more likely Bruton wanted to make the entire book an elegant sequence of pictures from cover to cover. Thanks to Betsy Shirley, Bruton's original pen and ink drawing for this innovative cover is now held at the Beinecke.[15]

Bruton used his formidable design skills to create the highly atmospheric illustrations for *Johnny Headstrong's Trip to Coney Island*, a home-grown travel story about a rambunctious boy's trip to New York's Coney Island.[16] A barrier island off of the Long Island coast, Coney Island was fast becoming a trendy destination for people of all classes in the 1880s. The newly established Iron Steamboat Company provided mass transit from Manhattan, making Coney Island an attainable day trip for many potential child readers of Johnny Headstrong's adventures. All of Bruton's drawings for this picture book are available at the Beinecke and they offer fascinating insight into Bruton's developing genius as an illustrator. Just as in his *Pantomime* cover design, Bruton incorporates the title into the visual design, drawing the viewer into the story before the cover is turned. The first two words of the title (Johnny

Headstrong's) are emblazoned across the horizon, summoning the eye to the ocean below it. "Trip to" is lettered within a lifesaving ring that serves as both a nautical symbol and frame for the face of the story's hapless hero. And what about that face? Unlike the idealized children appearing in Richard Andre's cover design for *By Land & Water*, Johnny Headstrong looks like an average, unassuming boy of about ten or eleven wearing clothes in keeping with his status as a middle-class child going on a summer holiday, with his broad brimmed hat and button-down middy blouse that looks like an adaptation of the naval garb worn by Andre's androgynous sailor child.

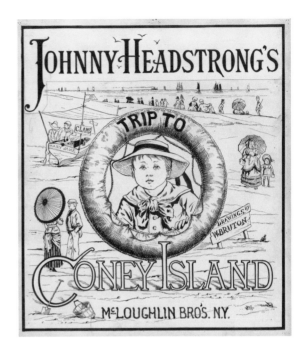

Original front cover design for *Johnny Headstrong's Trip to Coney Island*, ca. 1882.

The words "Coney Island" are drawn like an elegant sign announcing the destination to eager visitors. Bruton also provides small sketches around the periphery of the design to offer visual clues to various scenes that one could encounter on the Coney Island beach: a woman walking with a child; a young couple conversing, the woman's face discreetly hidden by a fashionable parasol; a clam vendor selling his wares under a canopy; and the miniscule figures on the horizon taking in the cool refreshing beauty of the ocean. Last, but certainly not least, the illustration credit "drawings by W. Bruton" is drawn on a sign posted right next to the hapless hero.

The story of Johnny Headstrong's trip to Coney Island is simply one comical mishap after another. Told in what now seems stilted verse, Johnny's father, the top-hatted "Neighbor Brown," takes Johnny, his younger sister Sue, the baby, and the household's nursemaid on a summertime trip to Coney Island. Unlike Andre's sophisticated traveling

Original illustration of Johnny riding the horse across the crowded beach, ca. 1882.

children, Johnny is prominent in every illustration as a cutup whose adventure quickly turns into accident. Johnny gets into trouble almost immediately; he falls overboard from the Iron Steamboat ferry while trying to fish. He himself is literally fished out of the ocean, and is brought down to the furnace room to dry off. Once at Coney Island, Johnny gets separated from the adults almost immediately, and ends up crying before a motley crew of strangers including tourists and street vendors. One man offers the weepy boy a horse in order to give the child more visibility so he could be spotted by his father, but mischievous Johnny goads the horse to take a gallop on the beach, a scene which Bruton captured in a panoramic spread over two Bristol boards, and it commands the coveted center fold of the published book.

At first glance, Johnny might seem to be the central focus of this expansive scene. Bruton shows a frightened Johnny on the runaway horse just after it knocked down a woman apple vendor on the beach. Bruton's drawing does not follow the text, as it shows both Johnny and

184

his sister Sue behind him on horseback. Johnny's hair and hat blow in the wind and his mouth is wide open, as if saying, "Oh, no!" Both of them are terrified and seem to be riding among a cast of thousands, with the ocean view ever present in the background. Two boys run beside them, as if cheering them on, and probably goading on the horses with their crops. Most of the figures immediately in back of Johnny are adults who have their backs turned, as if they are more interested in viewing the ocean than witnessing Johnny's predicament. The only two adults in the background who seem to be actually watching the galloping children are their father (in his formal suit with top hat), and the ever-smiling nursemaid holding the baby. Surprisingly, neither one seems particularly worried about the runaway children, as though it is an expected part of a sunny day at the beach. Just to the left of these bemused adults is a trio of figures in the foreground that does not seem to have any direct connection to Johnny's misadventure or the other figures turned toward the ocean.

These figures, a grown man and woman in bathing suits and a little boy carrying a pail, who might comprise a family bring a jarring presence to this scene because they are facing away from everything else going on, and because they are drawn with better detail than Johnny and his family, which is puzzling. The man and woman are portrayed in the most modern (even avant-garde) beach dress of the time. They are both wearing new-fangled bathing suits and swimming hats. The woman, her eyes downcast as if expressing self-modesty for wearing this unaccustomed dress in a public place, wears a long swimming blouse with shorts underneath coming to just above her knees. Remarkably, her legs are bare, which would have been quite unusual for a grown American woman in the 1880s. According to *Percy's Pocket Dictionary of Coney Island* (1880), "Bathing-dresses . . . are no longer considered indelicate if they follow the outline of the form to some little extent. . . . With a pair of . . . bathing-shoes over the stockings the drawers need only reach the knees . . ."[17] Townsend Percy also notes the relatively new existence of "free swimming-baths for both sexes," remarking that "females can and do learn to swim as easily as males."[18] Her male companion looks dreamily off into the distance, away from the woman, and from the runaway horse action nearby. He wears a horizontally striped swim suit of a similar cut as his companion, and the boy with the shovel and pail seems to be waiting upon them expectantly, as if wanting to go to the water's edge.

As it turns out, two figures of this trio were transplanted into Bruton's composition. The drawing in the Betsy Shirley collection reveals that the man and woman were drawn on separate board and pasted into the picture! The rendering of this trio, especially the man, is so purposeful, so detailed, that it begs the question of whether William Bruton might have inserted his own likeness into the scene—the ultimate form of artistic branding.[19] Bruton's drawing was faithfully reproduced, bathing-suited couple and all, in the published picture book, perhaps reflecting the fact that the potentially racy image of a bare-legged woman was diffused by its incorporation into a large comic scene in a children's book. In the end, Johnny's misadventures play out predictably enough: after getting his hair pulled by monkeys at the Coney Island zoo and falling off of a swing, a bruised and battered Johnny returns home with his family to be lectured by his father about proper behavior at the beach.

Unlike Richard Andre, William Bruton did not enjoy a lengthy career as a celebrated illustrator doing commissioned work for a variety of publishers. He died in 1885 at age 30, so these drawings collected by Betsy Shirley provide important evidence of a talented American artist who is more than worthy of rediscovery.[20] Both Richard Andre and William Bruton came into their own as illustrators during the latter half of the nineteenth century when the market afforded the mass publication of folio picture books produced with multi-color processes like chromolithography, allowing opportunities for a high standard of detailed and personally defined illustration. These developments, along with improvements in transportation and the growth of a child-centered consumer market influenced illustrators like Andre and Bruton to create picture books celebrating the child as an independent traveler. However, their approaches to that child traveler differed sharply. In *By Land & Water*, Andre drew almost mythical child travelers on the cover that can ride horses through oceans and nimbly step on top of the world without getting dirty or cold. But it is the machinery of travel, be it a boat, or an elephant, a train, or a bicycle that commands the central focus. In contrast, Bruton's naughty Johnny Headstrong blazed a hapless trail from the cover and onto every illustration in the book. Although he exudes personality and independence, his poor choices brought him bruises, bumps, and constant dependence on his father to fish him out of trouble.

As these drawings from the Betsy Beinecke Shirley Collection so beautifully reflect, Richard Andre and William Bruton flourished in a competitive, trans-Atlantic market where illustrators aggressively studied the competition and copied each other while developing their own unique voice, and the road between London and New York definitely went two ways, as seen in Bruton's adaptation of Andre's fairy tale figures and Andre's marketing his work directly to McLoughlin Brothers for an American audience. Ultimately, both artists used their skill and opportunities as emerging players in this trans-Atlantic world of the picture book to go beyond the fairy tale to create new books celebrating children engaging with the modern world, both close to home and far away. These marvelous drawings conceived by two masters of illustration also reveal how both Andre and Bruton navigated their relationship with McLoughlin Brothers to forge their unique artistic voice, beckoning our rediscovery and recognition.

POST-SCRIPT

I was honored to be invited to write an essay honoring Betsy Shirley and her collection at the Beinecke Library; I realize I have known both the woman and aspects of her collection for a long time. I first met Betsy in October 1988 when she came to my library, the American Antiquarian Society, to speak about her collection during a collectors' roundtable session held during a symposium on children's literature. Looking back nearly thirty years later, I marvel at my good fortune; I had recently been hired to catalog the Society's magnificent but little explored collection of nineteenth-century children's books, and I was assigned the exciting but daunting task of speaking about the collection in the presence of a great pantheon of collectors, including Justin Schiller, Lloyd Cotsen, Herbert Hosmer, Jack & Linda Lapides, Ruth Adomeit, and Betsy Shirley. I was taken by Betsy's astute prowess as a collector, and her down-to-earth affability. She was a devoted member of the AAS, and as I later found out, gave valuable financial support to our American Children's Books Cataloging Project when it was most needed. After I delivered my presentation on my discoveries working with this largely untapped collection, Betsy responded with cheerful good will, and I was relieved that I had passed muster. In the ensuing years, I received occasional phone calls from Betsy asking about specific editions of early American children's books; her questions clearly reflected the command of both the subject matter and her collection.

1   For clarity's sake I will refer to William Snow as "Richard Andre," as this was the pseudonym he was using when he corresponded with McLoughlin Brothers about the drawings for *By Land & Water*.

2   McLoughlin Brothers' *Aunt Louisa Series* competed against the original Frederick Warne & Co. issues imported from London by Scribner, Welford, and Armstrong—a branch of Charles Scribner & Co. It is probably no accident that Crane's vitriolic letter attacking McLoughlin's gaudy and unauthorized reproduction of his Baby's Opera picture book appeared in the September 1877 issue of *Scribner's Monthly* (v. 14, p. 721). But until the American copyright law of 1891 guaranteed some rights for foreign holders, McLoughlin Bros. was a prolific publisher of pirate picture book editions.

3   Thomas E. Blom, *The Secret Lives of Richard Andre* (1834–1907). (Toronto: Toronto Public Library, 1990).

4   Ibid. p. 14.

5   Ibid. p. 20.

6   *By Land & Water* mockup, Betsy Beinecke Shirley Collection, GEN MSS 764, Oversize Box 34, Folder 530.

7   "Deerstalker" Wikipedia, https://en.wikipedia.org/wiki/Deerstalker, Oct. 13, 2015.

8 Ibid; the story was "The Silver Blaze."

9 Bold striped pants were fashionable in the 1880s. See Landscape Change Program, University of Vermont website; https://www.uvm.edu/landscape/dating/clothing_and_hair/1880s; Photographs provided by Joan L. Severa; see also her *Dressed for the Photographer, Ordinary Americans and Fashion, 1840–1900* (Kent, Ohio: Kent State University Press, 1995).

10 "Spats (footwear)" Wikipedia, https://en.wikipedia.org/wiki/Spats_(footwear), Oct. 13, 2015.

11 Richard Andre to McLoughlin Brothers, Aug. 2, 1887, Betsy Beinecke Shirley Collection, GEN MSS 764, Oversize Box 34, Folder 530.

12 Besides these Santa products expressly credited to Andre there is a series of watercolor drawings of Santa for an 1888 edition of *Santa Claus and His Works* shelved in the Betsy Beinecke Shirley Collection, GEN MSS 764, Oversize Box 34, Folder 532, that are attributed to Andre by an anonymous hand on the versos. This Santa is shown in his workshop and at his desk with his ledger of children's names, and is depicted as a dignified gentleman in a red vest. These drawings do not appear to be signed by Andre.

13 He might be the William F. Bruton listed as a lithographer at 55 Liberty in *Goulding's Business Directory of New York* (1877). The 1880 United States Federal Census lists William Bruton as being a 25-year-old artist living in Brooklyn, N.Y. The earliest known illustration that I have located signed by Bruton is a cover design for *The Pet Lamb and Other Tales. Willie Winkie Series.* (New York: McLoughlin Bros., ca. 1878).

14 *Aladdin. Dean & Son's Children's Pantomime Toy Books* (London: Dean & Son, ca. 1880). Viewed on the Baldwin Library, University of Florida website, ufdc.ufl.edu, Nov. 11, 2015.

15 Back cover design for *Pantomime Toy Books*, Betsy Beinecke Shirley Collection, GEN MSS 764, Box 2, Folder 45.

16 *Johnny Headstrong's Trip to Coney Island* mockup, Betsy Beinecke Shirley Collection, GEN MSS 764, Oversize Box 42, Folder 616; *Johnny Headstrong's Trip to Coney Island* (New York: McLoughlin Bros., 1882).

17 *New York Herald*, May 31, 1880, quoted in *Percy's Pocket Dictionary of Coney Island* (New York: F. Leypoldt, 1880), p. 83.

18 Ibid, p. 85.

19 I have not located any image of William Bruton.

20 Family Search, June 4, 2008: William Bruton; son of John Bruton, Sr. and Ann M. Hart; b. about 1855, New York; died 3 Jan. 1885, Jersey City, N.J.

LEONARD S. MARCUS

Seen & Heard

Margaret Wise Brown & Leonard Weisgard's *The Noisy Book*

In the fall of 1938, a charismatic 28-year-old Yale graduate named William R. Scott went into business with his wife and brother-in-law with the goal of publishing innovative children's books inspired by the revolutionary insights of American progressive education. Scott had come to this lofty work following a series of less than inspiring publishing jobs that had broadened his knowledge of typography, book design, and illustration but without setting him on a long-term professional path. He and his wife Ethel lived in a Greenwich Village townhouse (the barn of their second, southern Vermont home would serve as the company's warehouse), and had enrolled their children in a nearby progressive nursery school, one of only a handful of such experimental preschools then in operation in New York City. The school's parent institution, called the Bureau of Educational Experiments, was an unorthodox but increasingly influential center of child development research and training housed in a shabby-chic former warehouse building located on Greenwich Village's industrial western fringe. A fateful encounter with the Bureau's founder, Lucy Sprague Mitchell, convinced Scott of the groundbreaking importance of the work in which she and her colleagues were then engaged as proponents of a developmentally sound new approach to writing and book-making for children of the youngest ages. When Mitchell, a visionary thinker and keen strategist, learned of Scott's background, she and a colleague, nursery school director Jessie Stanton, boldly suggested to him that he

(*opposite*) Unpublished interior illustration by Leonard Weisgard for *The Noisy Book*, ca. 1939.

become the first publisher of the kinds of books Mitchell had in mind. Mitchell sweetened the proposal by offering him an office at the Bureau and the help of a former student and protégée, a brilliant intuitive writer and editor named Margaret Wise Brown.

Mitchell's Bureau—known today as the Bank Street College of Education—brought together three carefully interwoven experimental ventures: the Harriet Johnson Nursery School, the Cooperative School for Student Teachers, and a core staff of child development researchers, psychologists, sociologists, and others. Empiricists in the William James-John Dewey progressive tradition, Mitchell and her colleagues favored learning from direct experience, a principle they applied equally to themselves as theoreticians and educators and to the young children in their care.

The nursery school provided the Bureau's future teachers with their first hours of in-class training and researchers (who routinely watched from behind two-way mirrors) with the chance to study entire groups of children of a given age as they developed over time. Student teachers were also prompted to re-experience aspects of their own childhood by means of a battery of sensory-based exercises involving dance, pantomime, painting, and, in one instance, simply standing still at a busy street corner with their eyes closed, the better to take in the city soundscape with something like a young child's heightened awareness.

Mitchell founded the Bureau in 1916, and within a few years' time her studies of early language development had prompted her to question whether the available literature for young children was in fact as developmentally appropriate as the experts claimed. Concluding that this was not the case, she formulated a wide-ranging critique not just of the books but, more fundamentally, of the criteria by which the field's self-appointed arbiters—library specialists led by The New York Public Library's Anne Carroll Moore—determined which books were good and prize-worthy. Mitchell observed that Moore and her colleagues favored "timeless," "once-upon-a-time tales" of make-believe and high adventure, and took it as a given that children wanted vicarious escape from the modern, industrial-age world to some other, less prosaic, imaginary realm. Mitchell's research suggested otherwise: that contemporary children responded best to stories about the electrified urban wonderland of planes, trains, telephones, and skyscrapers they knew. Stories about castles and kings meant little to them. It was the librarians, Mitchell concluded, who were living in a fantasy world.

Not satisfied merely to share her findings within her small professional circle, Mitchell produced a book-length collection of age-graded model "Here and Now" stories and poems of the kind she thought of greatest value. Part story-hour read-aloud and part manifesto, Mitchell's *Here and Now Story Book* was published by Dutton in 1921 and became a much-discussed bestseller, stirring controversy through the sharpness of its attack and Mitchell's dramatic claim of quasi-scientific authority. The book's success did little to undermine the public librarians' dominance as literary gatekeepers, or to fundamentally alter juvenile publishers' editorial direction. Still, Mitchell had not meant for her book to do more than serve as a foundation for more gifted writers to build on in the future.

That future arrived in 1936 when it became apparent that Bank Street had gathered enough talented trainees and staff members within its ranks to warrant serious thought about ambitious new literary projects. Acting decisively, Mitchell arranged with Dutton for a sequel to the *Here and Now Story Book* with the stipulation that the new collection would not be another solo work by her but rather a collaboration open to everyone at Bank Street with the requisite talent. To further spur her colleagues' creative efforts, she launched the Bank Street Writers Laboratory as an informal weekly workshop where members might critique each other's manuscripts in a supportive atmosphere over a glass of sherry. Finally, with a view to establishing a permanent publishing base, Mitchell enlisted Scott in her cause.

The time would not have been right for any of this had not a most remarkable candidate for admission to Bank Street's school for teachers breezed into the Bureau's headquarters one day in the spring of 1935.

A graduate of Virginia's Hollins College, Margaret Wise Brown was a spirited 25-year-old with film-star good looks and a self-dramatizing manner that set her apart from her more earnest Bank Street colleagues. "Brownie," as Mitchell took to calling her in a sunny attempt at reining in the glamorous new arrival, had spent the last three years gadding about New York and, between parties and hunting weekends, laboring over a series of short stories that *The New Yorker* regularly declined. Teaching had become Brown's default option. Writing for children, it seems, had never occurred to her. But as an enrollee in Bank Street's Cooperative School for Student Teachers, she was required to try her hand at the genre, the better, Mitchell explained, to understand what children at different stages of their young lives wanted and needed in books. Brown proved to be an exceptionally quick study and, far exceeding the writing class's stated objectives, prompted Mitchell to comment in her student evaluation file first on the breathtaking magnitude of Brown's raw talent and, mere months later, on the possibility that this mercurial student of hers might one day become the "real writer" she had dreamed of: the literary standard bearer of a Here and Now-based literature for young children of the highest order.[1]

Brown became the Writers Laboratory's central figure after Mitchell and the second-most prolific contributor after her to *Another Here and Now Story Book*, which Dutton published in 1937. Having discovered that she had no patience for teaching small children, Brown thrilled at the chance to edit books for Scott, and especially at the opportunities the new role implied for working closely with artists and writers. "Collect[ing]" illustrators at the chic parties she frequented became a favorite pastime, as Scott would recall with a smile decades later for an interviewer.[2] Clement Hurd, the future illustrator of *Goodnight Moon*, first came to her attention in this way, as the artist responsible for a wealthy Connecticut friend's bathhouse murals. Having found her voice and vocation with Mitchell's help, Brown now wrote quickly and from a seemingly endless supply of smartly original ideas. Now, whenever she met an illustrator with whom she was eager to work, she simply composed a manuscript to order.

The fall 1938 inaugural Scott list consisted of five illustrated books, each representing a distinctive bid at translating Mitchell's Here and Now philosophy into action for young children. *Bumble Bugs and Elephants*, for example, introduced the board book as an unconventional but eminently practical format for toddlers. Illustrated by Hurd in his debut effort in the field, the book's sturdy cardboard pages and plastic spiral binding sensibly accommodated the developmental reality that children at two and three years of age are sensory learners who bite and grab at whatever catches their attention. The content was equally anchored in developmental considerations, with each double-page illustration designed to suggest the setting for a different story, and with Brown's minimal text meant to serve as a prompt for the stories that the parent and child might improvise on their own. It was a Bank Street article of faith that children learned best when playfully coaxed into becoming full collaborators in their education. *Bumble Bugs and Elephants* left ample scope for children to complete what the author and illustrator had merely started, leaving skeptics to wonder whatever had happened to the time-honored tradition of the well-told picture book tale with a beginning, middle, and happily-ever-after ending.

The influential New York Public Library chose not to purchase or endorse the Scott titles—a response that surprised no one considering the ferocity of Mitchell's well-known diatribe against the librarians' point of view. Scott's philosophical mentor had moderated her position since 1921 but hardly enough for the comparable passages of *Another Here and Now Story Book* to be mistaken for a peace offering. On the contrary, Mitchell declared in the new volume, "We stand by our analysis of children's language and interests as stated in the Introduction to the original book, though perhaps we should now state some of our conclusions less hesitatingly."[3] Meanwhile, Scott and company were hard at work preparing a new round of experimental offerings

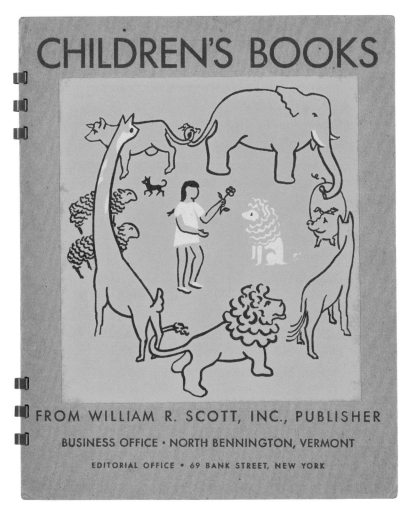

CHILDREN'S BOOKS

FROM WILLIAM R. SCOTT, INC., PUBLISHER

BUSINESS OFFICE • NORTH BENNINGTON, VERMONT

EDITORIAL OFFICE • 69 BANK STREET, NEW YORK

Cover of the 1939 Scott catalog featuring an illustration from *The World is Round.*

for 1939, including a picture book by Brown that the author, perhaps with an impish wink for the golden rule of library silence, had titled *The Noisy Book.*

Brown wrote *The Noisy Book* in a rush of excitement after meeting a talented 22-year-old artist named Leonard Weisgard. "It was on a late summer afternoon," Weisgard recalled, "that I was asked to show my portfolio to Scott's editor. "The sun was shining into a basement window of a Greenwich Village brownstone house. The editor was seated at her desk with her back to the window. The sunlight gave a golden greenish glow to her hair. Her eyes twinkled with a humorous, mischievous look. She started looking at the things in my portfolio, and that mischievous look twinkled all the more...."[4]

Weisgard had stopped by Brown's West 10th Street apartment to place his name in contention for a plum assignment that Scott, with a sharp eye for publicity, was trumpeting around New York as an open competition: the chance to illustrate fabled expatriate Gertrude Stein's first children's book, *The World Is Round*. Stein had written the manuscript in response to a letter from Scott's brother-in-law and partner John McCullough, one of a handful of such feelers he had sent out to famous American authors known for clear, unadorned narrative writing or (as in Stein's case) playful prose. Ernest Hemingway and John Steinbeck had both declined the obscure little firm's quixotic invitation. Stein, however, feeling at a loose end several years after the outsized success of *The Autobiography of Alice B. Toklas*, had responded with an expression of tentative interest, and after a prickly negotiation with McCullough and Scott, had delivered an idiosyncratic fantasy about the adventures of a girl named Rose—a text that the author specified must be printed on rose-colored paper.

Stein ranked at the top of Brown's literary pantheon and was doubtless the writer from whom she had learned the most about creating the impression of a buoyant, free-flowing, conversational presence on the page. It must have thrilled Brown when her idol unexpectedly agreed to join the Scott list, even if McCullough, a garrulous, droll New Englander who minded the business side of the company's affairs, insisted on conducting nearly all of the firm's correspondence with the skittish author himself.

As it turned out, Clement Hurd, not Leonard Weisgard, won Stein's approval and received the commission to illustrate *The World Is Round*. But Brown had other plans in store for Weisgard, with whom she shared a broad interest in contemporary literature and art, a restless passion for experimentation, and the conviction that children were not well served by the genteel, emotionally crimped "strawberries and cream" school of picture-book art and writing that publishers and librarians of the time often favored.[5] *The Noisy Book* would be the first of their more than twenty picture-book collaborations, a professional partnership that soon extended beyond Scott's list to encompass projects undertaken for Harper & Brothers, Doubleday, and Simon and Schuster—all publishers whose greater reach into the marketplace did much to propel the collaborators' innovative ideas—and Lucy Sprague Mitchell's—into the children's literature mainstream.

In *The Noisy Book*, Brown and Weisgard created the quintessential Here and Now book. Brown's playful, script-like read-aloud text gave children chances not only to respond to the direct questions posed to them, but also—and better still—to generate round after round of uproarious noise. How had Brown done this? As the story (such as it is) opens, a little dog named Muffin is found to have gotten a cinder in his eye and is taken to the "dog doctor," where a bandage big enough to cover both his eyes leaves the poor puppy to make his way around town guided only by his sense of hearing. Muffin—much as Brown was once assigned to do during her student teacher days—must listen carefully to each of the city sounds he experiences in turn:

> *"MEN HAMMERING*
>
> *Bang bang bang*
>
> *AUTOMOBILE HORNS*
>
> *Awuurra awuurra*
>
> *HORSES HOOFS*
>
> *Clop clop Clop clop . . ."*

Sensory learning!

> *"Then the sun began to shine*
>
> *Could Muffin hear that?"*[6]

The Noisy Book

By Margaret Wise Brown, illustrated by Leonard Weisgard. Age: 3–5, four colors, 7¼ x 8¾ inches, paper over boards, 48 pp. $1.00

For *The Noisy Book*'s listeners and readers, the little dog's adventures became a lively guessing game and let's-pretend game almost certain to dissolve any grownup participant's solemn attitude, and to end with adult and child sharing in the unfettered fun of the moment on an equal footing. So much for library silence, and for the séance-like atmosphere of traditional library story hours: *The Noisy Book* was a clarion call to raucous, sticky-fingered progressive-school-style self-expression, and a foretaste, in its way, of other picture-book rumpuses to come.

"I submitted it," Brown later recalled of *The Noisy Book*'s enviably smooth road to publication, "and we [referring once again to herself] accepted it."[7] It was an article of faith at Scott that work in progress should be tested on groups of children of the appropriate ages, which in the case of *The Noisy Book* meant children of 3 to 5. As readers of the company's lavishly produced 1939 catalogue learned, the effort had prompted the author to revise at least one line of text.

Interior spread from the Scott catalog showing an illustration for *The Noisy Book*, 1939.

"It's surprisingly difficult for grown-ups to keep seeing things freshly as children do," the elaborate insider anecdote began. "This is partly because the child's world changes but the adult's remembrance of his own childhood stays static. Margaret Wise Brown, our experienced editor, found, when she tried out the manuscript of *The Noisy Book* on a group, that children no longer recognized what she thought of as an automobile horn, and she had to delete 'honk honk' in favor of the 1939 model. Perhaps this changing world accounts for the cold shoulder that greets many of our childhood favorites when we read them to the child of today."[8]

Brown had a strong visual sense and almost certainly would have liked to illustrate her own books had she been capable of doing so. Editing allowed her to do the next best thing: match her own and other writers' manuscripts with the illustrator best suited to interpret them visually, and have a substantial say in the outcome. While Clement Hurd required extensive direction at the start of his career, Leonard Weisgard had arrived fully formed, a wunderkind with a *New Yorker* cover design to his credit by the age of 20. One of Weisgard's major appeals for Brown was his ability to rapidly size up a manuscript, mentally sketch out a plan for its illustration, and then to swiftly execute that plan, sometimes in a mere matter of days.

An only child of European Jewish immigrants, Weisgard had been born in New Haven and raised primarily in the Bronx. He met Martha Graham and Doris Humphreys as a teenager and was training for a career in dance when an injury forced him to redirect his energies. Pivoting to graphic design and illustration, he enrolled in Pratt Institute and began selling his modernist-inflected drawings to national magazines while still a student. In 1937, the year in which Weisgard first appeared in *The New Yorker*, he also published a children's picture book called *Suki, The Siamese Pussy*. Not long after that, he and Brown met and became fast friends.

Weisgard was lanky, shy, and a bit formal, even with friends. (Not one to mince words, Brown once pointedly told him that he spoke

English as though it were his second language.) But he had a keen intellect, absorbed everything that was new and exciting in the realms of theater, dance, and art, and enjoyed sharing his enthusiasms. His sleek, nimble illustrations were a skillful brew of contemporary influences: Soviet Constructivist book illustration, the avant-garde graphics of E. McKnight Kauffer, and the Cubist cityscapes of Stuart Davis, among others.

Working closely together, Weisgard and Brown approached the picture book as an synesthetic art form: an opportunity to combine words and images in such a way as to amplify the expressive power of both media, thereby creating an intensely immediate sensory experience for children that was greater than the sum of its parts. Recalling one of the key design elements of *The Noisy Book* and the six later volumes he illustrated in the series, Weisgard wrote: "As a Noisy Book would develop, I designed shapes that would frame the objects that were to be contained in the pictures. Within a jagged frame a fire engine would appear, making its own special sound. A curving, swishy shape brought the sound of a hissing radiator to the illustration. Not even the most astute book critic ever caught on to this pictorial trick."[9]

Several unpublished examples of fully rendered color art for *The Noisy Book* in Yale's Betsy Beinecke Shirley Collection offer rare glimpses of Weisgard experimenting with basic compositional matters and degrees of abstraction. Placed side by side with these preliminaries, the finished art reveals a preference for images in which Muffin or some human character is made to serve as an emotional focal point for the reader and in which the subject of an illustration, whether animate or not, is re-positioned in the foreground for maximum effect. Scott's catalog aptly describes the illustrations as having been "splashed" across *The Noisy Book*'s pages. "All the pictures are plain, strong and unmistakable."

By the fall of 1941, as her writing career took flight and offers to publish with the larger, established New York houses multiplied, Brown found herself rethinking the value of Bank Street-style empirical research for her writing and the extent to which she shared Lucy

Sprague Mitchell's interest in the waking, cognitive aspects of childhood experience. Increasingly, she found herself drawn inward instead for inspiration, to her own emotional memory of childhood. The book that most clearly signaled the change was *The Runaway Bunny*, illustrated by Clement Hurd, and published not by Scott but by Ursula Nordstrom at Harper & Brothers, in 1942.

Brown gave up her editorial work at about this time as well but continued to publish an occasional book with Scott. *The Noisy Book* had not only far outsold the much-touted *The World Is Round* but had proven to be the young firm's hands-down bestseller, and she was happy to satisfy the continuing demand by periodically writing a pithy sequel, starting with *The Country Noisy Book* of 1940 and *The Seashore Noisy Book* of the following year. The series ran to five volumes when in 1949 Brown generated a different sort of noise by selling "The Ridiculous Noisy Book" to Nordstrom in direct violation of her contract with Scott. The out-of-court settlement that resolved the dispute provided for Harper to assume ownership of the entire Noisy franchise. At the time of her sudden death in 1952, at the age of 42, of a blood clot following a routine operation, Brown had notes for four more installments, including one to be tantalizingly called "The Smelly Noisy Book," its pages to be impregnated with a variety of scents for the reader to investigate.

The seven Noisy volumes that Brown and Weisgard did see through to publication (and an eighth volume, *The Winter Noisy Book*, illustrated in 1947 by Charles G. Shaw) represent an important cultural legacy as the books which, more than any others, introduced the spirit of modernism into American writing and illustration for children. Heeding the modernist imperative to "make it new," Brown, Weisgard, and their like-minded colleagues succeeded in bringing kinetic language, stylized abstraction, and an urgent immediacy to the words and pictures of books intended for people for whom the world itself was a brand new experience. The streamlined building-block city Muffin explores resounds with echoes of blaring car horns, propulsive jackhammers, and of the author who had written, "We are always the same age inside"—Gertrude Stein.[10]

1 Lucy Sprague Mitchell, student evaluation of Margaret Wise Brown, 11 April 1935; quoted in Leonard S. Marcus, *Margaret Wise Brown: Awakened by the Moon* (Boston: Beacon Press, 1992), p. 63.

2 William R. Scott, interview with author, New York, N.Y., 10 September 1981; quoted in Marcus, p. 90.

3 *Another Here and Now Story Book*, edited by Lucy Sprague Mitchell (New York, E.P. Dutton, 1937), pp. xvi-xvii.

4 Leonard Weisgard, "Patchwork Memory," in *Something About the Author Autobiography Series*, Volume 19, edited by Joyce Nakamura (Detroit: Gale Research, 1994), p. 261.

5 Leonard Weisgard, interviews with author, Traelløse, Denmark, 26 October–5 November 1982; quoted in Marcus, *Margaret Wise Brown*, p. 109.

6 Margaret Wise Brown, *The Noisy Book*, illustrated by Leonard Weisgard (New York: William R. Scott, 1939).

7 Margaret Wise Brown, "Leonard Weisgard Wins the Caldecott Medal," *Publishers' Weekly* (5 July 1947), p. 4; quoted in Marcus, p. 111.

8 "Children's Books from William R. Scott, Inc., Publisher" (catalogue) (New York and North Bennington, VT: William R. Scott, 1939).

9 Weisgard, "Patchwork Memory," p. 262.

10 Quoted in *The American Treasury, 1455–1955*, edited by Clifton Fadiman (New York: Harper & Brothers, 1955), p. 946.

PATRICK KILEY

This Page is Fallow
A One-field Survey of Agrarian Rhetoric in American Children's Literature

Today's farming movement owes some of its strength and momentum to books for children and young adults published in the last two centuries. Printers, publishers, authors, and illustrators have used rhetorical strategies to persuade young people that farming is a worthy vocation and to teach them how to do it better. In this essay I survey a selection of books published in the United States in the nineteenth century aimed at juvenile audiences. I try to establish a kind of taxonomy of the most prevalent rhetorical themes and devices in this tradition of encouragement. This chronological overview of a specific type of rhetorical development is given with very spare analysis; I do not approach questions of readership and circulation, watershed events, or the ways this rhetoric has operated in our public history (i.e., these books' modes of action in the hands of readers). Indeed, this can be read as a one-field survey. Most of the works cited are from the Betsy Beinecke Shirley collection of American Children's Literature.

The U.S. government spends approximately $20 billion annually on farming subsidies.[1] The vast majority of this amount goes to support agricultural practices and economies that exhaust human and ecological health. How can this be turned around? One point of leverage is to change kids' attitudes towards food and farming so that they are hungry to participate in responsible ways. The fortunate fact of *publication*

(*opposite*) "The Farm Yard,"
The Farm, 1854.

is that books can be far cheaper to make and have greater impact than Monsanto's GMO corn seed. Books blow into towns through many pathways; language is notoriously promiscuous. Rhetorical language in particular is a supple set of tools that can be adapted to fit new ideas and new ways of speaking and thinking. Rhetoric is like seed broadcast on the blank page—and a fallow field can become fertile again.

My theory is that the overarching strategy behind the nineteenth century style of rhetoric was to appeal to readers of the day with a vision of America and what is meant to be "American" and then to position farming inside that vision. This is what an agricultural conglomerate does when it superimposes its brand logo at the center of a bucolic panorama. Through stories, the rhetorical themes are organized and the devices carry out this strategy on the field of the page. American authors have discovered that narrative is the most effective form for persuading readers, and they refined their techniques to embed beliefs about agriculture into their storytelling. The child's idea of America and being American became a canvas for agrarian rhetoric.

Current agrarian rhetoric in children's books may be enhanced if we examine how it was used a century ago. Much, but not all of it has worked to encourage rural values and interest in farming. Most of this rhetoric is bound up with writing that had additional aims, the points of intersection clouding over the text like a plague of locusts or an inscrutable weather anomaly. But sometimes the corners are clean, the lines are straight, and we can see clearly how a message grows out of the page. Contemporary writers, illustrators, publishers, and speakers can also persuade young people that agriculture is worthwhile, and thus refine our own understanding and convictions in the process.

Below are some rhetorical themes and techniques that were frequently employed to influence attitudes towards agriculture in American children's books in the nineteenth century. Their purpose was to instill cultural memes that promoted the positive values of food and farming. Authors also wielded them to suggest motives for action and belief: Economy, Profit, and Entrepreneurism; Survivance and Health; Morality & Religion; Youth & Innocence; Industry and Family & Community Values; Sensuality and Pleasure; Personal Refinement; Patriotism; A Sense of Wonder; Environmentalism and Beauty; Adventure; and Humor

EXAMPLES OF NINETEENTH CENTURY BOOKS FOR CHILDREN ABOUT FARMING

The older books in this survey are more often instructive and didactic than later ones, which employ a different array of rhetorical strategies to fit the periods in which they were written. At the time of these early books' publication, particularly in the first half of the nineteenth century, two cultural conditions prevailed that resulted in this bias towards the instructional and the edifying (usually religiously).

In the earliest days of the United States of America, waves of religious revival swept a nation that was predominantly Christian. Chasteness, industry, and modesty were the principal Puritan virtues proclaimed in religious messages, even if they were not always practiced faithfully in everyday life. More importantly, the majority of Americans in the early nineteenth century were farmers. Young people would most likely be destined to become farmers. It was more important to improve their knowledge of agricultural practices and work processes, and to inculcate its philosophical and moral foundations, than to persuade or recruit young people to the work. These were early primers and textbooks for kids with dirt-scraped hands and morning chores. Today we would call them homesteaders. The kind of rhetorical writing seen in these early works, then, is one that seeks to effect an end result (better-trained, God-fearing farmers) more than persuade readers to think or act in a different way.

A third angle of rhetorical approach that we find widely throughout the early history of agrarian children's literature is the celebration of youth and beauty, particularly that of the natural and the pastoral. This theme matches well with the didactic and instructive themes discussed above. A toy book such as *Summer* (discussed below) can wax Arcadian while also offering light treatments of farming subjects—mowing, shearing sheep, and cradling (an archaic word for scything).

———— ❦ ————

Husbandry Moralized; or, Pleasant Sunday Reading for a Farmer's Kitchen, Philadelphia : Printed by B. & J. Johnson, no. 147 High-Street., 1800. In this work, the author prevails on the reader in didactic language with a clear message: religious and agricultural practices are two sides of the same coin, i.e.: Agriculture is a form of religious practice.

> No wise Husbandman will neglect a fit opportunity of gathering his Hay and Corn, upon a presumption of much fair weather to come…And no wise Christian will lose present opportunities of studying his Bible, upon the hopes of more time in the future…"

———— ❦ ————

The Farm-Yard Journal : also, the Histories of the Dog, Cat, Mouse, Marten and Squirrel : ornamented with plates. By John Aikin, New-York : Published by T. B. Jansen, book-seller, 1806 (New York : L. Nichols)

The frisky tone and first-person narrations of this entertaining series of farm stories stands out from the often stiff, admonishing, and cloying kids' books of the period. In the copy held at Beinecke, a girl named Mary Ellcott, who once owned this collection of rural escapades, has sketched birds and practiced her signature in the front pages. What must have been pure amusement for Mary was also a neat vehicle for moral fables. The recipe here is one folly after another, followed by narrow escapes and strokes of good luck, which themselves are the kind of providential outcomes that spring from good children (or animals) who make the right choice at the last minute. A fox steals a rooster, the bull gets loose, the cow kicks over the milk pail, hogs get into the garden. What fun!

The best character may be Grimalkin, the talking cat: "I got one day locked up in the dairy…Having climbed up a shelf to get at a bowl of cream, I unluckily fell backwards into a large vessel of butter-milk, where I probably should have been drowned…"

The Cries of New-York, New-York : Printed and sold by S. Wood, at the Juvenile book-store, No. 362, Pearl-Street, 1808.

The message of this noted little book from 1808 (one version of a frequently-reprinted title) might be summed up by a quotation taken from the middle of its pages: "Industry will produce wonders." The "cries" described in each short chapter catalog the voices a child might hear on the streets of New York. Three quarters of the cries are from vendors selling foods (although the first entry is "Fire! Fire! Fire!"). In fact, a booklet like this served to introduce thousands of young Americans to foods they had never seen or tasted before. The author's moral approach warns against idleness and encourages humility, but the book more effectively appeals to the child

reader's imagination by arousing the sense of wonder and the pleasures that are essential to eating:

On cherries: "The children are quite blithe and merry, / when summer brings the crimson cherry." Sweet potatoes are "brought from South Carolina by water, several hundred miles" while pineapples come from the West-Indies and have a smell that "resembles very much that of the strawberry." Corn is "boiled in the husks while green, and, with the addition of a little salt, which the children carry with them, is very pleasant eating." Milk is a "choice and wholesome liquid…one of the good things with which the Promised Land was said to abound…"

Sometimes the mixture of sermonizing, dietary advice, and descriptions of exotica make funny impressions. One gathers that sugar, not to mention alcohol, were as popular then as now:

"They [oranges, limes and lemons] are much used to make a liquor, by the English called Punch...made of...sugar and the sour juice of the fruit. Punch is a palatable liquor, but very dangerous in its tendency, so that people, by its taste, are tempted to drink too much, which frequently deprives the wise of understanding; lays the strong prostrate; reduces man below the level of the beasts; qualifies for many evils; and is a great sin."

———∞———

The Farm, or a Picture of Industry, Philadelphia : Sold wholesale by P. Price, Jr., 66 Lombard St., [1813?]

Like so many of these early nineteenth-century toy books, *The Farm* celebrates scenes of nature, farm operations, and farmers by using a series of discrete tableaux, with Utopian poetic descriptions:

And see, behind the sloping hill,
The morning clouds grow brighter still,
And all the shades retire;
Slowly the Sun, with golden ray,
Breaks forth above the horizon gray,
And gilds the distant spire.

With ruddy cheeks and cheerful mien,
Haymakers in the field are seen,
At work from morn till night;
A pleasing sight is here display'd,
The Father, son, and youthful maid,
Toiling with all their might.

———∞———

Summer, New York : Printed & sold by Samuel Wood, at the Juvenile Book-store, No. 357, Pearl-Street, 1814.

The subtitle of this book is "Youth—The Summer of Life." It is the companion of another short allegorical work, *Winter*.

Down far in the valley where bubbles the spring,
Which soft through the meadow land glides,
The lads from the mountain the heavy sheep bring,
And shear the warm coat from their sides.

Summer suggests that the right life of hard work and industry are inseparable from the enjoyment of the pastoral. In fact, they are two integral factors in a process of life that God, time, and the seasons preside over:

> When the herds and flocks retire into the cool shade, and the pretty songsters of the grove take shelter from the scorching sun among the branches; the industrious farmer has to ply his business late and early.

Some readers now might find the tone moralizing, though at the time of its printing most readers would have accepted it as a sensible and necessary work ethic, a simple fact of life.

Dame Partlet's Farm: Containing an Account of the Great Riches She Obtained by Industry, the Good Life She Led, and Alas Good Reader! Her Sudden Death; : to which is Added, a Hymn, written by Dame Partlet, just before her Death, and an Epitaph for her Tomb Stone, Philadelphia: Published and for sale by Johnson and Warner, 1810.

The story of Dame Partlet is a good and grave example of how moral virtues, piety, and ruralism ("The Life of Rural Innocence") redeem the kind and industrious farmer. Ms. Parlet tragically expires at the end, released to carry on in the Christian afterlife. It's likely not an ending

She daily in the garden walk'd
   (But always took her dog and book)
And told the gardener to cut
   Some vegetables for the cook.

In rows along the orchard stood
   Her fruitful stalls of bees;
And in the store-room tow'rds the north
   She rang'd her stock of cheese.

that readers of *Mrs. Piggle-Wiggle's Farm* would have liked nearly a century and a half later.

> She every morning rose at five,
> And ne'er forgot her pray'rs;
> But thanked God for her good night's rest
> Before she came down stairs.

⸙

The Arts of Life, Described in a Series of Letters : 1. Providing food. 2. Providing clothing. 3. Providing shelter. : For the instruction of young persons. / By the author of Evenings at home. By John Aikin, Boston : Carter & Hendee, and Waitt & Dow., 1830.

> For although in the state of society in which we live, persons of superior rank are seldom called upon to exercise the common arts of life themselves…how precious to them would be a little knowledge of those arts, which they may perhaps have disdained as beneath their notice! What would a mere scholar, or fine gentleman have done in place of Alexander Selkirk, when left alone in the island of Juan Fernandez?

The reference to the hero Selkirk, a real-life stand-in for Robinson Crusoe, drives home the survivance argument Aikin uses to convince his readers in this homesteading book that might have been popular with back-to-the-landers in the 1970s. Farming here is profound lifework and noble art, but also a bridge into a world of exotic wonders, and a world of stories. Food and the discipline of agriculture bring faraway lands and the world of adventure into focus.

We can see that Aikin was testing out themes of moral behavior and exotic adventure already, with books like *Letters from a father to his son, on various topics, relative to literature and the conduct of life*; and *Geographical delineations; or, A compendious view of the natural and political state of all parts of the globe*. This latter work satisfied a young reader's craving to discover the "natural history" of foreign lands and peoples.

(*opposite*) A walk in the garden with Dame Partlet, 1810.

In *Arts of Life*, thumbnail descriptions of ordinary foods like pota-toes ("they do not answer well without previous boiling") and honey ("the sweet juice of flowers") join more peculiar ones such as bread-fruit, cassava root, palm sago, and cherry-tree gum. A young New Englander in 1830 would likely never encounter subtropical foods beyond sugar and molasses, and certainly wouldn't have reason to know how to grow them. But to read their descriptions is to glimpse the far ends of the world where American commerce had increasing attachments, and where expansion would soon follow. At the same time, readers could here learn through instructive passages the prac-tical arts of tillage, trench making, hedging and ditching, fallowing, manuring, soil fertility management, pasturage, and feed crops. The imagination is lured while the memory is stamped.

Rhetoric adapts to new cultural values and ideas. Authors for young people today struggle to make broad-based claims for farming based on survivance. They avoid the harsh word survival, preferring well-being, standard of living, and quality of life. Arguments in favor of robust citizen agriculture fail on the radically reformed definition of survival alone. In a world where average life expectancy has jumped twenty years forward compared with the nineteenth century and comfort is a widely-accepted middle-class standard, well-being is largely a factor of a person's relationship to the products and services of a commercial economy, not a gamble with mortality based on their relationship with land or other people. Public opinion is changing quickly, as visions of the apocalypse dance around the mounting evidence for global environ-mental failure. The rhetorical theme of survivance has been subsumed by the theme of environmentalism, and rhetoricians are shifting their language accordingly.

Rollo at work; or, The way for a boy to learn to be industrious. By Jacob Abbott, Boston: Weeks, Jordan & Co., 1838.

Father, you were right, after all; I *don't* know how to work any better than Elky. [italics in original]

Here's a story where a well-meaning but naïve child protagonist has a lot to learn. In the *Rollo* series and its broader genre, experienced elders (usually fathers) correct mostly innocent mistakes and venial sins of their sons, and we watch character and behavior develop integrity. Rollo plants his beans twice in a row because the first time they don't grow fast enough. He claims to be tired before beginning to work and has little fits of insubordination. Through many trying incidents, Rollo admits to his frivolity and learns to do things right the first time around. The arc of events lends itself better to storytelling than the brief morality-building episodes of the preceding decades.

As the nineteenth century progressed, we find authors using more sophisticated and illustrative narratives to instill discipline, humility, and similar virtues embraced by Christianity and agrarian society. Americans flocked to cities, and the familiar trope of *moral corruption* in urban society advanced apace (see *Farming for Boys*, below). Authors created richer narratives to promote moral virtues that, if the theory was to be believed, young readers were increasingly tempted to ignore. We see the story itself—its more elaborate characterizations and its serializing of these characters, its embrace of dialogue more familiar to the modern ear—become a nuanced tool of indoctrination.

As Rollo's father says:

> A boy works steadily when he goes directly forward with his work, without stopping to rest, or to contrive new ways of doing it, or to see other people, or to talk. Now, do you think you could work steadily an hour, without stopping for any of these reasons?

The Farm: or, a new and entertaining account of rural scenes and pursuits, with the toils, pleasures, and productions of farming.: For young readers in the town and country. By Jefferys Taylor, Philadelphia : Lippincott, Grambo & Co., 1854.

A certain class of instructional book in the nineteenth century was transparent in its aim to recruit and train young and aspiring farmers.

The Farm was published fewer than ten years before Lincoln signed the first of the Morrill Acts that designated land-grant universities for the education of young farmers. The author addresses his reader directly, lays the foundation of his argument, tempts the reader with a question, and proceeds to answer it.

> I have…two classes of readers in my view—the one belonging to the city; the other to the country. It is my design to benefit both. But, pray, what interest can one born in the city, and who expects there to spend his days, have in farming operations? Let us see.

The ensuing chapters deploy a series of rhetorical themes, including arguments that rest on economic/entrepreneurial, patriotic, and ethical subjects. Economic and patriotic subjects suggest that love of country supports an integrated American economy in which we all depend on the good work of each other:

> Now, you have an interest in your country—have you not? You desire her prosperity? But that prosperity depends greatly upon the fact, whether farmers flourish or not. Suppose you become a *merchant*…if the farmers flourish not, the merchants will not flourish.

It's a short hop in reasoning from here to urge young readers to support farmers based on an ethical obligation:

> You will encourage him by every means in your power, and on a wet day, or a cold morning in January, when he has come some ten or a dozen miles to bring you the rich productions of his land, you will not be so disposed to get a '*good bargain*' at *his expense* [italics in original].

The tactic that holds up best today may be one that rests on personal pleasure, refinement, and consumer agency:

> Besides, with some knowledge of farming you will be better able to urge of the *qualities* of the products which are brought to market… And lastly, I would set forth to my city readers the value of some acquaintance with farming on the score of *pleasure*.

Country Sights for City Eyes. Published by the American Sunday School Union, Philadelphia, [ca. 1860?].

This book and others like it from the period create the sense that the authors have a further goal in mind than recruiting new farmers onto the land, or improving their work. They celebrate farmers as pioneers of a movement. It is a nascent PR campaign stitched with implicit political messaging: temperance, educational and market reform, infrastructure improvements, and free development of western lands (two years later formalized in the Homestead Act). Civic virtue and public engagement are well positioned in these arguments. Seven years after this book was published, the National Grange of the Order of Patrons of Husbandry was founded. The Grange began as a fraternal order and a Union with a dedicated investment in these and other political issues affecting farmers.

Also found here are some familiar rhetorical themes: religious morality, patriotism, and entrepreneurship:

> Whoever causes a blade of grass to grow where there was none before, is a benefactor to his race. Then surely those hardy and enterprising men and women who make their way into the forest, open large tracts of rich land for cultivation, and found villages to be filled with industrious, temperate and enterprising people, are great benefactors…That which makes our country prosperous and happy will soon become the cause of ruin, if a single generation grows up in ignorance and irreligion.

> How pleasantly he [the farmer] must feel, in returning home from market, to reflect that what he has sold there is not to be employed—like tobacco and intoxicating drink—to madden the brain and poison the blood of his fellow-men.

The Farmer Boy, and How he Became Commander-in-Chief / by Uncle Juvinell [Morrison Heady]; edited by William M. Thayer. Boston : Walker, Wise, and Company, 1864.

[Spoiler alert: The farmer boy is George Washington.]

This book's introduction makes explicit what the author is going for: "…he hopes to awaken in your mind a desire to imitate the example and emulate the virtues of this greatest and wisest of Americans."

This is a tale of ultimate social mobility predating the formulaic rags-to-riches stories of Horatio Alger. (Although the Alger books show kids moving to the city, whereas *The Farmer Boy* is about preserving the nobility of country life. Farmer boy eventually returns to become farmer man.) Washington is the king who came from the country. Honest, exacting, bold, and industrious, he climbs to mythic rank. This book really isn't *about* farming at all, but about nostalgia, patriotism, and heroism. Nevertheless, the story's plot structure—the rise from farm boy to great statesman—puts forward some key agri-rhetorical themes. As we have seen in other books, honesty, precision, a strong work ethic, and self-reliance were some of the formula virtues of American farmers. Here, they are defining traits in the lionizing description of Washington's character. *The Farmer Boy* tells us that farming prepares a young person for a life of patriotic service, which is just what America needed in 1863, on both sides of the Mason-Dixon line. Farmer boys reading about the great achievements of farmer boy Washington may have thought about becoming eager soldiers.

Washington at war is the dominant subject of the book. "Farmer" is used here as a nostalgic pivot point—ironically, a pivot into war. The author presents them as wars of freedom, rather than wars waged over territory, natural resources, and arable land. This is a case where the rhetoric becomes truly problematic. It takes a certain deftness to convince frontier readers that farming is merely coincidental with the realities of open hostility and even warfare. In fact, the relationship in American history is one of causality, with the drumbeat of land acquisition preceding inevitable territorial battles. Pioneers pulled Westward expansion from the east, which led to wars with Native Americans, and the Spanish, Mexicans, French, and British.

But in *The Farmer Boy*, we find a different story:

> This grateful duty duly done, he once more sought the shelter of Mount Vernon, to whose comforts he had been for so many months a stranger. The toils of a soldier's life were now exchanged for the peaceful labors of a husbandman. Nor did this change, to his well-ordered mind, bring with it any idle regrets; for the quiet pursuits of farmer's life yielded him, young, ardent and adventurous as he was, scarcely less delight than the profession of arms, and even more as he grew in years.

<hr>

Farming for Boys : What They Have Done, and What Others May Do, in the Cultivation of Farm and Garden : How to Begin, How to Proceed, and What to Aim at / by the author of "Ten acres enough"; with illustrations. by Edmund Morris, Boston : Fields, Osgood & Co., successors to Ticknor and Fields, 1869.

> It is a great mistake to suppose that all who exchange the farm for the city become either good, or great, or even rich… Examples of friendless adventurers from the country to the city, who there rose to fortune, have been largely set before the youthful mind, while no proper notice has been taken of the much more numerous class of

boys who, beginning as rakers in the hay-field, thence rose to the position of successful farmers, and subsequently to that of statesmen or public benefactors.

To persuade his young reader, Morris takes advantage of the popular dichotomy between city and country, posing them side-by-side in direct contrast. Here's a rhetorical theme that has currency today, though the terminology has changed.

> The charm of city life has been unduly magnified, while the greater one of country life has been overlooked. Our boys have thus too generally been taught to think the former preferable to the latter.

The really special feature of *Farming for Boys* is the way that education in agricultural techniques is encoded in the story the way morals are encoded in a fable. That is to say: not subtly. Here is an author cramming instructions into a narrative as thickly as weeds come up in a garden. When a cat dies we learn how it could be used as compost:

220

As directed, Bill took up the grains of corn from the last hill, dug a hole some ten inches deep, in which he placed the animal, then covered it with earth, on which the grains were replaced and again covered, as before.

⁓∞⁓

OBSERVATIONS

Taken together, the children's books examined here approximate a sort of public relations campaign rolled out over the course of a century and directed towards American youth and their parents. Its message: farmers are true Americans, and the heart of America is found in its rural population and their labors. The rhetoric of advancing the American story supported the rhetoric of farming, and vice versa. We peer back from our contemporary moment and see that this collective effort in publication evolved in parallel with the economic and political realities of nation-building in the nineteenth century, mirroring its developments. Thus, religious exhortation was increasingly replaced by the instantiation of secularized moral values and the language of popular democratic movements. But at the center of the implicit argument, couched inside stories that more and more resemble twentieth century children's classics, a familiar character began to emerge: that of the virtuous agrarian citizen.

1   "American farm subsidies are egregiously expensive, harvesting $20 billion a year from taxpayers' pockets" *The Economist*: http://www.economist.com/news/united-states/21643191-crop-prices-fall-farmers-grow-subsidies-instead-milking-taxpayers

HEATHER KLEMANN

Mo Willems & the Poetics of Parenthood

All the kids from day care are in dreamland.
The froggie has made his last leap.
Hell no, you can't go to the bathroom.
You know where you can go? The fuck to sleep.[1]
— Adam Mansbach and Ricardo Cortés,
   Go the Fuck to Sleep (2011)

Children's picture book parodies intended for adult audiences such as Adam Mansbach and Ricardo Cortés's viral bestseller *Go the Fuck to Sleep* and Lisa Brown's *Baby, Mix Me a Drink* (2005)[2] develop a shared pathos of parental frustration. Each page of the former work, for example, offers the cathartic refrain of anger and exhaustion that parents may think but never say during the bedtime routine: "Go the fuck to sleep." The popularity of these works indicates the precision with which they strike a collective cultural nerve, one frizzled by a lack of outlets for anxiety and exasperation, and propose coping mechanisms, if only in jest, through profanity and alcoholism. To suggest that Mo Willems's picture books, too, provide an unexpected form of support for parent audiences is the purpose of this essay.

Pressure on parents stems in no small part from the Darwinian idea that "controlling and ordering" the development of the child is a critical means of establishing order in society at large.[3] The postwar era of permissive parenting exemplified in the work of Dr. Benjamin Spock moved toward a more child-centered approach in which "the

(*opposite*) *I am Going*, Mo Willems, 2010.

223

natural development of the child and the fulfillment of the child's desires are ends in themselves."[4] Instead of the adult training children to align their routines and behaviors with adult needs, in this Copernican shift in parenting, the child, whose needs are interpreted increasingly through experts such as Freud and Piaget, now trains the parent.[5] More recent expansion in the role of experts across a range of fields and institutions—developmental psychologists, policymakers, pediatricians, global and single-issue advocacy organizations (for example, La Leche League International)—has affirmed the widely held conviction that effective parenting does not merely suggest, but rather requires, raising children in accordance with expert advice.[6] This is a radical change, as sociologist Frank Furedi notes, in that it moves away from the belief that "there were limits to what parent could do" but "that with sound advice most problems could be solved" toward an assumption "not only that parents haven't a clue but also that they are unlikely to be able to cope on their own." Most contemporary child-rearing advice, Furedi states quite simply, "inform[s] parents that they can't cope alone."[7]

Alongside these developments in the sociology of parenting, the trials of parenthood have become a popular subject of modern picture books, and not only in the form of parodies for adults. Daniel Zalewski of *The New Yorker* asserts that contemporary picture books reflect a twenty-first century child-centered, "confrontation-averse" shift in parenting, one that diminishes disciplinary roles of parents through softened language and enfeebled punishments. Mothers and fathers illustrated in the pages of such picture books dramatize the experience of their parent reading audiences, who "harried and befuddled, [scurry] to fulfill a child's wishes and then hesitantly [draw] the line."[8] The presentation of parental challenges in the safe space of a children's book may provide a "palliative for guilty parents"; such works occasionally include small asides or wisecracks that buoy parents by acknowledging the shared struggle to keep calm as they carry on.[9]

If Zalewski is right that the "newspaper-burrowing fathers" of the twentieth-century picture books have been replaced by "eager, if bumbling diaper-changers,"[10] Trixie's father in Mo Willems's *Knuffle Bunny: A Cautionary Tale* (2004) may present the chary, blundering dad *par excellence*. Notably, this Caldecott Honor book does not begin as many classic picture books for child audiences do, by establishing the absence or departure of parents from the scene of action.[11] Rather, Trixie's father plays a supporting role to her throughout the tale, both inadvertently causing and perseveringly correcting the oversight that creates the central conflict in the plot: the disappearance of Trixie's beloved transitional object, a stuffed rabbit, during their trip to their neighborhood Laundromat. Willems plays out what Zalewski calls "variations on the theme of parental subjection" as Trixie in the company of her father devolves into curbside tantrum, going boneless and attracting the pointed glances of passersby. Trixie's father endures not only exasperating toddler behavior, but also the superbity in Trixie's and his wife's looks at the moment when they mutually identify, alongside Trixie's father, the evident cause of Trixie's outburst. Willems counterbalances subjection with heroism as the father recovers Knuffle Bunny at the conclusion of the work, an act that is duly and poetically rewarded with Trixie uttering her first words: "Knuffle Bunny."

Beginning with the book cover on which the subtitle, "A Cautionary Tale," advertises the didactic function of the work, *Knuffle Bunny* throws the purposiveness not only of parental authority but also of genre into question. Cautionary tales as a subgenre of children's literature typically foreground the child as the target audience for discipline and instruction while interpolating warnings for grown-ups as well. At first glance, however, the classification of *Knuffle Bunny* as a cautionary tale appears ambiguous. If the young reader identifies primarily with Trixie, the principal owner of and imaginary caregiver to Knuffle Bunny, he or she learns from Trixie's negative example to bear responsibility for the loss of a beloved toy: in her Knuffle Bunny's absence, Trixie suffers accordingly for her neglectful behavior. Yet Trixie's protests and her mother's castigating look, which are both directed at Trixie's father when the bunny is determined to have gone missing, suggest that her father is the one even more answerable for Knuffle Bunny's loss. The force of the message to children to "take care of your property" is sapped by the helicopter-parent presumption that parents are obligated not only to do all in their power to ensure the safety and happiness of their children, but also to protect and preserve their children's favorite things. The message, then, might be a satirical charge, poking fun at hyper-vigilant parent culture: "Keep track of your child's property, or else." Indeed, Trixie's father also suffers—unknowing of the cause at first—for the loss of the toy and is perhaps more completely and triumphantly rewarded than his daughter is upon the restoration of Knuffle Bunny.

As Trixie engages the reader's sympathy with her childlike reaction to loss, Trixie's father provides parodic reassurance to parent readers, reflecting and exaggerating "conflict-averse" parent culture. The picture book's failure of genre—as the alleged cautionary tale reveals itself as parody—provides an objective correlative to the parental collapse of authority in the text as the confident, authoritative father becomes a hapless, bumbling child-handler. Moreover, for the parents outside of the text who share *Knuffle Bunny* with preliterate and early literacy audiences, Trixie's father's ineptitude becomes their own: despite their pretensions to self-assured child rearing, when the work miscarries as a decisively cautionary tale, well-intentioned parents find themselves without a didactic tool that positively extends their control. Instead, they are left with the salutary humor of parental deficiency and the comforting reminder—encapsulated in Trixie's triumphant exclama-tion—that children develop, one milestone at a time, in spite of, or even thanks to, parental shortcomings. In ways that are hardly subtle or hidden, *Knuffle Bunny* is for the understanding, enjoyment, and edi-fication of parents. And Willems's motives for addressing parents have in part a biographical explanation: in describing the 2010 project to adapt *Knuffle Bunny* into a musical theater show, he adds, "it became a personal touchstone for the sort of parent I hope to be—determined even if I'm befuddled, concerned even if I'm exasperated, helpful even if I'm hopeless."[12]

Children's books, of course, have always been at least in part for parents. Since the emergence of the earliest print publications for children in the late seventeenth and early eighteenth centuries, adults have been a target audience whether explicitly stated or not. The savviest of early publishers for children, Thomas Boreman and John Newbery, understood well that "children do not buy books, adults do" and in this period of unprecedented class transition and educational opportunity books became a consumable good that reassured parents and provided them with the confidence that they, too, could teach children to read in the home.[13] Many of these early works have prefaces outlining the importance to parents of the content that follows, offering tips for how to use the work. Some works even refer to parents or parent-child relationships in their titles. For example, nursery innovator Lady Ellenor Fenn designs *The Mother's Remarks on a Set of Cuts for Children* (1799), and the celebrated Romantic-era novelist and author of tales for children Maria Edgeworth unambiguously titles her works *The Parent's Assistant* (1796), asserting the value and practicality of her writing for parent audiences. In keeping with this long tradition, Willems has published works, such as *Time to Say "Please!"* (2005) and *Time to Pee!* (2003), that tout their usefulness to parents and other adults in raising children.

Yet Willems's work seems more in tune with the twenty-first century need for adults to "cope" with parental responsibilities and pressures. Each vignette in *Time to Say Please!*, for example, dramatizes a scene in which the child's utterance of "please," "excuse me," or "sorry" is prescribed by the illustrated situation such as a girl looking longingly at a cookie or a boy wanting to try a rollercoaster for the first time. In these scenes, the parental role of educator and enforcer has been divided up: Willems's parent figures here serve to permit or forbid the child's

"And Sorry is useful,"
Time to Say "Please"!,
Mo Willems, 2005.

wished-for outcome, and at the same time Willems channels parental id through a peppy chorus of mice that goad and cheer the child towards the wished-for behavior while holding up the word bubbles of the text. The busy, unsteady mice not only embody the kind of eagerness and bumbling that Zalewski ascribes to modern-day parenting, but they also redirect attention away from the straightforwardness of the work's plainspoken guidance in courtesy, such as: "There are all kinds of reasons to say 'Please.' When you want a turn. When you want a toy, or to borrow someone's truck," and "'Please' isn't hard to say. Just go try it!"[14] As preliterate children hear the unequivocally instructional message of the text read aloud, before them appear anywhere from one to four dozen mice holding signs, parachuting, bathing, snorkeling, swinging, flying, or sipping tea. Much like Keith Baker's *LMNO Peas* (2010), in which Baker enlivens the alphabet through an infestation of anthropomorphized and professionalized peas, the joy and whimsy of Willems's work plays out in the details and activities of the minutest figures. The mice invite readers to linger and explore the page visually, providing much of the entertainment in the Horation balance of entertainment with instruction. Moreover, the mice and the peas underscore the larger social motives behind the alphabetic or courtesy instruction. Each capering pea or mouse may have his or her own antics, but they are all loosely gathered on the page as part of a larger group, reinforcing the role of alphabetization and manners in establishing community membership.

The tension that connects various vignettes of *Time to Say Please!* has as much to do with whether or not the child will use the proper form of supplication as it does with whether or not the parent will give in to the request being made. Parents offer some of the most expressive looks in the work, and their faces most often avow uncertainty. For example, the slightly submissive, bowed posture; upward-raised eyebrows; and down-turned lip of the bespectacled father as his eager son leads (or drags) him toward a formidable rollercoaster that the child desires to ride indicates the need for especially congenial supplicating terms in order for the father to acquiesce. In the editor's mark-up of the work, Willems debates his editor over the size of the roller coaster with Willems asserting that the amusement ride needs to be big and intimidating, perhaps even to the adult. The emotional dynamics of the page establish discord between the enthusiasm of the child and the hesitation of the parent. Willems treats the perspective of the parent and the child with equal seriousness in this illustration, suggesting that uttering "please"

"B" and "C",
LMNO Peas,
by Keith Baker, 2010.

involves stakes for both parties: here, "please" becomes the negotiating tool in a parental decision between a protectionist stance that the rollercoaster is too scary for the young child and an interest in rewarding and reinforcing the socially acceptable behavior of the polite request. Willems reveals the word "please" as an emollient for the difficult parental decisions, one that eases adult reasoning through conflicting

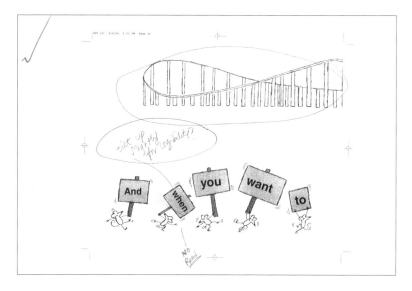

advice, for example, that rides are unsafe for children of a certain size or that permitting cookie consumption can establish bad eating habits and promote obesity.

In *Time to Say Please!*, Willems sustains a negotiation between parental control and child agency, staging it both on the page and through the live performance of an adult reading the book to a child. The hesitation of the parent figures in the picture book extends to the parents beyond the printed page as Willems *scripts*—to borrow Robin Bernstein's term—reading performance.[15] Willems utilizes capitalization, punctuation, and shifts in font size and orientation to indicate where pauses and emphasis should go in the work as it is read aloud. The layout of the text in word bubbles and the scattered or cluttered organization of the bubbles on the page, forces the reader to stumble over the utterance by preventing the reader's eyes from scanning automatically and steadily from left to right. Instead, readers must search locally for the next word in the grammatical sentence, which has the effect not only of slowing the pace of reading aloud, but also of inducing jerky, hesitant expression. What one understands

about parenthood through the text, then, is in part a product of what Stanley Fish calls "affective stylistics," which treats the texts "no longer as an object, a thing-in-itself, but as an *event*, something that happens to, and with the participation of the reader."[16] The stilted, scripted expression debilitates the firm, authoritative tone of the narrator's voice as it is ventriloquized by the parent reading to the child. For example, the sentence "When you want to try" appears with each word on its own sign held in place by a mouse. To the editor's comments to turn a tilted sign "slightly for legibility" in the Beinecke collection's page proofs of the text, Willems replies, "No Read." Willems's purposeful arrangement of the printed text not only slows down the delivery of the reading performance so that each word may be taken carefully into consideration, but by addling parent utterance it also levels a little the disciplinary relationship between parent and child, making "pleases" and "thank yous" more accessible coinages of a shared community rather than just the verbal mechanisms of parental control. Willems agrees to turn more upright a sharply titled "a" on a different page only when the editor suggests that doing so would make it easier for a child

Two versions of a proof page for *Time to Say "Please"!*, Mo Willems, 2005.

"Yore show spa shell."

"End pert tea."

to read or when the small size of the word on the page runs the risk of it being skipped over.[17] For Willems, it is not merely the content of the work or the codex form in which that content appears, but the nature of the live performance through which we read his works that gives them meaning. As Willems explains, "What I love about books is they're dependent on us. They need us to turn the pages. They can't turn the pages for themselves."[18]

Through an emphasis on the performance of reading Willems makes adult readers vulnerable to the contingencies of live and embodied performance. Willems's boldest experiment with the performance of reading may be his sketchbook for adult readers, *Beligerent* [sic] *Bunny in "Olive Hue Show Mutts": An Intoxicatingly Hard Reader* (2011), in which an inebriated bunny implores the reader for a kiss through a series of nearly illegible slurs; for example, the title "I Love You So Much" is printed as "Olive Hue Show Mutts," and instead of "how about a kiss?" the bunny asks "Flower bout hay kitch?" On the inside back cover of the work Willems notes that the sketchbook is "an attempt at recreating for adults the decoding process that children must go through when they

"Flower bout hay kitch?"

"Jest hay griddle kitch..."

first learn to read."[19] Although the adult subject of the work suggests that Willems does not intend for this work to be read to children or alongside children, it does indicate the attention that he pays to how children encounter picture books. As Philip Nel explains of the work, "For the literate adult, being forced to sound out each word is a rare and disruptive experience that makes us conscious of the tenuous link between spelling and sound."[20]

As with the tilted letters of *Time to Say "Please"!*, the quasi-phonetic spelling of *"Olive Hue Show Mutts"* seeks not only to defamiliarize reading acts that adult take for granted, but also to revise and recast relationships between adults and children. The kind of experience of learning to read that Willems seeks to create in *"Olive Hue Show Mutts"* has compassionate ends, as he explains in an endnote:

> I think we often forget how hard and slow-going learning to read can be when you're at its cusp, and I wondered what it would be like to go back to that point. The result is this "hard reader," a drunken diatribe of words that merely sound like what they mean. This story almost requires that you read it aloud, much like

Beligerent Bunny in Olive Hue Show Mutts: An Intoxicatingly Hard Reader, Mo Willems, 2011.

children must do when reading their first books independently. I hope you find it funny and that it gives you empathy for all those young readers out there.[21]

The parental act of reading Willems works towards is not one of control over the child, but rather one of understanding for the child, as he explains: "There is no such thing as a good childhood…There is no other time in one's life, after all, when one must ask permission to use the bathroom and when that permission can be denied."[22] Likewise, in another interview he explains of childhood, "The furniture isn't made to your size. If you are having a hard day, they can pick you up and move you to another room….It's just one indignity after another."[23] In such moments Willems establishes his authorial persona as a benevolent friend to children, much like picture-book icons John Newbery and Dr. Seuss have done before him. On one hand, such a persona helps to grow his brand, and indeed the Beinecke collection of Willems's works and various "Mo-iana" illustrates the breadth of his publications globally and the commercial success of his franchise. The Beinecke Library holds not only first editions, sketches, and page proofs, but also stuffed dolls, plastic toys, and Harper Collins press kits that indicate the new markets and revenue streams into which his most popular pigeon, pig, and elephant characters can tap. On the other hand, such comments are an extension of Willems's ethos-ridden mantra — "Always think of your audience, but never think for your audience"—that makes his works so appealing because they talk to and not down to audience members who vary in age, moral understanding, and literacy. Willems's reviewers, too, note his "Pixar-esque knack for speaking to parents and children at the same time, without over- or under-estimating either."[24]

Although Willems claims that he does not see his child and adult readers as two different audiences,[25] the empathy with children that Willems seeks to cultivate in his works offers a unique benefit for modern-day parents, who, as Furedi notes, are "coping" with their social and biological roles. Some of Willems's most empathetic works include those in his Gerald and Piggie series, which, though devoid of explicitly parent or child characters, often narrate moments of crisis only to reassuringly and humorously reveal and re-inscribe them as mis-understandings or lower-stakes issues in ways with which both young and old constituencies may identify. *I Am Going!* (2010), for example, dramatizes Gerald's anticipation of Piggie's positive assertion that she is leaving, with the implication that she will never come back. By the end of the book, however, the reader discovers that Piggie goes merely to lunch, Gerald has grossly overreacted to her simple statement of "I am going!" and Piggie has spent much of the book failing to recognize (or choosing to overlook) Gerald's mistake. Readers readily apprehend Gerald's separation anxiety as he allegorizes the confusion of a child coming to terms with the rules and happenings of day-to-day life in which preschoolers are separated from parents and caregivers and adults depart unexpectedly and in ways that are beyond the child's control. Gerald's overreaction, too, may be uncomfortably familiar to parents who practice irrationally calling to mind the worst possible outcome of any situation for their young child in order to prevent it. Indeed, mod-ern day parenting requires adults to grapple with and recover from their own fearful imaginations and tendencies toward overprotectiveness; by raising an incident to an extreme of crisis only to joke that the situation[26] was misunderstood or never really existed at all may help adults, too, to identify and reframe unreasonable parental panic. Furthermore, as psychologists know, empathy works two ways: providing emotional support to others not only aids the person with whom one empathizes, but it also develops the self-regulatory processes in the one who empa-thizes, making it easier to cope with his or her own situation.[26] If parents empathize with children as Willems hopes they will, then the bene-fit may be as much for mothers and fathers wrestling with the high demands of parenthood today as it is for the youthful recipients of parental empathy.

1   Adam Mansbach and Ricardo Cortés, *Go the Fuck to Sleep* (Brooklyn, NY: Akashic Books, 2011), n. pag.

2   Thank you to Beinecke Curator Timothy Young for directing me to this reference.

3   Ellie Lee, "Experts and Parenting Culture," *Parenting Culture Studies* (Basingstoke, UK: Palgrave Macmillan, 2014), 57.

4   Sharon Hays, *The Cultural Contradictions of Motherhood* (New Haven: Yale University Press, 1996), 45.

5   Hays, *Cultural Contradictions*, 45.

6   Lee, "Experts and Parenting Culture," 67, 68.

7   Frank Furedi, *Paranoid Parenting: Why Ignoring the Experts May Be Best for Your Child*, 2nd ed. (London: Continuum, 2008), 177.

8   Daniel Zalewski, "The Defiant Ones: In Today's Picture Books, the Kids Are in Charge," *The New Yorker*, October 19, 2009, http://www.newyorker.com/maga zine/2009/10/19/the-defiant-ones.

9   Zalewski, "The Defiant Ones."

10 Zalewski, "The Defiant Ones."

11 See, for example, Maurice Sendak's *Where the Wild Things Are* (1963), Don Freeman's *Corduroy* (1968), Ezra Jack Keats's *The Snowy Day* (1962), Dr. Seuss's *The Cat in the Hat* (1957), and Crockett Johnson's *Harold and the Purple Crayon* (1955).

12 Mo Willems, "Notes from the Playwright," Kennedy Center Theater for Young Audiences on Tour 2010–2011 Season, brochure

13 J.H. Plumb, "The New World of Children in Eighteenth-Century England," *Past & Present* 67 (1975): 66–67.

14 Mo Willems, *Time to Say "Please"!* (New York: Hyperion Books, 2005), n. pag.

15 Robin Bernstein defines to "script" as involving "a set of invitations or prompts" relating to a certain set of behaviors that is open to "resistance and revision"; see "Dances with Things: Material Culture and the Performance of Race," *Social Text 101* 27.4 (2009), 68, and "Children's Books, Dolls, and the Performance of Race; or, The Possibility of Children's Literature," PMLA 126.1 (2011), 165.

16 See Stanley Fish, "Literature in the Reader: Affective Stylistics," *New Literary History* 2.1 (1970), 125.

17 Mo Willems, *Time to Say "Please"!*, original manuscript with editorial comments, Beinecke Library, GEN MS 1003, Box 2

18 Lindsay Deutsch, "Trailer and Q & A: *That Is Not a Good Idea!* by Mo Willems," *USA Today*, March 7, 2013, http://www.usatoday.com/story/life/books/2013/03/07/mo-willems-trailer-reveal-not-a-good-idea/1965173/.

19 Mo Willems, *"Beligerent Bunny in "Olive Hue Show Mutts": An Intoxicatingly Hard Reader,"* sketchbook (2011).

20 Philip Nel, "Surrealism for Children: Paradoxes and Possibilities," *Children's Literature and the Avant-Garde*, ed. Elina Druker and Bettina Kümmerling-Meibauer (Amsterdam: John Benjamins, 2015), 274.

21 Willems, *"Olive Hue Show Mutts."*

22 Monica Hesse, "Mo Willems Is the Go-To Author for Children—And Their Parents," *The Washington Post*, January 6, 2012, https://www.washingtonpost.com/lifestyle/style/mo-willems-is-the-go-to-author-for-children--and-their-parents/2012/01/06/gIQAFLztfP_story.html.

23 Patti Hartigan, "Mo Willems Aims to Inspire Kids to Write Their Stories," *Boston Globe*, June 15, 2015, https://www.bostonglobe.com/arts/books/2015/06/14/mowillems/WfFwJPU2ruPT7nozMPLtKK/story.html.

24 Pamela Paul, "You're a Big Girl Now," *The New York Times*, December 17, 2010, http://nyti.ms/1F1Luxi.

25 Mo Willems, interview by Ophira Eisenberg, February 12, 2015, "Ask Me Another," NPR, http://www.npr.org/templates/transcript/transcript.php?storyId=385546965.

26 Peter Salovey and John D. Mayer, "Emotional Intelligence," *Imagination, Cognition and Personality* 9, no. 3 (1990), 194.

BRIAN ALDERSON

Across the Wide Atlantic
The Reciprocal Nature of Children's Book Publishing between Great Britain and the United States, A Discursive Essay

[*It was Justin Schiller who, inevitably, introduced me to Betsy Shirley round about 1989. At that time I was working on an essay about the serial publication of Kipling's* Just So Stories *and she invited me down to Bernardsville to talk about it and to look at her collection. She had there, of course, the Christmas number of St Nicholas for 1897, with its banner headline "Rudyard Kipling's First 'Just So Story'", and alongside it was a duplicate copy which, with typical generosity, she presented to me. (It is beside me as I write, along with several sheets of shocking pink paper, bearing the legend "This note comes from a beautiful, rich, famous, thin, chic person" which she gave me to write memoranda on.)*]

Rudyard Kipling and *Just So Stories* are in themselves a good subject with which to beg these brief reflections. Leaving aside the post facto presence of the Beinecke Library's tremendous Kipling collection, home base for David Alan Richards's equally tremendous bibliography of the author, those stories are symbolic of the complexities of the bridge built across the ocean for the two-way traffic in the making of children's books. Kipling, a British author married to an American, is beginning to write a sequence of stories while living in Vermont—eleven tales when the first book edition comes out will have been previously published in American magazines and illustrated by the American artists Oliver

(*opposite*) This is the cat..., detail from *The House that Jack Built*, 1833.

Herford and Frank Ver Beck. However, the first collected edition will be (memorably) illustrated by the author himself and published in London in 1902 with the New York printing done in the same year from the English copy-text. Significantly though, in the context of differences in commercial promotion, the pictures with their essential authorial commentary may have been found too severe for American eyes and ten years later Doubleday found it necessary to augment them with pointless color plates by Joseph Gleeson.

As is well known, such to-ing and fro-ing of texts across the wide Atlantic is a foundational feature of children's book publishing in America. A sixteen-page catechism can be accounted one of the earliest texts for children printed there and exhibits a very tangled relationship. Its author was the minister John Cotton, a former rector of Boston, England, who had emigrated to Boston, Massachusetts, in 1633 (the conjunction of that date with the renaming of the town from Trimountaine to Boston in 1635 may owe something to his arrival there). The book was first published in London in 1646 under the title of *Milk for Babes, Drawn from the Breasts of Both Testaments. Chiefly for the Spirituall Nourishment of Boston Babes in either England*, but when it finally appeared from the Massachusetts press eleven years later it was S*piritual Milk for Boston Babes . . . for their Soul's Nourishment*. Given the temper of Puritan New England it would have more market appeal there than in Cotton's homeland. Further, it would also find itself incorporated into one of the most celebrated of all early American children's books: *The New-England Primer.*

The Primer too is of old English origins, first being announced in the register of the Stationers' Company in London in 1683 and including *Milk for Babes* as an alternative title. From this it would seem to be intended for export (and indeed, down to the nineteenth century copies were printed in England and Scotland both for home consumption[1] and for filling orders from booksellers across the water) but its immediate history is murky. It emerges from the powerful evangelical movement in England at this time that had many equivalences to

what was happening in New England and hence made the children's books that were generated in the East very acceptable to customers in the West. In the case of the London bookseller and writer Benjamin Harris, who had published his vehemently anti-Papist *The Protestant Tutor* in 1679, serious legal wrangles led him to follow his book to Boston in 1686 where it had been published the year before. His book-trade experience in London and his native energy drew him into several editorial ventures in Massachusetts (not least the introduction of news-sheet publishing) and in 1690 he is found advertising in an almanac that "There is now in the Press, and will be suddenly extant, a second edition of *The New-England Primer enlarged* . . . ," an event which, if true, further marks early Anglo-Colonial collaboration. (He returned to London in

The martyr John Rogers being burned at the stake, from *The New-England Primer*, Boston, 1767.

1694/5 where, soon after, he wrote and published *The Holy Bible in Verse* "for those of weaker memories [including children]," a tiny volume printed in Boston by John Allen in 1717. (It must have appeared in an earlier edition though because it carries a "caution" to readers signed by Benjamin Harris's son John about a spurious edition dated 1712).

A thrilling copy of this exemplum of the transatlantic relationship formerly belonged to two great authorities on American children's books, Wilbur Macey Stone and Justin Schiller, and now resides at Yale in the Betsy Beinecke Shirley Collection. It is supported there by at least twenty-one editions of the *New-England Primer* dating from 1734 to 1813 (one with the charming imprint: "Massachusetts. Printed for the Purchaser") and more than twenty variants hailing from other parts of the nation. Those show America accepting its own, but two editions are also present of another primer, the *Royal Primer*, both printed at Worcester, but originating in London from John Newbery's shop round about 1750. Of his edition, which must ultimately have been printed over a period of more than thirty years in tens of thousands of copies, fewer than a dozen have survived, a quantity probably outdone by the editions still found in the Colonies.

The British supply of earnest and Calvinistic children's books to the publishers of New England included other predictable titles. John Bunyan's *Book for Boys and Girls* (London, 1686) under its later title of *Divine Emblems*, put in only a late appearance (Welch[2] lists only three editions, one of which is in Shirley) but James Janeway's mournful accounts of early death in his *Token for Children* (1671) would have found favor with the God-focused communities under any circumstances, but was augmented for the locals with an additional section for the children of New England. It was vastly more popular in America than in Britain (Welch lists no fewer than thirty-five editions before 1821 and there must have been more thereafter), while Isaac Watts's *Divine Songs attempted in Easy Language for the use of Children* (originally London, 1715) ran to over a hundred printings in the same period, varying its English title from publisher to publisher.

An explanation for such popularity does not lie only in the mind-set of the parents, teachers, and ministers who were doubtless prominent among those "Massachusetts purchasers," but also in the outstanding difference in the requirements of the American market. The British Isles were no great size, and their long history of book publishing was centered on the single active hive of London with its multiplicity of cultures interacting with each other in an embedded literary tradition and under the control of the Stationers' Company. Whatever was produced could also be advertised and transported over a comparatively simple system of communication. In America, even at this early stage in its development, the book trade was necessarily fragmented both by the huge and growing geographical field of activity and the diverse government of individual states. Thus, although business was attracted to the commercial centers of Boston, Philadelphia, New York, and Baltimore (and, thanks to Isaiah Thomas, not least for his children's books: Worcester, Massachusetts), printers in many small towns were drawn to the reprinting (in whatever fashion their equipment permitted) of works—especially for children—of popular appeal.

The lack of a single center for the generating and dissemination of new ideas, together with limiting cultural inhibitions, were probably root causes in the dearth of a secular literature for the children of New England. It is difficult to believe that in both homes and schools there was not some measure of non-catechistical entertainment which would include the telling of jokes, riddles, household stories, and nursery rhymes, but for the provision of such fare in print purchasers were again dependent on works sourced from the other side of the sea. What's more, they had to wait for a few decades before Tom Thumb and Mother Goose and their comrades put in an appearance. In Britain, the French tales by Mme. D'Aulnoy were first translated at the start of the eighteenth century, often appearing later as the tales of Mother Bunch; the altogether more genuine and attractive effusions of Ma mère l'Oye, though, arriving in Paris in 1697 under the editorship of Charles Perrault, took nearly thirty years to draw up alongside her in Britain—in the translation by Robert Samber in 1729 as *Histories; or Tales of Passed Times by Mother Goose*. But in the United States (as it had become) the former seems never to have appeared in full at all while the latter—the foundation work in imaginative children's literature—did not arrive complete until 1794 in Haverhill, Massachusetts. A year later, in New York, a more distinguished bilingual edition came from Rivington's, garnished with nine plates by Alexander Anderson, and that, with its illustrations, was published in London a year later—perhaps the first contribution to flow from west to east. Betsy Shirley had both those books but the first, alas, without its plates, and the second with one plate and one of the tales missing.

Some individual stories from Perrault's collection and other, anonymous, sources look to have come out much earlier in chapbook form from American printers following copy from (primarily?) London's center for such popular, and often scurrilous, fare: Aldermary Church-Yard. The English chapbook, *The Most Delightful History of the King and the Cobler* is listed by Welch as being printed in Boston by Thomas and John Fleet, circa 1770, while Dr. Rosenbach lists a *Friar and Boy* from A. Barclay in the same place dated 1767.[3] Although excluded by Welch, presumably because of its farting episodes (the most enjoyable bit for children), it carried an advertisement which listed not only "Goose's Tales" (it doesn't say which) but also a not-further-defined History of Mother Bunch, along with such Aldermary treasures as *Arabian Tales*, *Jack and the Giants*, *Jack Horner*, and *Tom Thumb*. (The Rosenbach Library also has a broadside version circa 1770 of the sixteenth century cautionary ballad *The Children in the Woods* which may well be the first in a long line of American re-fashionings of *The Babes in the Wood*.)

It was around the latter part of the eighteenth century that John Newbery too enters the consciousness of American publishers. *The Royal Primer* was published in Boston in 1768 (an earlier Philadelphia edition had been much altered) and although Welch excludes it from his survey on the grounds that it was an educational work, its arrival stands close to what looks like a concerted import of Newbery titles by

The careful *Mother* Inftructing her Children.

Hugh Gaine in New York. His selection of titles ("London printed, New York re-printed") has to be tallied through advertisements—for they are very rare (Betsy Shirley had only a mutilated copy of *The Fairing*, dated 1778)—but these titles mark a venture which would be later repeated with much greater vigor by Isaiah Thomas at his Worcester premises.

Despite his fame as some kind of founding father of American children's book publishing, Thomas's involvement with them was only a part of his protean activities. He had first met with a juvenile title (originating from Britain) during his prentice years at Boston when he printed a *Tom Thumb's Play-Book* for Barclay in 1764 and did some unskilled woodcuts, not least for his own edition of *The Prodigal Daughter* in 1771 (illustrated as no.70 in Rosenbach's *Early American Children's Books*). It was only some time after his move to Worcester in 1779 that he latched on to some London successes published by the two Newbery firms and by John Marshall. He ordered a bundle of copies and set about reprinting them *en bloc* over 1786–1787. Here was a more thorough-going American exploitation of the books that were establishing a lively

The Prodigal Daughter, 1787.

The Prodigal Daughter,
1787.

and variegated tradition in Britain. What have come to be regarded as classic titles such as Watts's *Divine Songs*, *A Little Pretty Pocket-Book* (probably edited by John Newbery), *The History of Little Goody Two-Shoes* (probably by Giles Jones) and the enduring nursery-rhyme collections of *Mother Goose's Melody* and *Tommy Thumb's Song-Book* must have made a dramatic impact, not just in themselves as bringing a new look to children's books but also in their concerted appearance over so short a period.

Thomas edited these titles in a fairly casual way for his American market, but their importance lay in their display of the commercial possibilities of using the rapidly developing London scene as an instant source of novelty. With the coming of the new century and the explosion of new comic and pictorial and literary ideas among London publishers such as John Harris, the Dartons, Benjamin Tabart, William Godwin, and a transformed John Marshall, their American confrères may have felt like fishermen when the trout were rising. The impetus is most noticeable in a shift of activity from Massachusetts to Philadelphia where Jacob and Benjamin Johnson in Market Street are found building on an initial interest in Newbery titles towards what looks like a sustained exploitation (if not collaboration) with work from William Darton senior in London's Gracechurch Street. The many books drawn from his lists (Rosenbach lists some thirty-eight items from Jacob Johnson alone) tended towards the moral and the educational, while John Adams's briefer career saw a liking for the new jokiness—merely endorsing the attractions of Perrault with the title of *Bluebeard* changed to *A New History of Blue Beard*, written by Gaffer Black Beard, *for the Amusement of Little Lack Beard and his Pretty Sisters* (first use in a Hartford edition from Babcock in 1800), or introducing the famous apple-pie with the rhyme:

> *The letters on a time agreed,*
> *Upon an* Apple-Pye *to feed.*
> *They all agree to stand in Order*
> *Around the* Apple-Pye's *fine Border.*
> *Take turns as they in* Horn-Book *stand*
> *From Great A down to* &.

Whether these are local embellishments or owe their presence to some British original is not known, but they are symptomatic of a publisher siding with the likings of his audience, an attitude found *par excellence* in the brief publishing life of William Charles on Chesnut Street.

Charles was an immigrant from Scotland, where he had trained as an engraver, and his earliest appearance was in some New York imprints where he seems to have founded, or had connections with, a certain Porcupine Office. There he produced copies of the newly developed English engraved picture books, a skill which he carried to Philadelphia where in his short life (he died in 1820) he published many examples—the plates for which were subsequently used by his widow, Mary, and by collaborators William Morgan and a Mr.[?] Yeager. Thus, those two pet-lovers portrayed in John Harris's *Comic Adventures of Old Mother Hubbard* (1805) and William Darton's *Dame Trot and her Comical Cat* (1804/5?) came out in America barely a year later (the first had a Porcupine printing advertised as "25% cheaper" than the London one.) Harris's similarly successful *The Butterfly's Ball* (1807) by William Roscoe came out allied to its successor, *Mrs Dorset's Peacock at Home* (1808) with similar speed, and the take-up was such that hardly a page-opening in Welch does not have one or more entries for books originating in England. An alternative endorsement of the prevalence of London texts may be seen in the publishing activity of a single publishing house: John Babcock in his premises first at Hartford up to 1804 and then, as Sidney's Press alongside Increase Cooke at Church Street, New-Haven (about one minute's walk from where the Beinecke Library now stands), and later with his sons William and Sidney at Charlestown, South Carolina. An immensely detailed bibliographic study of the Babcock businesses by Jane Ellen Carstens shows them publishing and regularly reprinting both nursery and chapbook titles from London and also reprints of children's books from British authors.[4]

Two salient questions arise from this view of the dominance of British examples in the publishing of children's books in eighteenth- and early nineteenth-century America, the first concerns the form that the home-grown tradition was taking. The dominance of religious and educational works for local consumption, though inhibiting, is unarguable, although one title may be accounted as the first wholly American bestseller for children. This was *The History of the Holy Jesus*, assumed from an advertisement to have been first published in Boston in 1745, although known only from its second edition of 1746.[5] From

Herod flaying the innocent Children.

the exact equivalence of main titles it might be thought to relate to a London publication of 1703 by one William Smith, but the resemblance stops there. That book was a mostly prose work of nearly two hundred pages, bringing in the evangelists and apostles, whereas the "Lover of [children's] precious Souls" who compiled the American book (in one portrait of The Author he looks a bit like Gaffer Black Beard) offered 30-odd pages of verse, accompanied often by woodcuts of a surpassing crudity. The book could also be bulked out by the addition of prayers and hymns, Dr. Watts's *Cradle Hymn* being prominent. (Welch lists some 55 varied editions; Betsy Shirley has twelve, not always in finest trim.)

There were of course American editorial intrusions into imported popular titles, especially after the Revolution when kings and their royal arms fell out of favor and when a heightened national sensibility might cause Charlestown rather than London Bridge to have fallen down, but Jacob Blanck, the author of that listing of emergent "classic" titles, *Peter Parley to Penrod* (1938), got the chronology right when he

Woodcut by Isaiah Thomas
The History of the Holy Jesus, 1787.

ascribed the status of a first properly American classic to Samuel Griswold Goodrich's *Peter Parley's Tales about America* (1827). It and the many effusions from "Peter Parley" that followed it were hardly literary classics, but along with the related periodicals, *Parley's Magazine* (beginning in 1831) and *Robert Merry's Museum* (in 1841[6]), they exploited the attractive name and character of the eponymous narrator whose "tales" arose almost entirely from the factual content of his books.

The frequency with which title followed title was a component of their success, and it was a publishing ploy that was refined by Goodrich's contemporary, who also figures in Blanck's pantheon, Jacob Abbott. He was among the first to recognize, as Maria Edgeworth did in Britain, the pull of sequences of stories that feature the same characters. It was a technique that he came to gradually after introducing the young boy Rollo at the end of his first set of stories, *The Young Scholar Learning to Talk* (1834), designed intentionally with the educational purpose of encouraging children to read with their mothers. Education and religion were preoccupations of Abbott, who ran a Preface in various books on his wish "to furnish useful and instructive reading to young children" along with similar high-flown hopes, but these contrasted with some very convincing storytelling not without an accurate ear for dialogue and much gentle good humor. His runs of stories about Rollo, and Caleb and Jonas, had much greater imaginative potential than Peter Parley's didacticism and, as tales with sequels, were harbingers of such later bestsellers as the Ellen Montgomery books of "Susan Wetherell" and the stories of those little women at Concord.

Viewed from later times, there is nothing remarkable about these foundation works of American children's literature. Often unnoticed, however, were the activities of G. S. Peters of Harrisburg, Pennsylvania, of whose works Betsy Shirley had a particularly desirable and important collection. Peters was a publisher for the American-German community in Harrisburg who, after some conventional output for local use, issued in 1832 a copy of *The Comic Adventures of Old Mother Hubbard* "with numerous colored engravings." Colored they were, but not by hand, as was customary, but color-printed, thus pre-dating the arrival of this process for popular works in England by some dozen years.

Peters had perfected a method of letterpress printing from wood blocks in three colors (which also allowed for some color-overlaying to take place) and from then on a succession of English texts: *John Gilpin*, *The House that Jack Built*, *The Children in the Wood*, were issued in uniform orange-colored wrappers as entirely successful picture books. Some were also very competently translated into German for the local community, but such was the obscurity of this American provincial effort that its achievements have never been universally acclaimed.

The ramifying social and technical developments that impinged radically upon the American book trade prompt the second salient question: how far might the growth of a home-grown literature feasibly offer a commercial return to publishers in Britain whose output had so noticeably underlain that of the U.S.? As has been noted, perhaps the first transatlantic crossing eastward was made by the blocks that Alexander Anderson cut for the American bilingual Perrault, published in London by T. Boosey a year after the American edition. So far as written work is concerned, however, we must again be guided by Jacob Blanck who, in singling out Goodrich and Abbott for their early success among American readers, gives a clue to their potential in a wider market among London publishers.

As might be expected in a country with an already thriving and very diverse children's literature, the impact of American material was muted—a response that was to persist for about a hundred years—although there were bouts of contention on the part of the British

This is the cat…,
The House that Jack Built, 1833

recipients. The arrival of Peter Parley occasioned the foremost of these. The first to light on Parley's British possibilities was the publisher Thomas Tegg, a regular dealer in children's books during the 1830s, who had branches in Scotland, Ireland, and Australia. His editions followed the Boston model with their dumpy format, and short, plentifully illustrated and chatty chapters, which despite the catechising questions at the bottom of many pages would have had more appeal than dry schoolbooks. They were, however, something of an offense to those who sought to bring imagination into children's books. Edgar Taylor had complained that "philosophy is made the companion of the nursery" in the preface to his translation of the Grimm tales years before the advent of Peter Parley, while in the 1840s, after his arrival, Henry Cole set up the editing of his Home Treasury of traditional rhymes, ballads, and romances under the banner of "anti-Peter-Parleyism." Goodrich was offended by that—and even more so by the actions of editors at the Holborn Hill firm of Darton and Clark who not only pirated his texts but altered them and even produced Parley titles of their own. Indeed, Darton's regular *Peter Parley's Annual* that began its long life in 1840 under the editorship of William Martin was an entirely English production.[7]

The children's books of Jacob Abbott began a British career almost simultaneously with the onset of Parleyism when *The Little Scholar Learning to Talk; a picture book for Rollo* was published by James S. Hodson of Fleet Street (1836). He was a minor publisher who may have had hopes of developing transatlantic connections since he ran a Depôt for American Literature—but it seems to have been very short-lived.[8] *The Little Scholar* would have been something unusual on the English market (despite a possible influence from Mrs. Barbauld's *Lessons for Children*), each little section of text, as already noticed, consisting of a picture about which a mother is questioning her son William, sometimes asking him to point things out. The pictures though—some of which are a good way after Bewick—are too muddily printed to be of much service. On the very last page (as apparently also occurs in the

American edition), Rollo is introduced with a promise to have more said about him "in my next book." That indeed happens, for Hodson institutes an Abbott's Rollo Series with at least five more very scantily illustrated titles, and although the Depôt has disappeared there is an advertisement including *The Young Farmers; or the Franklin family* and a version of *Peter Parley's Method of Telling about the Bible*, adapted by one, S. Blair.

While that seems to be the end of Rollo (and Hodson?), Abbott goes on to a far more extensive availability under T.J. Allman, another smallish publisher, first in Holborn Hill, where during the 1830s he introduces the two Caleb books from the Jonas series and later in Oxford Street where he engages with *Abbott's Histories* and other titles. In the 1870s Abbott achieves his most august presence at the hands of Frederick Warne, who, in 1865, had started a company that would eventually publish *The Tale of Peter Rabbit.* But here the firm is found publishing three "Franconia" stories (*Stuyvesant*, *Caroline*, and *Agnes*) either separately for a shilling each or as a Gift Book at three shillings and sixpence. They are illustrated with attractive wood engravings and handsome full-page color plates. Beechnut, from the "Franconia" series, even found his way into the twentieth century with a neat little selection of stories in Methuen's series of "Little Blue Books for Children," *The Beechnut Book* (1901). It was edited by E.V. Lucas, who wrote and was something of an authority on children's books (he also edited the works of Charles Lamb in some seven volumes). He was married to an American and may have been led to Beechnut by her childhood reading.

Abbott's many books, often of only moderate size, contrast sharply with the tonnage that fell upon British readers (probably ninety percent female) with the arrival of the first and most famous offering from "Elizabeth Wetherell" (i.e. Susan Bogert Warner): *The Wide, Wide World*. First published in two volumes in 1851, a year after its American edition, but quickly reduced to one, its 592 pages of sentimental and religiose narrative seem to have presented no obstacle to the young readers of its time, and over twenty versions appeared down to 1950. (That last was a much-abridged edition of 288 pages edited and illustrated with excellent pen drawings by Joyce Lankester Brisley—famed creator of the "Milly-Molly-Mandy" stories. Her introduction carries the note that she undertook the edition through her own love of the original story when, as a child, she had been given her grandmother's copy.) Such was its success that many of Warner's later books—often almost as daunting in scale, but sometimes in the early years accompanied by attractive colored plates—had a similarly long life. Several dust-jacketed copies were published as late as the Second World War in Ward-Lock's "Prize Library," such series for school and Sunday School prizes being notorious dumping-grounds for the mechanical issue of unread "classics."

While many American titles (such as the dozens of stories about Elsie Dinsmore, written under the influence of Miss Wetherell) would have been taken up by English publishers, the number of true "classics" were the few still-honored titles by such as Mark Twain and Louisa May Alcott. (Surprisingly, Roberts Brothers' girls' books about Katy—who *did* things—that were successors to *Little Women*—became more popular in Britain than in the U.S.) The *weltbuch* first published as *A Visit from St. Nicholas*[9]—admittedly a slow starter in the United States—was hardly known in Britain until the 1940s and, such were the riches of the Edwardian period, that *The Wizard of Oz* escaped proper notice until Judy Garland became its ambassadress.

There were also those two re-workings of myths from classical times by Nathaniel Hawthorne (still in print today), of which the first, *The Wonder Book*, was responsible for the making of one of the great books of English children's literature. That came about not through any quality on its own part but through Charles Kingsley's antagonism towards it. Feeling (with some justice) that the storytelling background diminished the power of the mythic scenes, he was driven to a demonstration of how he thought the job should be done, thus creating a masterpiece, *The Heroes*. (It would seem that Kingsley did not care for what was being imported from the former colonies, and *The Water-Babies* contains digs at Peter Parley and what he calls *The Narrow, Narrow World* and *The Pumplighter*.)

In two other fields of activity, however, the United States outdid by many leagues an unformed, not to say dismissive, attitude towards children's books in the land where their history had been most distinguished. On the one hand it was perceived early on how vital a national library service could be in spreading through the land an opportunity for all children to meet the range of reading experiences that were being created by publishers not just in New England but the great cities beyond. As early as the 1890s, teachers and librarians were engaged in what for their English colleagues would seem the anomalous business of formalizing the critical assessment of children's books and their provision for young readers. This led, on the one hand, to a cadre of adult specialists in the field who engaged in such public activities as the Boston Bookshop for Boys and Girls, with its associated *Horn Book Magazine*, and the establishment of national awards such as the Newbery Medal (honoring an eighteenth-century London bookseller), and, on the other hand, to the treatment of children's literature as a subject fit for academic study. It took librarians in Britain more than thirty years to catch up with such unfamiliar practices, while the arrival of children's literature within the syllabi of universities, rather than schools of librarianship, only began to occur in the 1970s.

At the same time, in another part of the forest, adults, with no particular interest in children but perhaps only their own childhood, latched on to a desire to collect early children's books. This occurred on both sides of the Atlantic—a notable precursor being the London publisher A. W. Tuer, the auctioning of whose children's books in 1900 must be among the first of such events—but collecting was prosecuted with more fervor (and more willingness to furnish funds) in the United States. Stimulus was imparted there by the "Emperor of the Rooms," Abe Rosenbach, whose great-uncle had worked for the Philadelphia business started by Jacob Johnson in 1780 and whose own collection was the source in 1933 of his groundbreaking catalogue *Early American Children's Books* (upon which much of this essay has depended). Its readability and its sense of historical interweavings showed the richness of his subject, but it engendered a far greater interest in English children's books among Americans and was surely the start of the forceful migration of many of the treasures of the East to the shelves of the more discriminating (and richer) collectors of the West. How few of them had the courage of Betsy Shirley to focus on the less Romantic products of the New England states and the far less easily traceable activities that spread across the Continent. How much is still to be learnt and how much her collection can teach us.

POSTSCRIPT

Almost coincidental with my theme in this paper a connection across the centuries comes to the fore. A direct descendant of the John Cotton, he of both Bostons, is Elizabeth Hammill. She was born Elizabeth Laurence Masten in Washington D.C. in 1943 and was a reader from her earliest years. (Her uncle was Cass Canfield, president and editor at Harper & Row.) After her marriage to Thomas Hammil, she came to England with her young family in 1971, eventually working in a specialist department for the Waterstone's chain. While there, she conceived the idea for a British children's book archive—a facility that, unlike provision in her native United States, was sorely lacking in Britain. After tremendous administrative labor, this was, with the assistance of a colleague, Mary Briggs, to result in the foundation in 2005 of Seven Stories in Newcastle upon Tyne, now designated the official British Centre for Children's Books—yet another fruitful return on the milk supplied so long ago to the Boston Babes.

1   cf. a copy in my collection: *The New-England Primer Improved*...Glasgow, 1827.

2   d'Alté A. Welch's *Bibliography of American Children's Books Printed Prior to 1821* has been a necessary crib in the writing of this essay. I have tended to use the first published version issued in fascicles by the American Antiquarian Society between 1963 and 1967.

Their subsequent gathering of the material there into a single bound volume (1972), issued after the author's tragic murder, contains important additions and corrections but suffers from the excision of many marginal titles and, sadly, many details of the original British printings of American editions. Confusingly, the Society renumbered the contents without supplying references to equivalents in the fascicles.

3 *Early American Children's Books*. . . Portland, Maine, The Southworth Press, 1933. No.59

4 Jane Ellen Carstens, *The Babcocks; Printers, Publishers, Booksellers* Diss. Columbia University, 1975. (Facsim. Ann Arbor, Michigan. University Microfilms, 1985. 2vv. 936ff.)

5 Probably in 1737 an earlier bestseller was published: *The Prodigal Daughter*. Although first published in England, its popularity in the Colonies was so much greater than on its native heath that it could be regarded as an American publishing success.

6 As with many magazines, their histories are complicated. Parley relinquished editorship of the *Magazine* after only a year but it continued, sustaining his name in its title, until 1845 when it was absorbed into his second magazine: the *Museum*. There are Alcott connections in both; the *Magazine* was edited for a time by her uncle William, and she herself edited what had become *Merry's Museum* for a year or so before the success of *Little Women* brought her financial security.

7 Much detail can be found in the relevant entries in Lawrence Darton's bibliography of his ancestors' children's books, *The Dartons* (London: The British Library, 2004).

8 An advertisement at the rear of *The Little Scholar* includes two traceable Boston books (both at the American Antiquarian Society): *Sarah and her Cousins* by a Mrs L. Larned, 1831 from Carter, Hitchcock & Babcock and *Edward and Ellen, A Tale* by the author of *Mary and Susan* (which is also listed), 1833 from John Allen.

9 Rather unseasonably in the spring of 1987, a small exhibition of Betsy Shirley's books was mounted at the Grolier Club in New York City with a hand-list (anonymous, but presumably by Betsy) *Mirth and Mistletoe*. The theme was St. Nicholas, and some eleven variant copies of the poem were shown either under its original title or "The Night Before Christmas."

TIMOTHY YOUNG

Happy Deaths & Urban Dangers

In *Cruel Jack*, a little book issued by the Sabbath School Society in Boston, Massachusetts, sometime between 1839–1842 as part of their Infant Series, we are introduced to the title character, who climbs trees to snatch eggs out of a bird's nest and destroy them. We learn that Jack tortures other animals with no sense of remorse. "God does not love a cruel boy," the book tells us, "No one loves him." The 8-page tale ends with a bizarre statement from an unnamed 19-year-old criminal confessing his impulse to kill. The final image is a woodcut of a man hanging from a gallows—possibly Cruel Jack's final reward.[1] The lesson of this book is simple: The wages of sin are death—and that inherent sin, if not addressed at an early age, will lead to evil behavior. Present-day readers may be shocked by the image of a dead body hanging from a noose, considering it a dark image to show a child, but such blunt imagery can be found throughout the history of children's literature.

A prime example is *The Children in the Wood*, the tale of an evil uncle who schemes to possess the money left in trust to his nephew and niece, in his care after they have been orphaned. The uncle sends the children out into the woods, where they freeze to death: "A robin covered them with leaves / And thus he made their grave." Versions of this old English ballad that were fashioned into books for children often prominently featured an image of the two poor children, huddled together and frozen in the forest. *The New-England Primer*, the most often reprinted educational book in the British colonies in the eighteenth century, was also part of this dismal tradition, owing to the fact that the one image that appeared in all variant versions of that book was of a man being

(*opposite*) "And thus he made their Grave," *The Children in the Wood*, John Wiley & Son, [between 1865 and 1874].

259

8

"Better than any thing else?"
"Yes," he said, "I think I
did." "Did you ever wish to
kill people, if they opposed or
vexed you?" "I don't know
that I did,—I used to want to
kill the cattle, when they didn't
act to suit me." To what a
dreadful end that boy's cruelty
brought him!

The final image in
Cruel Jack, 1839.

burned at the stake: John Rogers, the English Protestant martyr of the sixteenth century.

Why were books made to deliberately frighten children? The direct answer is that fright is a powerful method for grabbing attention and for teaching lessons. In a broader sense, scary stories demand that children pay attention, become aware of the world around them, and learn of its dangers—both obvious and hidden. That world can be spiritual, as was the focus in the early modern period—or physical, as seen in an increasingly secular society in the past 200 years.

We can discern some reasons by looking at how this intention to scare was manifested in a pair of themes that became extremely popular subjects for children's reading matter in the eighteenth and early nineteenth centuries in the English-speaking world. The first theme is "Happy Deaths of Pious Children," a phrase that may fill many readers with apprehension. The expression "happy death," itself, seems oxymoronic. It comes from a much older literary tradition, the *ars moriendi* (or art of dying), two related Latin texts dating from about 1415 and 1450 which offer advice on the protocols and procedures to "die well" according to Christian precepts of the late Middle Ages. These texts were in the form of rites and prayers to be used for a person who was dying. In addition, they included instruction on fighting off temptations that would come to a person on his or her deathbed. Thus, the ultimate instruction for a happy life was how to have a happy death.

These texts were widely incorporated into books on Christian religious practice, and in the seventeenth century these instructions on the proper way to live and to die were deemed applicable to children, thus the appearance, in 1671, of what would become an important book throughout the English-speaking world: James Janeway's *A Token for Children: Being An Exact Account of the Conversion, Holy and Exemplary Lives, and Joyful Deaths, of Several Young Children*. This book comprises a collection of brief narratives of thirteen children, seven boys and six girls, all who died during childhood, between the ages of 5 and 14. The causes of their deaths were varied, but at least a few succumbed to plague, smallpox, or measles. The author, James Janeway, was a Puritan preacher and author of a number of popular books, all of them about Protestant salvation. His *Token* anthology was often reprinted and became one of the most influential children's religious books in the Anglo-Saxon world.

In the introduction to the *Token*, Janeway asks the young reader: "...are you willing to go to Hell and to be burn'd with the Devil and his Angels? Would you be in the same condition as naughty children? O Hell is a terrible Place, that's worse a thousand times than Whipping; God's Anger is worse than your Father's Anger; and are you willing to anger God?" The introduction asserts the value of the book in hand—but only if the child pays close attention to the words of the individual narratives that follow.

The book reached America in 1700 when an edition was published by Cotton Mather, the colonies' own verbose Puritan zealot, who added several native stories to the volume in an addendum titled: *A Token, for the Children of New-England, or, Some examples of children, in whom the fear of God was remarkably budding, before they dyed, in several parts of New-England : preserved and published, for the encouragement of piety in other children.* A sample biography is that of Sarah Howley, a young girl who came to accept the gospel when she was but 8 years old. As her narrative states: "...this child was highly awakened, and made deeply sensible of the condition of her soul, and her need of a CHRIST." Her passion became so inflamed that "...she was exceeding desirous to die, and cried out, come Lord Jesus, come quickly, conduct me to thy tabernacle..." and, indeed, she died on February 19, 1670, to enter into "an everlasting Sabbath."

EXAMPLE IV.

ANN GREENOUGH, the Daughter of Mr. *William Greenough*, left the world, when she was but about five years old, and yet gave astonishing Discoveries of a Regard unto God and Christ, and her own Soul, before she went away. When she heard any thing about the Lord *Jesus Christ*, she would be strangely transported, and ravished in her Spirit at it; and had an unspeakable Delight in *Catechising*. She would put strange *Questions* about Eternal things, and make *Answers* her self that were extreamly pertinent. Once particularly, she asked, *Are not we dead in Sin?* and presently added, *But I will take this way, the Lord Jesus Christ shall make me alive.* She was very frequent and constant in *Secret prayer*, and could not with any patience be interrupted in it. She told her Gracious Mother, *That she there prayed for her!* And was covetous of being with her Mother, when she imagined such Duties to be going forward. When she fell sick at last of a Consumption, she would not by any sports be diverted from the
Thought

A more concise story is told about John Langham, the son of a knight and baronet, who was only 5 years old when he died in 1659. He is described as a prodigy, reading books and memorizing catechisms at a very young age. The final description in his short narrative is: "What an instrument of God's glory might he have proved? What a deal of service might he have done for God (in all likelihood) had he lived to old age? But it was God's doing."

Editions of these books stayed in print for over a hundred years in the United States and in England as religious fervor ebbed and waned. In the United States, their presence was seen most visibly during the "Second Great Awakening," a swelling of religious passion between 1800–1830 that gave rise to what we now refer to as the evangelical movement. During that period, a number of updated collections of deathbed narratives came into print, including several written by George Hendley. Beginning with *A Memorial for Children: being an authentic account of the conversion, experience, and happy deaths of eighteen children: designed as a continuation of Janeway's Token* (1805, London; 1806, New Haven), this collection was later expanded and split into two volumes: one for boys and one for girls: *A Memorial for Sunday School Girls: being the second part of an authentic account of the conversion, experience, and happy deaths of twenty-five children.*

An exemplary story from the girls' memorial is that of Sarah Aldren, who died at 12 years of her age. Like her precursors, she evidenced a keen understanding of religious teaching at an early age and like many young martyrs, preached to her peers: "When one day at the house of a neighbour, who was very fond of her, she heard him say some bad words; she went up to him, called him by name, and told him if he did not leave off such evil ways, God would not love him." Soon enough, though, "After suffering much pain with great patience, her happy spirit quitted the tenement of clay, to be for ever with the Lord, in the year 1802."

In these examples, we can see threads that run through narratives of happy deaths of pious children:

(opposite) A narrative from *A Token, for the Children of New-England,* 1700.

263

- > An early exposure to a sermon or religious teaching
- > A form of "awakening" to the truth of the gospel
- > A precociousness of spirit coupled with a keen intellect
- > The desire to evangelize and point out sinful behavior in others
- > And what may be the overarching character of these children—a kind of aura about them as being already divine—making their stories read like the lives of saints.

The moral of these stories is salvation, but one that came from a conscious, elective personal embrace of the savior. Children were responsible for their own religious destiny. This may seem harsh to our 21st century minds. To understand the position of the child in the very strict theology of seventeenth and eighteenth century Puritans, one can look to a pair of influential works.

Thomas White in his *Little Book for Little Children* (originally published in London in 1660, then republished for American readers in 1702) gives his opinion of proper reading material for youngsters. In Chapter IX, "Wherein is shewn what Books Children are to Read," White advises: "When thou canst Read, read no Ballads and foolish books, but read the Bible, and the Plain Mans Pathway to Heaven... The Book of Martyrs, etc."[2] His lesson is: waste no time in reading foolish books, for there are souls to be saved—namely yours!

A more fervent opinion was offered by Jonathan Edwards, the Calvinist minister who led the first Great Awakening in the United States in the mid-eighteenth century. In his work: *Thoughts on the Revival of Religion in New England* (published originally in 1742) he makes these observations:

> What has given offense to many and raised a loud cry against some preachers, as though their conduct were intolerable, is their frighting of poor, innocent children with talk of hellfire and eternal damnation. But if those who complain so loudly of this really believe what is the general profession of the country, viz., that all are by nature the children of wrath and heirs of hell—and that

everyone that has not been born again, whether he be young or old, is exposed every moment to eternal destruction, under the wrath of Almighty God—I say, if they really believe this, then such a complaint and cry as this betrays a great deal of weakness and inconsideration. As innocent as children seem to be to us, yet, if they are out of Christ, they are not so in God's sight but are young vipers—and are infinitely more hateful than vipers—and are in a most miserable condition, as well as grown persons. And they are naturally very senseless and stupid, being born as the wild ass's colt, and need much to awaken them. Why should we conceal the truth from them?

We can see that, in the worldview of pious preachers, there was no special dispensation allowed children in terms of religious salvation—even to the point that the printed "tokens" for children did not contain frivolous flourishes, such as illustrations. They were intended to instruct.[3]

While the "token" books had a bludgeoningly obvious goal, there was a related category of books for children that came into being in the early nineteenth century that conflated religious salvation and secular safety while exposing children to horrific and quite gruesome images: books on urban dangers.

Perhaps the best example of this genre is *The Book of Accidents*, published in New Haven, Connecticut, by S. Babcock in 1831. The intent of this work is stated in an introductory note: "In presenting to his little readers the 'Book of Accidents,' the Author conceived he cannot render a more important service to the rising generation and to parents, than by furnishing them with an account of the accidents to which Children, from their inexperience or carelessness, are liable." Among those dangers are: Playing with Horses; Crossing Streets; Worrying Dogs; Playing with Knives and Firearms; Climbing on Chairs; Falling out of Windows, and Troubling the Cook: "This little girl is seen rushing forward to tell some idle tale, perhaps, to the cook. Unless she is very

WORRYING DOGS.

Many children delight in teazing dogs, and without caution go too near them, by which they get miserably torn and mangled. Wicked boys sometimes hold a piece of meat towards the dogs and as they approach with demonstrations of joy, in hope of receiving it, they suddenly take it away. By repeating this the dogs become enraged, and often severely repay them for their trickishness. What these boys had been doing to enrage the dog we cannot tell, but suspect they had been tormenting him in some way, thinking that as he was chained he could not injure them. But they were mistaken in this, and one of them is likely to be bitten very severely. Dogs are celebrated for their sagacity, and their attachment to man; and many instances are recorded of their having saved the lives of their masters; but all dogs are not of this description. Some are cross and ferocious, barking at and biting all who come near them.

careful she may stumble over a pot of water, which is standing on the floor; or be scalded by the water running from the dish which the cook is carrying to the table. Children should beware of scalding water."

In *The Third Chapter of accidents and remarkable events: containing caution and instruction for children*, by William Darton and published by Jacob Johnson in 1807, there are accounts of equally horrible events, such as what may go wrong while "Travelling in Foggy Weather." But the short tale, "The Young Lamp-Lighter," is most interesting, because it tells of a uniquely urban danger, of a fellow who leaves his burner against a pole while going to get a beer. The burner is found by a pair of young boys who climb his ladder, become "giddy" and fall and are then scalded by hot oil from the lamp.[4]

The Beacon; or Warnings to thoughtless boys, published in New York between 1856 and 1857, begins with the tale of John Stevens, a "very reckless boy" who is prone to trouble and ends up being crushed to death by a horse cart after dashing out into a busy street to greet a chum. Later in this book, there is an account of a boy falling out of a tree after disturbing a bird's nest[5], and another bizarre tale that must be read in its entirety, *The Mask*:

The fate of "A Reckless Boy," *The Beacon*, 1856.

(*opposite*) "Worrying dogs," *The Book of Accidents*, 1831.

Here is a mask. It is employed to conceal the face. It is a pretty thing for amusement, when it is properly used. A heedless boy once put on an ugly mask to amuse himself by alarming some very small boys and girls, and one of them was so terrified that she died the next day.

The intent of these kinds of books is clear. Children need to be made aware of dangers that are present in the world—especially in the rapidly urbanizing world of the early nineteenth century. Growing cities were certainly full of danger, as were households that contained a number of scary threats.

Lest we think that such sermonizing was only active in the distant past, the impulse to shock and educate continued into our own era. Pamphlets promoting bicycle and traffic safety were widely distributed by police departments and civic organizations throughout the United States in the twentieth century. These were direct descendants of the earlier books of accidents—complete with illustrations that often closely echoed their nineteenth-century precursors. One overzealous example of the traffic safety book genre distributed to American school children sometime in the late 1950s or early 1960s was *It's Great to Be Alive*. Printed in garish red and black ink, it contained gruesome scenes such as: "Screeching brakes…but too late…Tommy is crippled for life" and "While hiding in a leaf pile you could be run over by a truck."

But whether books were from the nineteenth or the twentieth century, they shared a number of common features:

> Warnings about real threats to the body
> A child who is "heedless" to instruction—often with a willfulness of spirit.
> A child with an inherent attraction to sinful or bad behavior
> A gruesome death
> God disapproving of the child's behavior—[most often in nineteenth-century books]

In a very basic sense, these two categories of books for children, Happy Deaths and Urban Dangers, are related. They are about concern for the soul and for the body. These concerns overlap in some measure. The secular books about urban dangers often have religious morals embedded in them—not of the strict, evangelical type, but of the more broadly Christian stripe. However, when happy death books address threats to or the degradation of the body, this is usually treated as an inevitable step on the way to salvation.

The goal of these books can be summarized as: Happy Deaths concern the salvation of the soul; Urban Dangers concern the safety of the body. Together, they are about concern for the survival of children through the use of cautionary tales to teach them about the dangers of the physical world and the need for some system of moral and ethical behavior. To take a more broadly philosophical view, it can be argued that both genres are also concerned with awareness. Religious awareness is about learning about and abiding by the truth of the gospel of salvation; Secular awareness is about learning about the physical reality of the world—inside and outside the family home—and the extent to which this reality poses bodily harm. The overlap between the two genres happens when the question of agency is introduced.

What is meant by "agency" is the ability for a child to make a deliberate choice in how to act in a certain situation. In a story, if a child decides to act willfully in an unethical or immoral way, the child will be saddled with the burden of sin, in addition to the natural damage that the situation delivers (for example: falling out of a tree or being scalded by hot water). In short, badly behaved children will be punished and will be admonished that God does not love them. A child who acts merely out of ignorance or impulse is often afforded much more sympathy or comfort.

In another, more finely finessed sense,[6] while the texts and the images in these kinds of books may appear at first read to be overzealous, the subjects related by both genres—Happy Deaths and Urban Dangers—reveal much about our desire, as adults, to construct children as beings that must be saved. A pair of truths, competing and complementary, is at work in these stories. Childhood death is a tragedy, but we can deal with the pain of real dangers by being very blunt about them when interacting with children. We may want to laugh out loud when we read such stories, thinking (or hoping) that these dangers are so outrageous, they will never happen. At a safe, historic distance, reading them as parody or cliché pokes fun at our adult concerns and anxieties that remain very real.

Blunt words and explicit images in children's books are meant to grab the attention of the reader and to instill codes of behavior—goals that remain part of the intentionality behind many contemporary books for children. When we examine the history of juvenile literature, it is important to remember that books with disturbing messages have long played an important part. When scholars of children's literature discuss such books, they hope to bring a focus to the field in a fashion that is neither overly precious nor dismissive. We should keep in mind that all of our personal histories of literature start with books we read as children—books that entertained us and made us laugh—as well as books that scared us and made us think twice about venturing out into a busy street or into a dark night.

The books discussed in this essay remain ripe for investigation. A broader look into the creation and circulation of the "token" books could reveal why they stayed in print for so long and how the narratives they contained changed over time with the ebb and flow of religious fervor in Europe and America. Books of accidents, likewise, can provide ways of entry to understand the anxieties of urbanization and the evolution of approaches to child-rearing in the modern world. These paths of investigation can expand to observations about history, sociology, commerce, and psychology. In the same way that "The Child is father of the Man," then children's literature can be the key to understanding the big, scary world.

1 A companion volume in the same series was published in 1839: *Brave George*. In that book, the hero transgresses by spilling a bottle of ink—which he readily admits to doing. He is praised for his honesty, but only after being whipped. At least he didn't end up swinging from the gallows.

2   He also instructs his young readers to "mark in the margins, or by underlining the places you find most relish in ..."

3   However, the twentieth-century American humorist and artist, Edward Gorey, created a gimlet-eyed parody that captured the spirit of the original tokens: *The Pious Infant* (1966). Gorey's achievement is that his book barely differs from the actual pious death narratives. His longest reach into parody is the (very funny) scene that shows how young Henry Clump, the pious infant of the title, after achieving a heightened awareness of his sinful state, "used to go through books and carefully blot out any places where there was a frivolous mention of the deity."

4   Three volumes of *Accident* books were first published by the prolific English writer, William Darton, in 1801 in England. The texts appear to have been applicable enough to American disasters that they were republished wholesale by Johnson in Philadelphia.

5   In nineteenth century juvenile books, there are many cautionary tales centered on boys and birds nests. The nineteenth century afforded a limited palette of entertainments for frisky children.

6   Credit is owed to Dr. Pádraic Whyte for bringing to my attention many of the observations in this paragraph.

AUTHORS

BRIAN ALDERSON found himself accidentally involved in the field of children's literature in 1953 and has so far not escaped from it. He has been mostly a sort of odd-job man in his home country of England, but from the 1970s onward he has taken a more than passing interest in events in North America. Among other things this resulted in his taking up a Beinecke Fellowship in 2006 in order to work in the Betsy Beinecke Shirley Collection.

JILL CAMPBELL's essay on adaptations of *Robinson Crusoe* for young people will be published next year in the *Cambridge Companion to 'Robinson Crusoe'*, and her essay on Maria Edgeworth's children's tales appeared in *Imagining Selves: Essays in Honor of Patricia Meyer Spacks* (2008). She is a Professor of English at Yale University and the author of *Natural Masques: Gender and Identity in Fielding's Plays and Novels* (1995) and essays on topics ranging from newspaper advertising and the rise of the novel to eighteenth-century representations of female old age. She has taught children's literature by Mary Wollstonecraft, Anna Laetitia Barbauld, and Maria Edgeworth in graduate seminars and children's literature from the eighteenth century to the present in freshman courses. Her students have been thrilled to visit the children's literature collection at the Beinecke as part of these courses.

BEVERLY LYON CLARK is Professor of English and Women's & Gender Studies at Wheaton College in Massachusetts, where she teaches courses in children's literature, American literature, romantic fiction, and writing. She is the author of *The Afterlife of "Little Women"* (2014) and *Kiddie Lit: The Cultural Construction of Children's Literature in America* (2003). She has also edited *Louisa May Alcott: The Contemporary Reviews* (2004) and coedited *"Little Women" and the Feminist Imagination* (1999) and *Girls, Boys, Books, Toys: Gender in Children's Literature and Culture* (1999).

JOANN CONRAD is a folklorist and anthropologist. Her doctorate from UC Berkeley, written under Alan Dundes and John Lindow, was based on extensive fieldwork and study in Northern Norway, and analyzed the political and cultural negotiations between the Sami and Norwegian state. She currently teaches at California State University, East Bay, where her research is focused on the role of such ordinary cultural productions as mass-produced children's books, magazines, and advertisements in shaping a citizenry. Conrad was a Shirley Fellow at the Beinecke Library during December 2014 and January 2015.

ELIZABETH FRENGEL is the research librarian for the Beinecke Rare Book & Manuscript Library where she enjoys connecting scholars with world-class collections spanning seven curatorial areas and more than two millennia of cultural history. Her particular research interests are in twentieth-century children's literature and the history of the development of pictorial endpapers, two subjects that often intersect in interesting ways. She curated an exhibition on endpapers at the Beinecke Library titled "Under the Covers: A Visual History of Decorated Endpapers."

PATRICK KILEY is a writer and publisher based in Troy, New York. He steers Publication Studio Hudson, one in a network of such studios in the Americas and Europe. He worked as a curatorial assistant under Timothy Young at Beinecke Rare Book & Manuscript Library from 2004–07, focusing in particular on the Betsy Beinecke Shirley Collection of American Children's Literature and the book it inspired, *Drawn to Enchant*. Later he worked at New York Public Library, under independent scholar and curator Leonard S. Marcus, on the library's major exhibition in 2013–14, "The ABC of It: Why Children's Books Matter."

HEATHER KLEMANN teaches in the English Department at Yale University. Her current research project explores how children's books and material cultures of reading shape the circulation, reception, and development of Enlightenment-era moral philosophy and epistemology. Her work has appeared in *Eighteenth-Century Studies*, *Studies in Romanticism*, and *The Lion and the Unicorn*.

GREGORY MAGUIRE is the author of ten novels for adults and about two dozen books for children and teenagers. His best known work is *Wicked*, which inspired the Broadway musical; other recent books include *After Alice*, *Egg & Spoon*, and *Making Mischief: A Maurice Sendak Appreciation*. He lives with his family outside Boston.

LEONARD S. MARCUS is a children's-literature historian and critic. He is the author of more than 25 award-winning books about children's books and the people who create them, including *Margaret Wise Brown: Awakened by the Moon*; *Dear Genius: The Letters of Ursula Nordstrom*; *Randolph Caldecott: The Man Who Could Not Stop Drawing*; and *The Annotated Phantom Tollbooth*. Marcus is a regular contributor to the *New York Times Book Review* and a frequent commentator on radio and television. A founding trustee of the Eric Carle Museum of Picture Book Art, he curated the New York Public Library's landmark exhibition, "The ABC of It: Why Children's Books Matter," and the Rosenbach Museum's sesquicentennial exhibition, *Wonderland Rules: Alice at 150*. A graduate of Yale College, where he began his studies of children's books and cultural history, Marcus teaches at New York University and the School of Visual Arts and lectures about his work throughout the world.

SANDRA MARKHAM is the Lewis Legacy Archivist at the Lewis Walpole Library in Farmington, Connecticut, a department of Yale University Library. She has held positions as archivist, librarian, curator, editor, and registrar at institutions including the Beinecke Rare Book and Manuscript Library, the Library Company of Philadelphia, the New-York Historical Society, the Albany Institute of History and Art, University of Pennsylvania Archives, and Memorial Art Gallery of the University of Rochester. She has published more than a dozen articles on photographers, printers, collectors, and collections in *The Magazine Antiques*, *The New-York Journal of American History*, *The Ephemera Journal*, *History of Photography*, and *Printing History*.

MICHELLE H. MARTIN became the Beverly Cleary Endowed Professor in Children and Youth Services in the iSchool at the University of Washington in Seattle in the fall of 2016, where she teaches courses in children's and young adult literature. From 2011–2016, she was the inaugural holder of the Augusta Baker Endowed Chair in Childhood Literacy at the University of South Carolina. She is the author of *Brown Gold: Milestones of African-American Children's Picture Books, 1845-2002* (Routledge, 2004) and co-editor (with Claudia Nelson) of *Sexual Pedagogies: Sex Education in Britain, Australia, and America, 1879-2000* (Palgrave, 2003). Her current project, *Dream Keepers for Children of the Sun*, is a book-length critical analysis of the collaborative and individual works that Langston Hughes and Arna Bontemps wrote for children during their 40-year friendship and collaborative working relationship.

KATIE TRUMPENER is the Emily Sanford Professor of Comparative Literature and English at Yale, where she teaches courses on early children's literature, the picture book, and the graphic novel. Alongside longer projects on the history of the Anglophone novel, Central European film, and the history of the panorama, she has published essays on the early history of the picture book; urban picture books; emigré illustrators (H.A. Rey and Russian constructivist Alexandra Exter); the emergence of the British children's book trade; nineteenth-century child readers and the children's novel; and German and Anglo-American World War narratives for children.

LAURA WASOWICZ is Curator of Children's Literature at the American Antiquarian Society. Since 1987, she has worked to acquire, catalog, and provide reference service for the AAS collection of 26,000 American children's books issued between 1650 and 1899. She has written essays on various aspects of nineteenth-century American children's book publishing, picture book iconography, and child reading habits. She is also the editor of the *Nineteenth-Century American Children's Book Trade Directory*, available on the AAS website (http://www.americanantiquarian.org).

DR. PÁDRAIC WHYTE is assistant professor of English and director of the graduate program in children's literature at the School of English, Trinity College Dublin, Ireland. He delivered the 2012 Betsy Beinecke Shirley Lecture on American Children's Literature at Yale University. He is author of *Irish Childhoods* (2011) and co-editor of *Children's Literature Collections: Approaches to Research* (2016) and *Children's Literature and New York City* (2014). Forthcoming publications include an essay on children's literature in *The Oxford Handbook of Modern Irish Fiction*. In 2013, he received a major Irish Research Council award to establish a National Collection of Children's Book: nccb.tcd.ie.

TIMOTHY YOUNG is Curator of Modern Books and Manuscripts at Beinecke Rare Book and Manuscript Library of Yale University where he focuses on literature and modern cultural movements and oversees the Betsy Beinecke Shirley Collection of American Children's Literature. He is the author of *Drawn to Enchant: Original Children's Book Art in the Betsy Beinecke Shirley Collection* (2007), co-editor of *The Great Mirror of Folly: Finance, Culture, and the Crash of 1720* (2013), and he contributes regularly to *The Yale Review*, writing on music and books, and to DesignObserver.com, covering topics in book history.

IMAGES

JoAnn Conrad, *"Typical Norwegian": The d'Aulaires' Imagined and Imaginary Landscapes*

Images by Ingri and Edgar Parin d'Aulaire reproduced by permission of the copyright holders, Per Ola d'Aulaire and Nils M.P. Daulaire.

Image of Christmas card by Milly Heegaard reproduced with permission of the Norsk Folkemuseum.

Elizabeth Frengel, *Ludwig Bemelmans, from The Castle No. 9 to Madeline*

All images by Ludwig Bemelmans TM and © Ludwig Bemelmans, LLC, All rights reserved.

Heather Klemann, *Mo Willems and the Poetics of Parenthood*

For images by Mo Willems:
TIME TO SAY PLEASE! © 2005 by Mo Willems. Originally published by Hyperion Books for Children. Used with permission.

OLIVE HUE SHOW MUTTS: AN INTOXICATINGLY HARD READER from DON'T PIGEONHOLE ME!: TWO DECADES OF THE MO WILLEMS SKETCHBOOK © 2011 by Mo Willems. Used with permission.

"I AM GOING!" © 2010 by Mo Willems. Originally published by Hyperion Books for Children. Used with permission.

For images by Keith Baker:
Reprinted with the permission of Beach Lane Books, Simon & Schuster Children's Publishing Division, from *LMNO PEAS* by Keith Baker. Copyright © 2010 Keith Baker. All rights reserved.

Gregory Maguire, *The Haunted Stacks, or A Reader's Guide to Writing Fiction*

Image by Peter Boston used with permission of Diana Boston.

Study of Bilbo Baggins and Gandalf by Maurice Sendak. Copyright © 1967 by Maurice Sendak, used by permission of The Wylie Agency LLC.

Leonard Marcus, *Seen & Heard: Margaret Wise Brown and Leonard Weisgard's The Noisy Book*

Illustration on page 196 from *The World is Round* by Gertrude Stein and illustrated by Clement Hurd [used for the cover of the 1939 catalog of the William R. Scott publishing company]. Illustration copyright © 1939, renewed 1966 by Clement Hurd. Reprinted by permission of HarperCollins Publishers.

Illustrations by Leonard Weisgard:
Copyright and used with permission by The Estate of Leonard Weisgard.

Michelle Martin, *Black Childhood Abroad: Popo and Fifina, Children of Haiti*

Images by E. Simms Campbell, permission courtesy Liz Campbell-Moskowitz.

Katie Trumpener, *Nature in the Kitchen: Animals, Children, and Mothers in Robert McCloskey's* Blueberries for Sal.

For images by Robert McCloskey:
From *BLUEBERRIES FOR SAL* by Robert McCloskey, copyright 1948, renewed © 1976 by Robert McCloskey. Used by permission of Viking Children's Books, an imprint of Penguin Young Readers Group, a division of Penguin Random House LLC.

From *ONE MORNING IN MAINE* by Robert McCloskey, copyright 1952, renewed © 1980 by Robert McCloskey. Used by permission of Viking Children's Books, an imprint of Penguin Young Readers Group, a division of Penguin Random House LLC.

From *TIME OF WONDER* by Robert McCloskey, copyright © 1957, renewed © 1985 by Robert McCloskey. Used by permission of Viking Children's Books, an imprint of Penguin Young Readers Group, a division of Penguin Random House LLC.

Laura E. Wasowicz, *Headstrong Travels By Land & Water: The Transatlantic World of the Nineteenth-Century Picture Book*

Image from *Dean & Sons Children's Pantomime Toy Books* courtesy of Baldwin Library of Historical Children's Literature, George A. Smathers Libraries, University of Florida.

Padraic Whyte, *A Place in the Canon: Padraic Colum's Newbery Books and the Development of American Children's Literature*

Images courtesy of Trinity College, Dublin, and St. Patrick's College, Dublin.

The majority of the remaining images in this book were scanned from originals in the Betsy Beinecke Shirley Collection of American Children's Literature, Beinecke Rare Books and Manuscript Library. Special thanks goes to the staff of the Beinecke digital library for preparing these images for publication.